AF278725

The Signature of God

Confronts the

Forgeries of Men

The Signature of God

Confronts the

Forgeries of Men

*How Human Subjectivism
has Eroded Confidence in the Authority of Scripture*

EDWIN B. FOUNTAIN, PH.D.

AND

WILLARD A. RAMSEY

Millennium III Publishers
SIMPSONVILLE, SOUTH CAROLINA
2007

The Signature of God Confronts the Forgeries of Men
Copyright © 2007
by Edwin B. Fountain and Willard A. Ramsey

ISBN 0-9625220-7-4

Published by
Millennium III Publishers
P.O. Box 928
Simpsonville, SC 29681

Unless otherwise noted, all Scripture quotations are from the Authorized
King James version of the Bible.

All rights reserved. Except for traditional dialogue or scholarly criticism,
no portion of this book, electronic or otherwise, may be reproduced without
written permission of the publisher.

Library of Congress Cataloging-in-Publication Data

Fountain, Edwin B.
  The signature of God confronts the forgeries of men : how human sub-
jectivism has eroded confidence in the authority of Scripture / Edwin B.
Fountain and Willard A. Ramsey.
       p. cm.
  Includes bibliographical references and index.
  ISBN 0-9625220-7-4
  1. Bible—Evidences, authority, etc. 2. Subjectivity—Religious aspects—
Christianity.
I. Ramsey, Willard A.   II. Title.
BS480.F69 2007
220.1'3—dc22
                                                    2007003592

Contents

Foreword

Subjectivism is not a word I use everyday. Yet the authors, Edwin B. Fountain and Willard A. Ramsey, use the word to describe one of the major theological trends occurring among evangelical and fundamental churches today. This book is an analysis of the changing view of God's people toward Scripture. The authors make the case that Scripture is "God's unchanging, objective standard of absolute truth" and that "we know God only by faith – not by sight, sense or direct experience."

This view of Scripture has been a Baptist "core value." It has been an anchor for our souls for two millennia. Today, however, we are seeing a move from this view of Scripture as absolute, objective truth to one more consistent with the prevailing multicultural, postmodern relativism of our age. Increasingly, our churches are accepting doctrinal diversity, and "doctrinal ambiguity" (as evidenced by the "stealth church" trend). The new emerging church focus on "the worship experience" is impacting even conservative Baptists. The pollster, George Barna, now attends a "house church" and touts it as the wave of the future, admitting that its appeal is more relational than doctrinal. More and more it seems many are buying into the idea that people must "experience God" before we can effectively evangelize them. Many contemporary evangelism methods reflect this philosophy. While truth may not have "fallen in the street" among Baptists, it does appear to be reeling to and fro in some circles.

Several years ago, I read Willard Ramsey's book, *The Nature of the New Testament Church on Earth*. It has become one of my favorites on the subject of the local, New Testament church. Recently, we had the opportunity to meet and spend a few hours together. I found Willard to be an interesting, well-informed brother in Christ. Over lunch, I discovered I was talking to a real "rocket scientist" (he was an engineer with a NASA subcontractor in the early days of the space programs). When the discussion turned to theology, I discovered that while we have different views on eschatology (he is post and I am pre on our views of the millennium), we had common ground and genuine fellowship on our views of Scripture, the

local church and contemporary theology. This book has been helpful to me in clarifying the historic position of Baptists in regard to
the Scripture, and in showing the influence of Pentecostalism and
its spread of subjective thinking and emphasis on experience into
mainline evangelicalism.

Jerry Falwell recently asked, "Is the Culture Overpowering
Our Churches?" in his *Falwell Confidential* mailing to pastors and
Christian leaders. From all human observation the answer is, "Yes,
it certainly is." But we who hold that objective standard of truth revealed in Scripture know that the "gates of hell cannot prevail," and
that God will always have a people for His name. *The Signature of
God Confronts the Forgeries of Men* makes a significant contribution in clarifying the confusion of our age, and encourages Baptists
to hold to the "faith once delivered to the fathers."

— Pastor Bill Monroe

Preface

Judging by the appearance of euphoria in many of the huge evangelical or charismatic worship services, one might suppose "that the kingdom of God should immediately appear." But upon closer examination we find something quite different. We find that there has been a notable shift toward a new standard of truth among these euphoric throngs. To those who still hold to the historic Christian position, that the Bible is God's unique standard of absolute truth by which all other claims to revealed truth must be judged, this shift is a disturbing trend. The effect of this trend has produced, and continues to produce, a serious erosion of the authority of Scripture in the eyes of many Christians and especially in the ambience of our morally decaying culture.

In past decades evangelical leaders have seen some encouraging signs that the intellectual struggle for the inerrancy of Scripture has made progress. But now that progress, if progress it is, seems more and more to be a moot point. The Scripture today, everywhere acclaimed, is not so much denied but simply sidelined. It is one source of revelation among many others.

This book asserts that a serious multifaceted subjectivist trend has been growing for two centuries or more and has been steadily, almost imperceptibly, diminishing the historic regard for the authority of Scripture. Subtle streams of subjectivism (modern charismata, existentialism, postmodernism) have converged within our culture and the euphoric multitudes now tend to look elsewhere for their truth. They are looking within – a fatal flaw.

Those churches still focused upon the Gospel of the grace of God, going forth with weeping bearing precious seeds, preaching "repentance toward God and faith in the Lord Jesus Christ" from the objective pages of the authoritative canon of Scripture, can observe all too well the diminished sense of biblical authority within the population. The subjectivist trend has undermined the sense of urgency for doctrinal objectivity, including the Gospel, and has hindered progress toward Christian unity in truth which Paul commanded (1 Cor. 1:10) and for which Christ prayed (John 17:17-23).

In chapters two and three, we have looked at biblical and historical background showing a universal human quest for subjective experiences. We have documented the fact that this quest, in both paganism and Christianity, is a characteristic of fallen human nature, not a norm of Christian truth.

In chapters four and five we have examined the biblical doctrines of the baptism of the Holy Spirit and of tongues-speaking, which have been widely misinterpreted and used to support a ruinous subjectivism.

The final chapter makes the case that God has placed His signature upon the canon of Scripture so that it is uniquely confirmed as the one and only body of absolute truth available to mankind on earth. The Bible is shown to be the final Standard before which all other claims must be judged. Therefore we may be certain that God would not go to these lengths to produce His Word and then fail to preserve it. Though we have not dealt with the matter of translations and versions of the Bible in this book, the authors do not consider the subject a matter of indifference. God would have all nations receive His Word in language they can understand, and His divine providence is working to that end. "For ever, O Lord, thy word is settled in heaven" (Psa. 119:89).

An implicit theme laced throughout this book is that God is *transcendent* over all things. Nothing is beyond His jurisdiction; therefore, nothing is neutral. Pluralism is a temporary trend to be destroyed by the absolute truth of God's authenticated Word. All the Scriptures apply to every human, all the time, everywhere; whether in heaven, in earth, on the moon, Mars, or in distant galaxies.

We have written this book with the prayer that the contemporary subjectivist trend may be identified and forsaken, that all Christians may return to the objective authority of the completed, authenticated canon of Scripture and come together around it seeking real unity in truth. This alone will result in worldwide evangelistic power for which Jesus prayed: "that the world may believe that thou hast sent me" (John 17:17-21).

Edwin B. Fountain
Vidalia, GA

Willard A. Ramsey
Simpsonville, SC

Acknowledgements

It is probably safe to say that a book has never been written that is wholly the work of the authors alone. For this reason we want to express our gratitude for the help of numerous brothers and sisters in the Lord who helped in various ways. We especially want to thank the several persons who reviewed the manuscript and made valuable suggestions, without which this book would be far less valuable.

Then we want to acknowledge also the help of Miss Patti Fisher, Director of Library Services at Taccoa Falls Bible College in Taccoa Falls, Georgia, and Kevin W. Woodruff, Director of Library Services and a Professor of Bible and Greek at Tennessee Temple University, Chattanooga. Both gave valuable assistance with the research and encouragement with their wonderful friendship. And thanks also to the friendly library staffs at both Furman and Bob Jones Universities in Greenville, South Carolina.

We especially want to thank our respective church families: Lyons Sovereign Grace Landmark Missionary Baptist Church in Lyons, Georgia, with Pastor Paul Jackson; also Hallmark Baptist Church and New Covenant Baptist Church in Greenville, South Carolina. Thanks to all for your help, prayers, love and encouragement.

About the Authors

Edwin B. Fountain, Ph.D. In 1951, with an undergraduate degree from the University of Georgia, Dr. Fountain entered the Air Force as an officer in the Korean conflict. After returning to civilian life, he worked in New York as an actor. In 1974, he came to know Jesus as Lord and Savior and attended Lexington Baptist College (Th.B., M.R.E.). At the University of Kentucky he earned the M.L.S. degree and did most of the work toward his Ph.D. in education (Instructional Design), completing it in the American Bible College and Seminary. Dr. Fountain later taught various subjects at Lexington Baptist College, among which was Ethics and Research for Preaching and Writing. He also served as Director of Library Services, a position he later held at Tennessee Temple University, Chattanooga. Then, returning to his native Georgia, he was Reference Librarian in Statesboro. Now retired, Dr. Fountain resides in Vidalia, Georgia, and continues a ministry of writing. His skills and experience in research add a valuable dimension to this book.

Willard A. Ramsey, having supported his family as an engineer in the aerospace program and industrial control systems, was ordained to the ministry in 1968. Active in founding four Baptist churches and one foreign mission, Pastor Ramsey, though now officially retired, has spent 38 years in the pastoral service of Hallmark Baptist Church near Greenville, South Carolina, where he is still semi-active. A passion for writing has resulted in several books including *The Nature of the New Testament Church on Earth, Facing Eternity, Zion's Glad Morning,* and *The Dominion of God on Earth.* For twelve yeas he was editor of *The Pillar,* an internationally circulated magazine promoting Christian unity in truth, and currently is senior editor in a small publishing company. He and Nita, his wife of fifty-two years, have three children, numerous grandchildren, and presently reside in Simpsonville, South Carolina.

I.
Introduction

From Moses on Sinai to the Apostle John on Patmos – from Genesis 1:1 to Revelation 22:21 – God has delivered one authenticated canon of truth, clad in impenetrable armor, barricaded and buttressed, cross-braced and anchored, fortified by an indestructible bulwark of proof, unique and complete, bearing the signature of God. It is a veritable ocean of absolute truth, and no man can swim its full breadth nor fathom its complete depth. With this standard in hand, how could a person of faith ever feel "dryness" of soul? Or why would one agonize before God for yet another beggarly crumb of "revelation" when he has not yet mined the objective treasure from this mother lode?

But alas, millions are turning inward to the barren recesses of fallen emotions seeking excitement but finding only temporary highs.

This book will assert that a serious multifaceted subjectivist trend is growing and is steadily eroding the consciousness of the authority of Scripture from our culture. The already sparse Christian unity in truth, valuable spiritual energy, and precious time is being dissipated by Christians continuing to mine the shallow subjective swamps of internal emptiness in search of subjective personal religious experiences.

Since the advent and continued progress of postmodern thought over the last decades of the 20th century and the early third millennium, this very troubling trend within evangelical Christianity is becoming far more ominous. It appears to be a growing obsession with or quest for subjective personal experience and/or personal direct revelation from God that is undermining the unique authority of the Bible.

In this light, it is difficult to avoid the conclusion that certain recent evangelical trends, including a bourgeoning Pentecostal or charismatic progression, have in some significant ways paved the path or prepared the seed bed for the growth of the more menacing subjectivism of existentialism and postmodernism – and vice versa. R. Kent Hughes, in *The Coming Evangelical Crisis*, referred to contemporary attitudes of "…postmodernity which enthrones subjectivity and self-focus …."[1] And, in the same book, John Armstrong wrote, "…historically conservative denominations…are changing as postmodern influences shape them more and more."[2] The influence of postmodern concepts, having reached evangelical academia, has now had time to filter down to the street and to the pew in some cases. There it is mingling with a resident subjectivity in traditional churches, especially where the charismatic experience has been influential in late history. This has weakened the grasp on basic Christian doctrines and now

[1] R. Kent Hughes, "Preaching: God's Word to the Church Today," *The Coming Evangelical Crisis*, ed. John H. Armstrong (Chicago: Moody Press, 1996), p. 92.

[2] John H. Armstrong, "Introduction: Two Vital Truths," *The Coming Evangelical Crisis*, p. 18.

seems to be seriously eroding the historic backlog of Christian orthodoxy.

THE EVANGELICAL REGRESSION

The milder form of subjectivism resident in the traditional charismatic movements has been a contributing factor to the weakening of evangelicalism. Modern charismata, with its propensity toward subjectivism, has helped prepare the "soil" among evangelical Christians so that the more insidious doctrine of postmodernism, that truth is what every person makes it and that an objective body of absolute truth does not exist, has had more serious influence than is commonly realized. It is especially important, we think, at this time when major changes are taking place in evangelical thought, to reexamine the underlying issue of subjective personal experiences versus objective Christian doctrine as derived from Scripture. This is especially true in view of the rapid growth of the charismatic movement over the last few decades of the 20th and of the early 21st century.

The Spread of Modern Charismata

The charismatic movements (a.k.a. Pentecostalism, sinless perfectionism, tongues movement, Neo-Pentecostalism, etc.) reportedly gained more than 25 million persons over the age of eighteen in the twenty years from 1960 to 1980.[3] It is difficult to determine the current number of persons who would be called Pentecostal or charismatic, but since 1980 the movement has exploded throughout most Christian denominations. A little research on the Internet will show various estimates. The Swedish Pentecostal Research and Information Center placed the Pentecostal/charismatic movement worldwide at 523,767,000 in 2000, and projects a membership of 811,552,000 for 2025. A Catholic source, on the other hand, estimates the movement at 400 million. Despite the difficulty of obtaining a reliable account of the size of the movement, it is intuitively clear that the movement is huge and growing.

---

[3]Kenneth S. Kantzer "The Charismatics Among Us," *Christianity Today*, 22 February 1980, p. 29.

In this growth we can see that Henry Pitt van Dusen's prediction, "that the last half of the twentieth century would be remembered in church history as the age of the Pentecostal charismatic Christianity,"[4] has proved valid.

It is partially this fantastic growth and the constant swing of mainline evangelical churches to a charismatic orientation that has motivated this study.

A further motivation, however, is the inference that a large movement is influencing the whole of evangelical Christianity toward subjectivism trending more and more toward the belief that subjective personal experience is not only a valid source of religious truth but the most reliable source. Subjectivism is gradually deposing Scripture as the *ultimate standard* of truth. This is a deeply troubling trend. As the charismatic movement matures, and the deepening influence of postmodernism grows, there appears less and less a necessity to use the Bible as the basis for doctrine or as the final authority to test the validity of subjective personal experience. Thus the *experience* tends to become the ultimate authority for truth both for evangelicalism and the whole of our culture.

Experience: Trumping the Word of God

Moreover, charismatic and subjectively inclined men and women of today, not content that "the just shall live by faith," want rather to *"experience God"* directly. This is often sought either through an experience of ecstasy, through prophesying, by direct revelation from God, by signs and wonders, or by speaking in tongues. George Gardiner, a long-time charismatic who finally saw the light of Scripture truth and abandoned Pentecostalism, wrote:

> All [charismatics] have one common denominator, the search for experience. "I want to know – to feel – to have." Such phrases as "don't knock it unless you've tried it" and "a man with an experience is never at the mercy of a man with only an argument" are commonly heard.[5]

---

[4]Cited by Kantzer, p. 25.
[5]George E. Gardiner, *The Corinthian Catastrophe* (Grand Rapids: Kregel Publications, 1974), p. 51.

This clearly confirms, by one who knows, that in the mind of some charismatics *experience* trumps Scripture in authority. In view of Scripture truth, which we shall examine later in some detail on this issue, we must ask: should this thinking not be looked upon as cultish, as others who link themselves to the Bible yet do not embrace it as the final and complete authority? Here we are confronted, not merely with a modern aberration but with something more fundamental in human nature, reminiscent of the original desire of man to *experience* the forbidden fruit, to be "as god's" (Gen. 3:5).

The God-Shaped Void. There was a time when our original parents knew God's actual presence: "And they heard the voice of the LORD God walking in the garden in the cool of the day." But God withdrew from the presence of man, and ever since the Eden rebellion humanity has felt a sense of loss and still wants to experience *equality* with God – to be His *peer*. We still want Him to walk with us "in the cool of the day" as He did in the garden, to see, to hear, to feel, in a peer relationship. We want Him to make himself available to our *senses* again. We want to "experience" Him. Even though we have sinned against Him, we resent the fact that He took Himself away from our presence so that we cannot detect His presence by our senses.

We can know Him only by faith – "the *evidence of things not seen*," – or heard, or touched, directly. This fact leaves us a little humiliated and insecure in the physical separation which God chose to established after Eden.

Subjectivity and the Quest. Therefore, ever since the Eden rebellion, mankind has been engaged in a quest to find a god on his own terms, directly through experience. But there are problems: 1) the pagan's *god* does not actually exist; thus there can be no objective experience to the senses. And 2) the one true God is not available to human senses. Therefore, the only way to have such an "experience" is by *subjective* means within one's own psyche.[6] Since direct divine experiences can no longer come from

---

[6]We recognize that some experiences, especially pagan, are the result of demonic deceit. Still, it is wholly void of true knowledge or revelation.

external objective sensory contact with God, the only alternative is to conjure up from within, *subjectively*, something that *seems* like, or *feels* like, such an experience: emotional frenzy, hysteria, unintelligible speech, reckless abandon, letting go, falling "slain" in the spirit, etc. The truth is these things are "experiences" – psychic experiences – but not experiences of the true and living God, or of any god. There is no *source* of truth within the fallen human. *All knowledge* must derive from God. Thus, experiences and feelings not produced by objective truth from God have no epistemological value at all. This truth was expressed very concisely in a sermon by William C. Hawkins, a highly-esteemed brother and fellow pastor, who said: "Feelings should not mold your theology, but theology should mold your feelings." This truth expresses the central premise of this book very well.

Pagans since early history have been engaged in the quest to know their gods by experience. We should not be surprised that they seek such experiences, but the tragedy is that in more recent history, some Christians have been engaging in a similar quest to experience God illegitimately.

The quest for the subjective experience of God is one aspect of fallen human nature which, like many other sins, does not instantly disappear when we become believers. As long as the Word of God, the Bible, is fully embraced as the final recognized authority for Christian truth and behavior, the subjectivist can neither justify nor legitimately fulfill this subjective urge. Therefore, one goal of this work will be to demonstrate the finality of Scripture and its infallible and unchangeable nature as an objectively authenticated *body of absolute truth* (see final chapter). Thus we must challenge all forms of subjectivism from the Pentecostalism of well-meaning brethren to the hard core existentialism and postmodernism of academia.

God remains jealous of His transcendency and power, and since the close of the canon of Scripture, there has not been, and will not be, any more *direct* revelation from God. The mature Christian recognizes this as true and is fulfilled to walk by faith; but the gullible, being deceived, will follow false leaders happily along seeking to experience God or receive new and exciting divine revelation for themselves.

In today's religious atmosphere, it takes very little for a person to be led away by personal feelings and idiosyncrasies, turning his or her own subjective desires into "truths" for themselves. It is not likely that many, if any, charismatics set out either to deceive themselves or to be deceived, but it happens despite all good intentions: "When regard for truth has been broken down or, even slightly weakened, all things will remain doubtful" (Augustine, "On Lying"). It is perfectly possible to define "lie" so that it is identical with "deception." This is how expressions like "living a lie" can be interpreted. It is best to stay with the primary distinction between deceptive statements – lies – and all the other forms of deceptions.[7] James E. Gunn says that people like to treat truth as a cafeteria and take only what pleases them or mix and match until they have what they want to believe, leaving behind truth and purity to fend for themselves.[8]

SUBJECTIVISM: A HISTORICAL PHENOMENON

Because the quest to subjectively experience God is a characteristic of fallen human nature, we should not be surprised to find that it is a recurring phenomenon in history. Not only does it rise to extremes in some primitive religions and pagan cults, but there are clear and destructive manifestations of it, tempered somewhat by Christian truth, among the churches in history.

We will be able to show by historical examples in subsequent chapters, as well as by Scripture, that the subjectivism that pervades modern evangelicalism is a product of human nature that has not been brought under control of the Word of God. Far from being a manifestation of the Holy Spirit, it is rather a failure for Christians to bring every thought into obedience to Christ.

In this work one issue will stand out above the rest and will be the primary focus: That the Bible is the one body of absolute,

---

[7]Sissela Bok, *Lying or Moral Choice in Public and Private Life*, (Vintage Books, 1979), footnote p. 14.
[8]James E. Gunn, *Kampus*, 1977

unchangeable truth revealed to mankind, by which all claims of personal subjective experiences or direct revelation from God must be tried, and that human subjectivism undermines this vital truth.

We will show that by the early 20th century, as the misguided optimism of the older modernists was beginning to wane, the trend toward subjectivism was already on the rise. At the grass roots it took the form of Pentecostalism and eventually the modern charismatic movement, and in academia it took the form of existentialism and eventually postmodernism. Later, we will discuss more fully how these two categories of subjectivism are related and have fed upon each other. But in the last half of the 20th century, the pendulum began to swing rapidly toward a burgeoning subjectivism.

The status of evangelical Christianity in the late 20th and early 21st centuries shows serious signs of deterioration from many causes. Yet it seems to us that they all point to a lack of regard for the absolute authority of Scripture. Even the traditional orthodoxy concerning the uniqueness of Christ as the only Lord and Savior of mankind is crumbling. Daniel L. Akin wrote:

> Today the Church itself appears on the verge of insanity, having forsaken the exclusive claims of its Christ and the instruction of His Word. We have lost our way and abandoned our moorings. Tragically the deadly virus of modernity has even infected evangelicalism.[9]

Albert Mohler further explains that these evangelical problems:

> ... originated in debates over the formal principle of Scripture, it soon spread to material doctrines, including Christology, the Atonement, justification, and virtually every other major doctrine.[10]

We do not find it at all surprising that these grave divisions originated over "the formal principle of Scripture." An evangelical

---

[9] Daniel L. Akin, "The Never-Changing Christ for an Ever-Changing Culture," *Who Will be Saved*, ed. Paul R. House and Gregory A. Thornbury (Wheaton: Crossway Books, 2000), p. 61.

[10] R. Albert Mohler, Jr., "'Evangelical:' What's in a Name?" *The Coming Evangelical Crisis*, p. 33.

atmosphere where the Scriptures are not the final authority, fosters a growing belief that God also speaks directly to individuals in the "word freshly spoken from heaven."[11] In this environment, it seems inevitable that the very core doctrines of the Christian faith would eventually fall victim to new latitudes both in loose interpretations and in claims of personal revelation.

We do not contend the existing relapse in soundness of the traditional evangelical faith is the immediate and direct result of charismatic doctrine, or vice versa. It does seem obvious, however, that the convergence of two serious factors have fostered a low view of Scripture and its authority. These factors are 1) the quest for subjective experience with claims of personal revelation made by charismatics and others; and 2) existentialism and postmodernism.

In some measure they have worked to usurp the uniqueness of Scripture authority and opened the door for a spate of personal "revelations" and interpretations leaving many with no conviction that Scripture is the unique standard by which to "try" every claim and spirit (1 John 4:1). We must recover the biblical truth concerning the work of God in the revelation and authentication of His infallible and complete canon of truth to man.

---

[11] Jack Deere as cited by: R. Fowler White, "Does God Speak Today Apart from the Bible?" *The Coming Evangelical Crisis*, p. 78.

Lest We be Misunderstood

We know that subjectivism as a concept is a little abstract. And we are naturally concerned that someone may mistake our opposition to human subjectivism, as defined below,[12] as a denial of normative Christian experience, of assurance, intimate fellowship, emotion, and "joy unspeakable" resulting from communion with the Holy Spirit as He imparts God's objective truth from Scripture to the heart of every believer who seeks it. That would be a serious distortion of our intent.

Yet, Christians know God by faith, not by sight, sense, or direct experience. In our interface with God through faith our feelings and emotions, while realized internally, all have an external, objective cause: God's Spirit working in conjunction with His objective revelation. Only this validates our experiences.

God created us with both intellect and emotion. Intellect apprehends God's revealed truth, and only that truth applied by the Holy Spirit creates a valid emotional response or experience. Emotion moves; and intellect directs. Motivation without direction is dangerous, but direction without motivation is dead. Only as intellect is informed by revelation is it safe to move.

The authors of this book reject completely the image that Christianity is cold intellectualism. But we do insist that all valid emotions, feelings, and subjective experiences must arise as a result of God's objective revelation: either from creation (Psa. 19:1-3) or Scripture (Rom. 10:17). Subjective experiences must pass the test of Scripture; otherwise they have no validity at all and often sow serious error and discord among brethren.

The issue raised in this book is that millions of Christians are illegitimately seeking subjective feelings and experiences, not based on objective Scripture truth, and proclaiming them as truth. But no truth can arise within man that does not derive from objective revelation authenticated by God Himself.

---

[12] Subjective: "Of, affected by, or produced by the mind or a particular state of mind; of or resulting from the feelings or temperament of the subject, or person thinking, rather than the attributes of the object thought of; as, a subjective judgment." Subjectivism: "Any philosophic theory of knowledge that gives great importance to the subjective or a priori elements of conscious experience." – *Webster's New Universal Unabridged Dictionary*, 2nd Edition.

II.
Historical Background:
The Human Quest to
Experience God

The human passion to know God directly through personal experience, i.e., direct revelation from God, ecstatic utterances, to perform or receive miraculous wonders on a routine basis, or other sensory phenomena whether ancient or contemporary, is a characteristic of fallen human nature – not a normal biblical distinctive of the Christian faith. The validity of this statement will, in this chapter, be made abundantly clear by a look at the historical record. It will become clear also that Christians are not instantly immune to this sinful quest any more

11

than we are immune to any other sin, but this, and every sin, is to be corrected by an accurate understanding of Scripture and faithful obedience to it.

BIBLICAL BACKGROUND

The connection between the sin in Eden and the human quest for knowledge through direct personal experience is evident in the nature of the original sin. As we rethink this familiar passage, the true essence of Eve's sin, which was fundamentally insubordination, reflects features which are universally observed in fallen humanity. One of those features is the desire for a peer relationship with God.

Eve

Although God had enlightened Eve (through Adam) of the consequences of partaking of the fruit, she was not satisfied to know the effect of good and evil merely as an abstract principle, as God had taught them by words. She wanted the knowledge *experientially*. Not satisfied with her position as a subordinate; she wanted to be God's peer.

Satan led Eve to feel that she was right in doing as she did, but she was deceived. "God knows," Satan told her, "that in the day you eat of it your eyes will be opened, and you will be like God, knowing good and evil" (Gen.3:5, NKJV). Then Eve mused, the tree was "good for food" and "pleasant to the eyes," but that was rationalization. The real incentive was that the fruit was "desirable to make one wise," to put her, more or less, on a peer basis with God. Then they could talk things over person to person in an intimate way. But the fundamental sin was insubordination.

The Felt Need. Desire is a powerful emotion. According to *Strong's Concordance*, one translation for desire (as in Gen. 3:6) is "to covet," i.e., longing for that which belongs to another. Satan's suggestion had stirred dissatisfaction within Eve. Was God withholding wisdom and position from her? Was she inherently inferior to God? Could she somehow gain at least parity with God, if not superiority? There had to be some illicit desire to be more than a subordinate being, wholly dependent upon God's Word for knowledge. Thus she subordinated the authority of God's Word to her desire – the "felt need" to be like God.

On the surface, today, it sounds very spiritual and righteous to speak of one's hunger to "experience" God; but on second thought, maybe not. After the sin in Eden, God chose to put distance between Himself and humanity. We would know God only by faith, and reach Him through a High Priest, a Mediator: "For there is one God and *one Mediator between God and men,* [13] the Man Christ Jesus" (1 Tim. 2:5).

Faith: A New Norm. Thus any attempt to converse with God directly through immediate experience, through ecstatic language, or to bypass indirect revelation or the Bible to gain direct revelation from Him, or to escape from our dependency upon mediation during our temporary earth-bound sojourn, is a sinful attempt to circumvent the deliberate separation God established in Eden. It is an attempted contravention of God's choice of sensory separation. It is an attitude that God's perfect written revelation is not quite sufficient. No matter that He spoke to Moses "face to face"; that was His sovereign prerogative which He exercised in the process of bringing an objective, written revelation to mankind. The norm for mankind is that God chose sensory separation and mediation for the duration of our earth-bound sojourn. The subordinate saint is content to walk by faith, not by sight, or sound, or sense.

Cain and Abel as Prototypical

Many of the offspring of Adam and Eve, beginning with Cain, attempt to interface with God on a peer basis. Cain felt that he should be free to decide, and that God should be willing to accept his sacrifice despite God's former revelation. But God had no "respect" or "regard" for the fruit offering.

Abel, on the other hand, acknowledging his dependency on the mediatorial sacrifice of a substitutionary life, offered a lamb typifying the "seed" promised to Eve (Gen. 3:15). God regarded Abel's sacrifice, and in so doing He must also have reflected His satisfaction in the covering He had previously made for Adam

---

[13] Throughout this book, italics will often be added in Scripture quotations for emphasis or to highlight specific issues for further discussion.

and Eve in the Garden. After they had sinned and were in need of a Savior, He "clothed them," covering their sin and their shame after the shedding of the blood of an animal. We need not belabor what is now commonly known that these early symbols foreshadowed the mediatorial work of Christ:

> And for this reason *He is the Mediator of the new covenant, by means of death,* for the redemption of the transgressions under the first covenant, that those who are called may receive the promise of the eternal inheritance (Heb. 9:15).

Moreover, the Scripture says, *"... without the shedding of blood there is no remission"* (Heb. 9:21). He covered their shame, which their emotional desires had uncovered, by a mediator, and so will it ever be with all mankind in our earthbound condition. We will have no peer relationship with God, ever. Furthermore, until the time God is ready to "glorify" the believer, there will be no direct sensory experiential interface with God of the order that existed prior to the entrance of sin into the human race.

The Heart after Eden

When Scripture speaks symbolically of the heart of man, it is commonly understood as the seat of his emotions, his innermost being. As such, the heart or emotion is no reliable guide in righteousness. The Bible tells us that the unregenerate heart is the seat of all kinds of sin and covetousness. Jeremiah is very blunt: "The heart is deceitful above all things, and desperately wicked: who can know it?" (17:9). In Peter's second epistle we read, "Having eyes full of adultery, and that cannot cease from sin; beguiling unstable souls: an heart they have exercised with covetous practices; cursed children" (2 Peter 2:14). And Jesus said, "For out of the heart proceed evil thoughts, murders, adulteries, fornications, thefts, false witness, blasphemies" (Matt. 15:19).

As the heart is, so is the man: "For as he thinketh in his heart, so is he ..." (Pro. 23:7). "For out of the abundance of the heart the mouth speaks" (Matt. 12:34, NKJV). "Take heed, brethren, lest there be in any of you an evil heart of unbelief, in departing from the living God." (Heb. 3:12).

It is clear from these words that the heart, or emotion, is not trustworthy, but the natural man loves to live in his fallen emotions. He desires it; he reaches out for that unreachable star, the fulfillment of his emotions to be god-like just as the great deceiver: "I will ascend into heaven, I will exalt my throne above the stars of God" (Isa. 14:13).

A New Heart

Some will defend the modern charismatic practice on the grounds that the Christian has a new heart and may thus receive direct revelation or have direct experiential interface with God. The Scriptures do indeed teach that the heart is changed in regeneration. This has been a normative work of the Holy Spirit since the first sinner cried out for mercy – long before the baptism of the Holy Spirit was instituted:

> I will give you *a new heart and put a new spirit within you;* I will take the heart of stone out of your flesh and give you a heart of flesh. I will put My Spirit within you and *cause you to walk in My statutes, and you will keep My judgments and do them* (Ezk. 36:26, 27, NKJV).

Regeneration has long been the normal work of the Holy Spirit wherein He prepares the heart to receive His "statues" and "judgments" and to "do them" (More on that later). Jesus chided Nicodemus for not knowing this truth (John 3:10). God made this ancient truth to be the core principle of the New Covenant after the failure of the Mosaic Covenant based strictly on law-keeping. In Hebrews we read: "I will put My laws into their hearts, and in their minds I will write them" (10:16, NKJV).

The Word in a Regenerate Heart. The issue relevant to this discussion is: How does God put His laws into the regenerate heart? Does He do it instantaneously, directly, and completely? Does He "zap" the full knowledge of His commandments into every regenerate heart at the moment of regeneration so that we suddenly know the complete will of God? Does He do it by a "second work of Grace" giving direct revelation so that we may be sinlessly perfect? Should we ever expect to receive direct knowledge in the form of unintelligible language, or "unknown tongues"? Does

God speak personally or audibly as He did to Adam before sin entered the world, or to Moses afterward? Can every person claim to be "moved by the Holy Ghost" and authenticated by "signs and wonders" as were the unique writers of Scripture?

These are, of course, elementary questions to any nominal student of Scripture, and the answer to all of them is no. Even the changed, regenerate heart must be *trained by Scripture truth:*

> ... as newborn babes, *desire the sincere milk of the word*, that you may grow thereby ... (1 Pet. 2:2).

> For every one that useth milk is unskilful in the word of righteousness: for he is a babe. But strong meat belongeth to them that are of full age, even *those who by reason of use have their senses exercised to discern both good and evil* (Heb. 5:13-14).

> Study to show thyself approved unto God, a workman that needeth not to be ashamed, rightly dividing the word of truth (2 Tim. 2:15).

The heart of man, though made receptive to truth by regeneration, must still receive the knowledge of God's truth indirectly; he must still be shaped and molded by the objective Word of Scripture. "Now the purpose of the commandment is love from a pure heart, from a good conscience, and from sincere faith ..." (1 Tim. 1:5, NKJV). The normal Christian life is not to walk by sight or sensory experience, but the "just shall live by faith." There are no shortcuts.

Faith by the Word – Romans 10:17. Jesus responded readily to those who sought Him by faith but was very displeased with those who insisted on a more direct knowledge, such as signs and wonders or spectacular miracles:

> Then certain of the scribes and of the Pharisees answered, saying, Master, we would see a sign from thee. But he answered and said unto them, An evil and adulterous generation seeketh after a sign; and there shall no sign be given to it, but the sign of the prophet Jonas (Matt. 12:38-39).

"Now faith is the substance of things hoped for, the evidence of things not seen" (Heb. 11:1). Since God removed Himself from the presence of sinful man, deliberately making Himself *unseen*, we are shut up, not to direct experience of God, His glory and power, but to *faith*. "Behold the proud, His soul is not upright in him; But *the just shall live by his faith*" (Hab. 2:4, NKJV). This is the dominant and all-pervasive message of Scripture to earth-bound humanity. We must live by *faith* because God has removed Himself from our *sight*.

To live by faith requires that we observe and process evidence which was given to us indirectly by biblical revelation through a very few chosen individual writers. "So then *faith cometh by hearing and hearing, by the Word of God*" (Rom. 10:17). Therefore any attempt to short-circuit the process and attempt to gain the knowledge of the truth or to experience God by direct means is an affront to God: *"for whatsoever is not of faith is sin"* (Rom. 14:23).

Thus, the nature of Adam is still with us and must be brought under control by the life-long process of personal sanctification by the Word. There is still a proneness to seek out those things that please the emotions – that bring direct experiential gratification. We are often tempted and do trip and stumble from time to time. But today we have the words of Scripture, the truth of our Lord and Savior, and the empowerment of the Holy Spirit as Comforter, to lift us up again and set us back on the path of faith; thus we grow. Many regenerate people, however, dissatisfied with the less spectacular walk of faith, having been misled, still seek a direct experiential relationship with God before His time – before they are glorified. That dissatisfaction leads to sinful excesses.

PAGAN BACKGROUND

The identifying marks of non-biblical charismatic phenomena were evident in the historical background of the pagan and unbelieving world long before they appeared among Christians. Bear in mind that *subjectivist phenomena*, as used in this book, would include a wide range of activities and thought such as states of frenzy and ecstasy, ecstatic trances or "slaying in the spirit," mysticism, pietism, subjectivism, Gnostic traits, Pentecostalism, sinless perfectionism, ecstatic and unintelligible tongues, modern charismatics, pursuit of signs and wonders or sensationalist "miracles," and other religious phenomena such as dancing, spinning, the jerks, barks, and the like. The most extreme of these activities are most common to the pagan world and fringe Christian cults.

We readily acknowledge that no Christians known to us who identify themselves with any of the charismatic movements approve or practice *all* of these phenomena. Nevertheless many, if not all, of these activities have been observed among modern charismatics, and we believe it will become apparent in the pages ahead that they all stem from the same root sin: the fallen human quest or desire to know God by direct experience in contradistinction to knowing Him by a godly walk of faith which comes by hearing the Word of God (Rom. 10:17), the Scriptures, and maturing in them.

History is replete with mystics and "miracle workers" outside God's covenant people. Remember, for example, the magicians in Egypt who were able to reproduce several of the miracles that were done by Moses and Aaron. Recall also the "familiar spirit" of Endor, who brought Samuel up at Saul's request, and the frenzied antics and self mutilation of the prophets of Baal on Mount Carmel. Prophets and soothsayers have been known in all civilizations and to most religions as mankind has constantly, in every place and time, been trying to become "as gods"– to have the God-experience apart from faith.

Ancient Pagan Examples

We turn now to review a few historical examples of ecstatic activities, feelings, and tongues found to exist in ancient times, civilizations, religions, and philosophies. As previously discussed the fallen human heart will always seek to know right and wrong subjectively, from within, by the emotions or feelings. Mankind seeks out experiences so that he can feel, following after those who can produce exalted experiences for him. Human nature wants feeling, not faith. David W. Kling, a professor in the religious studies department at the University of Miami wrote:

> ... throughout the ancient world, possession by a divine spirit (pneuma) was a common occurrence among the many sects and cults, mystery and

Gnostic religions of the Roman Empire.[14]

Tongues, "miracles," and good feelings have been the stock-in-trade of various religions since the Eden event. With the fall of mankind in Eden came an almost insatiable taste for experience, feelings, and emotions ranging from mild subjective mind exercises to the frenzied gyrations of the savage.

Amon-Re, King of the Gods. An example of pagan religious subjectivism illustrating some of the features of today's charismata is found in an actual account of an Egyptian called Wenamon.[15] The account is an official document detailing the difficulties experienced by Wenamon on a voyage from Egypt to Byblos in Phoenicia for the purpose of obtaining pine "for the great and noble riverine barge of Amon-Re, King of the Gods." The account takes place toward the end of the New Kingdom Dynasties c. 1100 B. C. Originally a local god of the Egyptians, Amon was later identified with the sun god Ra and was known as Amon-Ra or Amon-Re, and was counted among the chief gods of Egypt.

The part of the account which is relevant to our purpose here involves a dispute between Wenamon and the prince of Byblos about the authenticity of Wenamon's identity as an official representative of Amon-Re. They would settle this dispute by an appeal to the gods.

Now when the prince offered to his god, "the god took possession of" one of his pages and "caused him to be ecstatic." He is said to have entered into a frenzied state and continuing in that state through a whole night. He is said to have gone through violent agitation and to have fallen into frantic and unknown speech.

The result was that the ecstatic page was able to "bring the god up" and verify: "It is Amon who dispatched [Wenamon]. It is he which caused him to come."[16] So the issue was settled in favor of Wenamon.

---

[14] David W. Kling, *The Bible in History* (Oxford: Oxford University Press, 2004), p. 234.

[15] R. O. Faulkner, et al., Tr., "The Report of Wenamon," *The Literature of Ancient Egypt* (New Haven: Yale University Press, 1973), pp. 142-155.

[16] "Wenamon," p. 146.

It is apparent from the account that the parties involved were true believers; they were deadly serious about the revelation from the ecstatic page. But as Christians, three thousand years later, we know there are mountains of objective evidence that the gods involved had 1) no actual existence, 2) no control over the frenzied activity and speech, and 3) conveyed no revelation.

Interpreting the Experience. Now, here we have an opportunity to examine the validity of these and other subjectivist experiences of this kind as phenomena which might confirm the authenticity of a worshipper's claim that his or her experience is due to the influence of a god or of God. It is self-evident at this point in time that the god or gods involved in this case had no actual existence, therefore they could not have been the source of either the tongues or the ecstatic spell or the revelation received during the spell.

The experience, however, was very real to the worshipper; onlookers also could verify the reality of the activity, even as the current charismatic experiences are also real experiences to them. That we do not deny. The issue with the claims of modern charismata is not the reality of the experiences; the issue is with the *interpretation* of the experiences. What do the experiences *mean*?

The Byblos worshipper, and apparently the onlookers, interpreted the experience as having been the result of the influence of a god upon his worshipper, thus establishing proof of the reality and deity of Amon and the credibility and claims of his worshiper and of Wenamon's credentials as a representative of Amon-Re. But the experience, though real enough, offers no such proof. The tongues and impulsive physical behavior must, in this case, be explained by other causes since the gods had no existence. Therefore, modern ecstatics, frenzied activities, falling into a trance-like state "slain in the spirit," or unintelligible speech – all subjective human reactions – likewise can offer no proof of divine influence or any honor to God. God, who is never the author of confusion, would not use such devices, obviously because they would attest nothing of value.

There are a number of very feasible interpretations of these experiences other than the influence of a god:

1. This illustration demonstrates that such phenomena can originate subjectively, wholly within the psyche of an individual, and produce the physical and visual results witnessed by observers. The individual can be *self-deceived by his own psyche*, and fully believe that his experience is caused by a direct interface with his god or with God. He argues that he knows: *"I experienced it; I know."*

2. Apart from Scripture truth, an observer can no more prove a worshipper wrong than he can prove himself right. Any claim of knowing or validating his god or his experience by this means is completely groundless and has no epistemological value. Nay, it is worse than useless; it is a reproach, whether claimed by a pagan or a Christian.

3. Subjective experience as epistemology is sterile. In this fact existentialism and modern charismata share a common principle. Such experiences and activities, born subjectively from within, prove nothing except that the God of the Bible is not the author and that the worshipper is deluded.

4. Such phenomena can also originate as the result of satanic influence or fallen demons. This is very likely in pagan religions, and probably occurs in some cases among professing Christians. And again, the experience in itself proves nothing except that the God of the Bible is not the influence behind it.

5. Then, rarely, such phenomena can also be faked. Some individuals may have the motive and ability to so convincingly act out such phenomena that an observer cannot distinguish it from one of the above causes.

Such pagan activities establish the fact that a worship experience, though very real to the individual and to the sympathetic onlookers, proves nothing to the worshipper himself and even less to observers. Neither should it impress another person to whom the worshipper may bear "witness" of the reality of his god, or God; "will they not say that ye are mad?" (1 Cor. 14:23).

Such experiences are not rare among pagan religions, as we might expect, for we should remember that the word frenzy comes ultimately from the Greek phrenitis, which means "madness, inflammation of the brain." Such phenomena are deceitful, useless, and dangerous; and, when ascribed to the Holy Spirit's influence, "who does all things decently and in order," they grievously dishonor His name.

Ancient Greek Examples

In Plato's dialogues he mentions several instances of religious ecstasy.

Phaedrus. One passage, from which we are able to gain valuable insight into the nature of religious experiences, is in Plato's Phaedrus. The passage is found within a discourse by Socrates concerning pagan rituals at Delphi and Dodona:

> ... but in reality the greatest of blessings come to us through madness, *when it is sent as a gift of the gods* [emphasis added]. For the prophetess at Delphi and the priestesses at Dodona when they have been mad have conferred many splendid benefits upon Greece both in private and in public affairs, but few or none when they have been in their right minds.[17]

The "madness" referred to here is very akin to many of the ancient pagan rituals that take the form of ecstatic frenzy. Socrates, in defense of the high value of this "gift" of madness in his discourse in Phaedrus, points to the name *prophet or prophetess*, saying:

> ... if they [the inventors of names] had thought madness a disgrace or dishonor, [they] would never have called prophecy, which is the noblest of arts, by the very same name (μαντικὴ, μανικὴ) as madness, thus inseparably connecting them; but they must have thought that there was an inspired madness which was no disgrace....[18]

---

[17] Plato, "Phaedrus," Rapheal Demos, ed., *Plato Selections* (New York: Charles Scribner's Sons, 1927), p. 465.

[18] Plato, "Phaedrus," B. Jowett, Tr., *The Works of Plato* (New York: The Dial Press, n.d.), p. 401.

Now, a remarkable comparison from Socrates' argument in defense of ecstatic madness may be made with certain observed contemporary charismatic characteristics:

Delphic Priestesses	**Historic "Charismata"**
1. Ecstatic, frenzied activities and speech were observed.	1. Ecstatic, frenzied activities and speech are observed.
2. This condition was regarded by true believers as a "gift" from the pagan Greek gods.	2. This condition is regarded by true believers as a "gift" from the Holy Spirit.
3. Messages from a Delphic priestess were regarded as the word of Apollo.	3. Messages from contemporary charismatic tongues or prophecy are regarded as the word of God.
4. Such psychic phenomena cannot be objectively authenticated and have no epistemological value.	4. Such psychic phenomena cannot be objectively authenticated and have no epistemological value.

We hasten to acknowledge that not all historic or contemporary charismatic claims would fit perfectly within this chart, but the comparison should give any Christian a reason to seriously examine the main premise of this book, that the human propensity for such religious experience is characteristic of fallen human nature, not biblical Christian truth.

That the psychic condition of these Greek worshippers 1) had much in common with what has been commonly observed among various charismatics in recent history is hardly debatable. And it is obvious from the words of Socrates, through Plato, that he regarded their state as a "gift" from the pagan Greek gods; and though it was a form of madness, he considered it was a good thing and beneficial to the whole nation. Moreover, according to Socrates, μαντικὴ or μανικὴ has the same meaning as *madness* which is also what they called their prophets.

In view of this, Paul's warning in 1 Corinthians 14:23, "will they not say that *ye are mad* [μαίνεσθε, (μαίνομαι)]?" is too remarkable to pass over. Was Paul's use of *"madness"* a deliberate allusion to the practices of the Greek prophets? The word used by Paul is but a different form of Socrates' word, but its basic meaning is insanity, to rave as a maniac, or madness (μανία) – the word from which we derive our words *maniac* or *mania*.

In light of this, Paul's statement may lend credence to John MacArthur's suggestion that the Corinthian tongues problem was that Greek "pagan activity kept creeping"[19] into the Corinthian church.

Delphi (the site of the Oracle of Apollo; words from a certain Delphic priestess were once regarded as the words of Apollo[20]) was a town on the north side of the Gulf of Corinth, less than fifty miles, as the crow flies, from the city of Corinth on the south.[21] Thus Corinth, and for that matter the whole of Greece, would still be heavily influenced by such religious practices when Paul wrote to the Corinthians less than four centuries after Plato's *Dialogues*, and surely Paul was well acquainted with these pagan religions as he was with Epicurean and Stoic philosophers and certain other Greek poets (see Acts 17:18, 28). So when Paul warned the Corinthians that people would say they were "mad," did they understand the statement as if he were saying: "They will say you are under the 'madness' of a pagan god"? It seems likely. And yet there is evidence that it was not the main problem in Corinth, which we will discuss in chapter V.

But Socrates continues, in the same discourse, to laud the qualities and values of this divine "gift" of madness:

> ... madness, lifting up her voice and flying to prayers and rites, has come to the rescue of those who are in need; and he who has part in this gift, and is truly possessed and duly out of his mind, is by the use of purifications and mysteries made whole and delivered from evil, future as well as present, and has a release from the calamity which afflicts him. There is also a third kind of madness, which is a possession of the Muses; this

---

[19] John F. MacArthur, Jr., *The Charismatics* (Grand Rapids: Zondervan Publishing House, 1978), p. 109.

[20] *Infopedia*, a Funk and Wagnalls multimedia encyclopedia, 1996.

[21] *Hammond Atlas of World History* (Maplewood, NJ, Hammond Incorporated, 1976), p. H-4.

enters into a delicate and virgin soul, and there inspiring frenzy, awakens lyric and all other numbers.… But he who, not being inspired and having no touch of madness in his soul, comes to the door [of the] temple … is not admitted; the sane man is nowhere at all when he enters into rivalry with the madman.[22]

So how different is that from certain charismatic claims of healing or sinless perfectionism, that through special works or miracles of the Holy Spirit they or others are "made whole and delivered from evil … and [have] a release from the calamity which afflicts him"? Neither Jesus nor the Apostles exhibited any of the symptoms of tongues, ecstatic trances, or frenzied activity to accomplish their mighty wonders or quiet miracles. Ecstatic tongues, hysteria, trances, or manias are wholly foreign to the Christian faith. But fallen human nature seeks them.

Ion. Another example is in Plato's *Ion* where he says good poets write by *possession*, that gods speak through diviners and prophets by *ecstatic speech*, and sometimes even when they are unconscious.

> … The Muse first of all inspires men herself … For all good poets, epic as well as lyric, compose their beautiful poems not by art but because they are inspired and *possessed.* And as the Corybantian revelers when they dance *are not in their right mind*, so the lyric poets are not in their right mind when they are composing their beautiful strains; but when falling under the power of music and metre they are *inspired* and *possessed*; like the Bacchic maidens … when they are under the influence of Dionysus, *but not when they are in their right mind* [emphases added]. [23]

This, Plato says, was an ordinary happening among the maidens of the Bacchic cult (Bacchus, the god of wine). And again, these supposed they were under the influence of a god; but we know they were not, since pagan gods have no actual existence. That means that the "influence" they felt was something else: either *subjective self-deceit, i.e., a self-inflicted psychic experience worked up from within*, or possibly drugs, or in some cases doubtless it was demon possession. An "experience" is not always what it seems.

---

[22] Plato, "Phaedrus," *Works*, p. 402.

[23] Plato, "Ion," *Selections*, pp. 238-40.

Euripides. The best description of the Bacchic revels is in Euripides' *The Bacchae*. We will not bring out the worst of this base work. But the following will be sufficient to show the antique and pagan character of the quest for "divine" experience:

> This god's a prophet, too, for in his rites – the Bacchic celebrations and the madness – a huge prophetic power is unleashed. When the god fully enters human bodies, he makes those possessed by frenzy prophets. They speak of what will come in future days.[24]

The quest which continues even today in the name of the Holy Spirit is not only similar to these pagan activities, but also similar to the Greek "theology": A god empowers a human to *exhibit unusual behavior* and *speak prophecies*. We must, however, acknowledge a difference in the degree of frenzy and debauchery. We have never witnessed among Christian charismatics the extremes that are described in *The Bacchae*, and yet some of the frenzy of the followers of Mother Ann of the Shakers (some of whom are said to have danced naked, see below), and other isolated cases, were not so different even in the extremes. *The Bacchae*, being pagan, reveals the worst in human nature; the reckless abandon to psychic (or demonic) spells looses the baser nature of the subject so that they do sub-human things.

In *The Bacchae* we have this statement: "You were made mad, and the whole land was possessed by Bacchic frenzy."[25] It is not far-fetched to suggest that some charismatic meetings we have witnessed must have resembled the revels of some of the Greek hysterics, trances, and frenzies. In the same play, the chorus is called "the maenads,"[26] which, the translator tells us, is literally "maddened women."[27] If we watch carefully on certain television broadcasts, we will eventually see a few "maenads."

Virgil. In Virgil's *Aeneid*, the Sibylline priestess of Delos

---

[24] Euripides, *The Bacchae*, Ian Johnston, Tr., (http://www.mala.bc.ca- /~johnstoi/-euripides/euripides.htm).

[25] Euripides, *The Bacchae*, Geoffrey S. Kirk, tr. (Englewood Cliffs, N.J., Prentice-Hall, Inc., 1970), p. 129.

[26] Ibid.

[27] Ibid.

prophesied by ecstatic speech. It is said that she would begin to speak in tongues, and that sometimes they could be understood and sometimes they were unknown.[28]

The Pythoness, or priestess, of Delphi (who spoke the word of Apollo) is described by the early church father Chrysostom as follows:

> … and she with disheveled hair begins to play the bacchanal and to foam at the mouth, and thus begin in a frenzy to utter the words of her madness.[29]

This quote from Chrysostom's *Homilies on First Corinthians,* uses the word *madness* which is consistent with Paul's statement (1 Cor. 14:23) as well as with Plato (above) and is another possible translation for the Greek word for *frenzy*.[30]

These few examples are sufficient to demonstrate that there is a predisposition in fallen human nature to seek a sensory experience with what one believes is deity. The inclination toward this sin, we will show below, does not necessarily disappear when one becomes a Christian, but it should be "put off" through obedience to the Scripture, just as any other sin.

Other Miscellaneous Observations

There are many reports in the old mystery religions of the past which are echoed in pagan religions of today. In Voodoo, a blend of tribal African religions with elements of Roman Catholicism, through the ceremonies of dancing, drumming, etc., the priest or priestess is possessed by a "god"; and in an ecstatic frenzy, hysteria, or trance are presumed to heal or give advice, etc.

In certain religions of the Eskimos are traditions of drumming, dancing, and nudity, all of which result in frenzied speech, unintelligible language, and "miracles" so called.

It seems that speaking in unintelligible tongues is frequently associated with frenzy or hysteria, sickness, or "madness." Mr. V. Raymond Edman of Wheaton College gave an account of such

---

[28] Virgil, *Aeneid.*

[29] Chrysostom, *Homolies on First Corinthians.* In the Ethereal Library at Calvin College. Available on www.ccel.org (2006).

[30] Euripides. *The Bacchae.* Geoffrey, tr., "Introduction."

things in Tibet and China. Born to missionary parents who lived on the Tibetan border, he told of hearing the rituals of Tibetan Buddhist monks dancing and speaking in languages of which they normally had no knowledge, such as English, even speaking quotations from Shakespeare. Sometimes their utterances were in the profanity of drunken sailors, sometimes German, French, or other tongues typically unknown to them. Other reports, from missionaries of no less credibility than those of the China Inland Mission, told of witnessing the same sorts of experiences.

We can only conclude that such pagan activities are worked up subjectively from the psyche of the worshipper; or if they actually speak other languages unknown to them, we see no other explanation but that they are under the influence of demons, clear examples of human forgeries of the signature of God.

Nothing resembling any of these cases cited above has any place in biblical Christianity.

Christian Background

We turn now to the Christian era to see if we find any examples resembling these pagan phenomena among Christians. We would not expect to find even a trace of such excesses among Christians. There are at least two major things within the Christian faith that should restrain the excesses observed within pagan religions. *First*, central to every authentic Christian movement is God's work of regeneration, and *second*, Christians have the Scripture.

These two things should wholly eliminate any trace of such phenomena among Christians, but unfortunately that is not the case. However, we would expect them, at least, to have a mitigating influence among Christians.

Nevertheless, one does not go far in research before it becomes obvious that many Christians also have been affected by the same quest for personal experience that we often find in pagan religions. Many still believe in, follow, and almost deify, self-styled prophets, tongue-speakers, and so called miracle workers even as non-Christian religions.

The Ante-Nicene Period (100 - 325)

One might suppose that the authentic Christian faith would instantaneously immunize the believer against the characteristics of fallen human nature. But that requires three things: the indwelling Holy Spirit in *regeneration*, Scripture *truth*, and *time*. To rid ourselves of the practice of the sins of the "old man" requires diligent study and growth in the Word. But for whatever reason, not everyone immediately grows in every area of Scripture truth, and that fact is reflected throughout history.

Gnosticism. One of the heresies that crept into some of the early churches with features of subjectivism is *Gnosticism*. In his book, *In the Face of God*, Michael Horton calls our attention to the "'gnosticization' of American religion"[31] and writes, quoting Wade Clark Roof:

> This new Gnosticism "celebrates experience rather than doctrine; the personal rather than institutional; the mythic and dreamlike over the cognitive; people's religion over official religion; soft, caring images of deity over hard, impersonal images; and the feminine and androgynous over the masculine"[32]

Though it would not be accurate to equate any modern movement with the Gnosticism of the second century, it is clear that there were some features common to several current trends. The evangelical movement today reflects a subjectivism toward the historic doctrines of Scripture that is Gnostic in nature. Horton also points out, "Pentecostalism represents an even greater dependency on gnostic tendencies."[33] It is not difficult to see that the above quotation identifies some features of the old Gnosticism that plagued the early church. Its tenets lacked objectivity; and though "Gnostics claimed to be in possession of the true Christianity,"[34] their system was based upon mystical experience and speculation drawn subjectively out of themselves. Shedd referred to Gnosticism as:

---

[31] Michael Horton, *In the Face of God* (Dallas: Word Publishing, 1996), p. 28.

[32] Horton, p. 29.

[33] Ibid.

[34] William G.T. Shedd, *A History of Christian Doctrine* (New York: Charles Scribner's Sons, 1897), Vol. 1, p. 115.

> ... that amorphous system of speculation which sprang up in the second and third centuries, with an ingenuity of speculation, and a perverse perseverance of mental power, never excelled in the history of human errours [sic].[35]

Montanism. Eusebius tells us that Montanus (126-180) prophesied, did miracles, and claimed to be the only man living who could speak for the Holy Spirit. He says that some of the Phrygians pretended that "Montanus was the Paraclete."[36] Eusebius describes Montanus' behavior as follows:

> "... he became possessed of a spirit, and suddenly began to rave in a kind of ecstatic trance, and to babble in a jargon, prophesying in a manner contrary to the custom of the church which had been handed down by tradition from the earliest times.... others were carried away and not a little elated, thinking themselves possessed of the Holy Spirit and of the gift of prophecy.[37]

Two things, at least, among the Montanists bear a close similarity to the charismatic movement of today: 1) unintelligible tongues, and 2) the prominence of women "prophetesses." But the thing in the above quote that is most informative to the issue of modern charismata, is its novelty in mid-Second century. The "charisma" of Montanus and others in his church was *contrary to the former tradition of the churches* since the "earliest times."

Since Montanus died in A.D. 180, this phenomenon arose earlier near the middle of the second century. This is easily within the life time of some who could remember the character of the apostolic churches. If therefore, as both Montanism and modern charismatics claim, "unknown tongues," or unintelligible speech, was a biblical Christian norm common to the churches of the first century, it could not have been looked upon so early as a new innovation. It was seen and treated as an aberration in the second

---

[35] Shedd, p. 114, 115

[36] Rev. S. Luchow, "Montanus: Spiritual Father of Charismatic Extremism." Available on Internet under Montanus: Early Church Fathers.

[37] As quoted by Henry Bettenson, *Documents of the Christian Church* (New York: Oxford University Press, 1943), p. 108. For Eusebius' full account of the Montanus controversy see Christian Frederick Cruse, Tr., *The Ecclesiastical History of Eusebius Pamphilus* (Grand Rapids: Baker Book House, 1955), pp. 195-199.

century, similar to or more extreme than the abuse Paul had re-
buked in the Corinthian church (1 Cor. 14). As we shall later see,
the only legitimate use of "tongues" in the apostolic churches was
the miraculous gift of communication in an ethnic language by a
person who had not learned the language – as at Pentecost (Acts
2) and on a few other occasions.

Moreover, the public prominence of at least two notable
women claiming to be prophetesses in the Montanist church, performing a type of public teaching ministry, is a clear violation of
the apostolic teaching relative to the ministry of women (1 Tim.
2:11, 12; 1 Cor. 14:34, 35).

Hippolytus, in *Refutatio omnium haeresium* (viii. 19), wrote:

> [The Montanists] have been deceived by two females, Priscilla and
> Maximilla by name, whom they hold to be prophetesses, asserting that
> into them the Paraclete spirit entered.... They magnify these females
> above the Apostles ...[38]

The public preaching ministry of women is clearly characteristic of the modern charismatic movement as anyone may verify
for themselves by simply surfing the cable channels at almost any
hour day or night. But to the early or mid-second century church,
such activity was a departure from apostolic Christianity, and so
it is today.

Aside from their charismatic doctrines and practices, the
Montanists, like many charismatics today, were orthodox in
other Christian beliefs, perhaps in some ways more biblically
sound than the developing Catholic[39] party. Hippolytus admits
that the Montanists "also acknowledge all that the Gospels tes-
tify of Christ." Tertullian (c. 160-220), a bishop of the church
in Carthage, in later life left the Catholic party and aligned himself with the Montanists. By his voluminous writings, however,
Tertullian proves himself to be generally orthodox in doctrine.

---

[38] Bettenson, p. 108-9.

[39] We must bear in mind that in the second and early third century, the descrip-
tive term *catholic* was not what later developed under that name. Though
doctrinal abuses were emerging, at that time the Catholic wing of a developing rift had not yet become integrated with the Roman state; and there was as
yet no papacy.

And yet Tertullian, by his own statement, claimed the gift of prophecy:

> For seeing that we acknowledge spiritual *charismata*, or gifts, we too have merited the attainment of the prophetic gift....[40]

This statement was written c. 210 after Tertullian became a Montanist saying, in effect, that since the church of his day recognized the spiritual gifts spoken of in the Scripture, that he had merited or deserved the attainment of being a prophet, whatever that meant.[41]

There is no question that the charismatic doctrine and practices were real and problematic among the Montanists, but the mere use of the word *prophet*[42] need not imply that Tertullian claimed for himself the supernatural gift to receive direct revelation from God, as claimed by some charismatic prophets today. But what Tertullian wrote about other Montanist activity suggests otherwise. He continued:

> We have now amongst us a sister whose lot has been to be favored with sundry gifts of revelation, which she experiences in the Spirit by ecstatic vision amidst the sacred rites of the Lord's Day in the church; she converses with angels, and sometimes even with the Lord ... at the conclusion of the sacred services, she is in the regular habit of reporting to us whatever things she may have seen.... "Amongst other things," says she, "there has been shown to me a soul in bodily shape ... such as would offer itself to be even grasped by the hand, soft and transparent and of an ethereal colour, and in form resembling that of a human being in every respect." This was her vision, and for her witness there was God; and the apostle most assuredly foretold [here a reference of 1 Cor. XII:1-11 was apparently inserted by Kidd] that there were to be spiritual gifts in the Church.[43]

---

[40] B. J. Kidd, ed., *Documents Illustrative of the History of the Christian Church* (New York: The Macmillan Company, 1933), p. 151.

[41] WWW.EarlyChurchFathers. A collection of works from several sources. *Fathers to AC 325*. Phillip Schaff, ed. Vol. II & III.

[42] D. A. Carson wrote: "The range of phenomena covered by this word group [prophecy] in the first century is enormous." Then he uses ten pages in discussing its meanings in the New Testament. See *Showing the Spirit* (Baker Book House, 1987), p. 91ff.

[43] Kidd, p. 151

It does not matter that this prophetess cited God as her "witness" and the apostle as the authority for her "gift"; every guru essentially does that. The point is that a subjective experience has no credibility. This woman's subjective experience can bring no credibility either to herself, her church, or her God.

The situation is reminiscent of the pagan Egyptian worshipper of Amon (see above). The Amonite worshipper and the onlookers misinterpreted the subjective experience of his own fallen psyche as having been the result of the influence of Amon, but Amon doesn't exist.

The Montanist woman likewise interpreted her own psychic experience as the influence of the Holy Spirit, as did Tertullian, yet a subjective Christian experience is no more verifiable than that of a pagan. There is no way a subjective human experience can add any credibility to the works of God or to His Word, which was a completed work at that time, and certainly not to the person having the experience; on the contrary, we must put such claims to the objective test of Scripture which debunks such activity (more on this later).

It appears that Tertullian and other Montanists stood pretty much where the typical charismatic Christian stands today. Aside from Montanus himself, the typical Montanist seemed to be sincere and generally orthodox in most other respects, but grossly failing to understand the temporary nature and purpose of certain of the gifts in the early church. Unwilling to part with the temporary explosion of signs, and exciting wonders beginning with the first advent of Christ and continuing to the close of the canon of Scripture, they failed to grasp the necessity and uniqueness of God's work of the *authentication* of Christ, the New Covenant church, and the writers of the New Covenant Scriptures during the formative years of this enormous undertaking. God's purpose to transition from the preparatory and imperfect nature of the *Old Covenant* to the more perfect *New Covenant* (Heb. 8:7-13) and to impart to the New Covenant the credibility it must have, by necessity required some *unique* and *temporary* measures.

But God cut off the real signs and wonders, including biblical tongues, leaving the Montanists and all subsequent charismatics to their own subjectively generated internal "experiences." The attempt to perpetuate these measures indefinitely is not only an exercise in psychic self-deceit, or satanic influence, but they would only destroy the *uniqueness* of God's authentic wonders and undercut His original purpose for them. Moreover, the flimsy attempt to perpetuate and repeat those wonders today has the effect of establishing the current charismatic persons, along with Moses and Paul, etc., as inspired recipients of on-going revelation from God. And if they were thus authenticated, we must likewise obey their word as Scripture!

This important distinction will be clearly established later, especially in the last chapter of this book.

Irenaeus (c. 140-202). According to Glenn Hinson,[44] one time professor at Southern Baptist Theological Seminary, Irenaeus refers to three occasions of tongue speaking. The first was referring to Acts 2. In the second, Irenaeus refers to the ability of some to speak foreign languages: "… we do also hear many brethren in the church, who possess prophetic gifts, and who through the Spirit speak all kinds of languages.…"

In the third passage we are told about an abuse of prophetic gifts by one Marcus who would deceive gullible women by promising them the prophetic gift. As they would protest that they didn't know how, he would say, "Open thy mouth, speak whatever occurs to thee.…" Irenaeus then continues:

> Then she, vainly puffed up and elated by these words, and greatly excited in soul that it is herself that is to prophesy, her heart beating violently [from emotion], reaches the requisite pitch of audacity, and idly as well as impudently utters some nonsense as it happens to occur to her, such as might be expected from one heated by an empty spirit.… Henceforth she reckons herself a prophetess, and expresses her thanks to Marcus for having imparted to her of his own Charis (Against Heresies, I.13.3; ANF, I, 334).[45]

This is doubtless an example of Paul's observation, "For of

---

[44] Frank Stagg, E. Glenn Hinson, and Wayne E. Oates, *Glossolalia* (Nashville: Abingdon Press, 1967), pp. 48-49.

[45] As quoted by Hinson, *Glossolalia*, p. 49.

this sort are they which creep into houses, and lead captive silly women laden with sins, led away with divers lusts" (2 Tim. 3:6). Also, it illustrates a practice where one charlatan can teach another how to attain the "gift" of the Holy Spirit, and this practice, though done perhaps ignorantly in good faith, amazingly continues among charismatics even today.

Unintelligible Tongues. The practice of unintelligible tongues (never exemplified in Scripture), which began to manifest itself among Christians in the second century was seen as a liability to Christianity well before the post-Nicene period. Some Christians who insisted on the use of unintelligible tongues provided opportunity for the pagans, among whom unintelligible tongues originated, to heap scorn upon the Christian faith. Again, we should not be surprised at this since we were warned by Paul: If we speak in tongues that are not understood (even if they are known languages), "and there come in those that are unlearned, or unbelievers, will they not say that ye are mad?" (1 Cor 14:23). For this reason it was necessary for Origen (c. 185-254) to answer the pagan philosopher, Celsus, who charged Christians of just such madness for using –

> ... strange, fanatical, and quite unintelligible words, of which no rational person can find the meaning: for so dark are they, as to have no meaning at all; but they give occasion to every fool to apply them to suit his own purposes (*Against Celsus*, VII.9; ANF, IV, 614).[46]

Post-Nicene Period (325-590)

In the Post-Nicene period reports of the use of tongues among Christians declined. This is not surprising, since Paul predicted they would cease and the special prophetic knowledge of the apostolic period would also vanish away, though no one knows the exact time (1 Cor.13:8).

Monasticism and Charismata. The Post-Nicene period, however, saw the rise of *monasticism*, a new movement among Christians though it was an ancient phenomenon. Pre-Christian ascetic influences surely contributed to rapid and geographi-

---

[46]Cited by Hinson, *Glossolalia*, p. 51.

cally extended growth of monasticism which continues to this day. Behind the ascetic phenomenon is the Platonic view that evil is identified with *matter* and goodness with the *spirit* world (a view also held by the Gnostics); and this pagan philosophy drove the monastic life of rigorous self-discipline[47] – unreasonable, useless, and hurtful self-denial, torturous treatment and abuse of the body – with a view to reaching a high plane of *spiritual experience*. "Clearly, the Christian monastic movement tapped into this broad stream of ascetic thought and practice."[48]

Though there are certain subjectivist characteristics common to both monasticism and the modern charismatic movement, we make no claim here that it is to be identified with monasticism; it clearly is not. The monastic life was a withdrawal from the world (into which the Christian is sent for ministry) to seek for a "higher plane" of spirituality through meditation and the contemplative life. The quest of both the monastic and the charismatic, despite the differences in method, is a direct experiential knowledge of and involvement with God.

Moreover, monastics like many charismatics are preoccupied in a misguided way with a quest for sinless perfection, driving themselves into an introspective subjectivism where some suppose they have attained a condition of perfect holiness. Paul warns against this error: "Do not touch; do not taste; do not handle … these things indeed have an appearance of wisdom in self imposed religion, false humility, and neglect of the body, but are of no value against the indulgence of the flesh" (Col. 2:21, 23 NKJV).

Not content to go into the world and "make disciples of all nations" in obedience to the objective commandment of Scripture, the monastics sought to rise above the struggle in the real world

---

[47] It has been suggested the monasticism and celibacy of Jerome (c. 345-419) and others of his day was the desire for a pure church in comparison to the official Catholic church of their day. Perhaps so, but in general the ascetic life was extreme beyond biblical standards.

[48] Kling, p. 26.

where, like the ministry of Christ, our ministries, if any, must take place.

Pachomius. Some of the monastics also exhibited other features of the charismatic movement. *Pachomius* (292-348), for example (who is often cited as the "father" of the monastic movement), is said to have had visions, worked miracles, spoken in tongues, and ruled over nature. He could handle serpents without harm and was "victorious" over the natural and supernatural because of his sinlessness.[49]

Mysticism. Another feature that many monastic Christians held in common with more modern subjectivists was their orientation toward mysticism. Kenneth Latourette tells us that "each new monastic order invariably gave rise to a deepening mysticism ... ."[50]

The mystic seeks a direct communion with God through internal meditation. Believing it is possible to attain knowledge of spiritual truth *intuitively*, he seeks to "experience God" and comprehend mysteries considered ordinarily to be beyond human understanding by searching *within*, not satisfied with the propositional truth revealed in Scripture.

Far from being features of biblical Christianity, both monasticism and the charismatic obsession, in every age, prove to be features of fallen human nature concerning which many otherwise good and sincere Christians have been deceived.

Augustine's Doctrine of Signs. Even as early as the time of Augustine (354-430) the gift of signs was recognized as being a temporary work of God formerly given to add credence to the infant church and the writers of the New Testament Scriptures. Augustine wrote:

> For the Holy Spirit ... was given in former days to be the credentials of a rudimentary faith, and for the extension of the first beginnings of the church. For who expects in these days that those on whom hands are laid

---

[49] "Pachomius," *Encyclopedia Britannica*. 1998. This list of gifts, particularly tongues and sinless perfectionism, is suggestive of many modern charismatic practices, and even snake handling continues today in some fringe Pentecostal groups.

[50] Kenneth Scott Latourette, *A History of Christianity* (New York: Harper & Row Publishers, 1953), p. 539.

that they may receive the Holy Spirit should forthwith begin to speak with tongues?[51]

Unintelligible ecstatic speech, which appeared among Christians in the second century and following, never gained much credibility among the more orthodox fathers as an authentic work of the Holy Spirit. As we have contended above, unintelligible babble, whether pagan or Christian, can have no corroborative value to authenticate a religious truth or act. Even though another person may claim to "interpret" the babble, it still adds no credibility to it because both the meaning of the original babble and its interpretation are wholly unverifiable.

Consequently, well before the middle ages, the authentic tongues phenomenon of Scripture, the gift to speak in other languages, had ceased because it had served its purpose, as Paul predicted (1 Cor. 13:8) and Augustine[52] verified. The counterfeit tongues practices, i.e., the unintelligible babble, had been rejected by most Christians because of the reproach it brought upon the faith (e.g., see quote from Irenaeus above).

The Middle Ages (590 - 1517)

Of this period Hinson asserts[53] that there was very scant evidence for tongue-speaking, and most of what was claimed was of the ability to speak in foreign languages – as the biblical accounts exemplify. However, since the phenomenon of unintelligible speaking is a recurring characteristic of fallen human nature that crops out even among Christians, we would expect to find some examples in this period. Sure enough, a quick glance in an encyclopedia reveals a couple of interesting tongue-speaking cases.

Hildegard. There was a nun named Hildegard (1098-1179) who was known as the Sibyl of the Rhine. She was a sickly person all her life, but during the worst times of her illness[54] she would

---

[51] Ibid, p. 52

[52] Both Chrysostom and Augustine wrote "as if glossolalia had not occurred since very early times." See Hinson, *Glossolalia*, p. 53.

[53] Ibid, p. 56.

[54] Recall the claims of pagan examples (above) that some of the greatest "gifts" are given in connection with sickness or madness. A sickly condition is men-

have visions, work "miracles" and speak in tongues. Some say that she invented a language, but in any case she would speak in an unknown tongue when she prophesied and worked her miracles.[55]

According to Latourette, Hildegarde was also somewhat of a mystic:

> At the tender age of three she began to see visions ... She also [later] prophesied, admonishing those in authority and speaking of Antichrist and the end of the world.[56]

Ferrier. Vincent Ferrier (1350-1419) was a Dominican monk of whom it was said that he performed miracles throughout Western Europe and had the gift of tongues and prophecy.[57]

Others. Hinson, citing J. J. Gorres' *Die Christliche Mystik*, lists the following names of this period as recipients of the gift of tongues: "St. Anthony of Padua (1195-1231), Ange Clarenus (in 1300), St. Stephen (missionary to Georgia [in Eastern Europe]), St. Colette (d.1447), Jeanne (sic) of the Cross, St. Francis Xavier (1506-1552)...."[58]

The Post Reformation Period

Although examples of subjectivism and charismatic activity in the former centuries just considered were sparse, the post reformation period is a different matter. In this era there was a revival of tongues and other charismatic features leading up to the modern charismatic era.

The Cevenol Peasants. The first outburst came following the revocation of the Edict of Nantes by Louis XIV in 1685 and a wave of severe persecutions of the Huguenots of southeastern France. The pressure of this persecution seemed to produce a sort of religious hysteria or frenzy, especially among the people liv-

---

tioned in connection with ecstatically "gifted" Christians enough times that the connection is hard to ignore as pure chance, as further examples (below) will confirm.

[55] "Hildegard," *Encyclopedia Britannica*.

[56] Latourette, p. 539.

[57] "Vincent Ferrier," *Encyclopedia Americana*, 1988.

[58] Hinson, *Glossolalia*, p. 56, (Hinson, however, discusses reasons why these accounts may not be reliable).

ing in the Cevennes Mountains. Abbe Duchayla, Arch-Priest of Cevennes, separated many of the children from their parents and forced them by severe chastisement to do penance for the heresy of their parents.

The results of this treatment included ecstatic speech that appeared to be in unknown languages, accompanied in some instances with other phenomena such as convulsions, foaming at the mouth, sobbing, etc.[59] It is said to have first happened to a ten-year old girl. A remarkable number of those affected were children, some as young as three are said to have been involved.

This reaction, however, is probably not a classic case of charismatic activity since many children were involved. This speech seemed to come about as a result of great terror as men, women, and children were killed for simply having been part of a Huguenot community.

The Jansenists. The name *Jansenist* is derived from the Flemish theologian, Cornelis Jansen (1585-1638). They were a reformed branch of the Roman Catholic Church during the seventeenth century. Though their main distinctive was Augustinian theology, similar to Calvinism, they announced that experience, not reason, was their guide and sought to experience God, or sought experiences that would prove that God existed.[60] This appears to be their only subjectivist tendency; Jansen "emphasized personal religious experience, the direct relationship of the individual soul to its Maker ..."[61]

The Quakers. The Quakers originated in England in the 17th century. They were originally the followers of George Fox, who preached the biblical concept of "Christ within" (Col. 1:27). But this concept was later distorted into the idea of an "inner light," and Fox's followers eventually grouped together under the name of Society of Friends. Among the Quakers, or Friends, the Bible was believed to be inspired by God, but it came to be viewed

---

[59] Hinson, *Glossolalia*, p. 60.

[60] "Jansenist," *Encyclopedia Britannica*, 1998.

[61] Kenneth Latourette, *A History of Christianity* (New York: Harper & Row, 1953), p. 879.

simply, and only, as a second rule of Christian maturity. The authority of Scripture became subordinate to the "inner light" which they regarded as something supernatural. Divine revelation, they believed, was directly and immediately given to the individual, and anyone could thus receive the Word of God in his soul. This degeneration in doctrine is an example of what can happen when a people turns in small increments from the objective Word of God to subjectivism, the "inner light." Over time the inner self becomes the source of knowledge and truth and the objective Word of God becomes optional. Modern evangelicalism has gone a dangerous distance down this slippery slope.

The Friends were popularly called Quakers because of the agitated motions they exhibited moments before receiving divine revelation. The Quakers came to believe that experience sits in judgment over the Word of God, rather than the other way around.[62] In addition to the trembling feature while waiting for the Holy Spirit to move them, speaking in unintelligible tongues appeared among some of their congregations.[63]

Quakerism, or a branch called the Shaking Quakers or Shakers, was brought to America under the leadership of Ann Lee (1736-1784). She was known among the Quakers as Mother Ann or Ann the Word. It was presumed among the faithful that Christ's second coming was fulfilled in her. She claimed the gift of tongues and led her followers into grievous excesses, which only worsened after her death. David R. Lamson gave the following account of the exercise of the "gifts and power of God" in a meeting he witnessed on February 23, 1845:

> As these exercises continue, the zeal increases, the whole company frequently clap their hands in concert. Some begin to turn around with great rapidity, some leap and shout, throw up their hands, and perform all manner of gesticulations, talk in unknown tongues, sing in unknown tongues. Sometimes, as to-day for instance, two or three times, all join in one concert of yelling, screaming, shouting, shaking with all their might.... When the din is not so great that one cannot be heard, there is preaching, prophesying,

---

[62] John R. Himmels, *Facts on File Dictionary of Religion* (New York: Facts on File, Inc., 1984), p. 169.

[63] "Shakers," *Webster's World Encyclopedia*, 2001.

speaking in unknown tongues, and singing songs by special inspiration. All this time the young sisters continue their turning so swiftly, that the air gathering under their garments ... exposes their person still more. But they must not be checked in their gifts, for it is by the inspiration of God.[64]

In a heartrending account, showing the severe psychosomatic disturbances which can sometimes result from extreme reckless abandonment to the human psyche in its quest to experience God directly, Dr. W. A. Hammond[65] gives us this melancholy account:

> There are many [visionists] among [the Quakers], who profess to see God, Christ, and Mother Ann .... [the visionist] calls on one to step forth and shake....while the visionist calls out at the top of his voice "Shake! Shake! Shake!"

The description of a frenzied scene follows. Then Dr. Hammond continues:

> Sometimes young men and women are exercised by what they call the "jerks," for two weeks at a time, during the whole of which period the head is kept in quick, convulsive motions of the shoulders and neck. The author of [the] little book from which these particulars were quoted says he once saw a young woman whose face was frightfully swollen, her eyes dilated and bloodshot, and who had been exercised by the "jerks" for three weeks. Directly after the "jerks" she began to talk in unknown tongues, and continued in short intervals for three or four days; then she stopped suddenly, and remained entirely mute for two weeks...

We do not contend that these extreme exercises in the name of the Holy Spirit are typical of all Quakers, many of whom live a quiet and peaceful life filled with good deeds and influences. But these are sad examples of the extremes of fallen human nature in seeking an illegitimate shortcut to direct revelation and to experience the Almighty in the flesh before the resurrection of the body.

---

[64] David R. Lamson, *Two Years Experience among the Quakers* (West Boyleston, 1848), pp. 85-88, as quoted by Alexander Mackie, *The Gift of Tongues* (New York: George Doran Company, 1921), p. 112. It should be noted that Lamson says not all Quaker congregations go to these excesses.

[65] William A. Hammond, *Spiritualism and Allied Causes and Conditions of Nervous Derangement* (New York, 1876), p. 242, as quoted by Mackie, pp. 113-115.

There are numerous non-Quaker examples of long-lasting anomalies arising from similar abuse of mind and body in the name of the Holy Spirit. Gardiner, a reformed charismatic, says:

> The desire for experience has subverted sincere people into involvement with a psychological phenomenon which they mistakenly think is "speaking in tongues." In the process, because the inhibitions are lowered, many emotional experiences are realized – euphoria, excitement, release, etc.… I have seen people run around a room until they were exhausted, climb tent poles, laugh hysterically, go into trances for days and do other weird things as the "high" sought became more elusive.[66]

That Christians groan in the flesh, desiring to be "clothed upon," there is no doubt. But we have the instructions of Scripture and the intercession of the Holy Spirit to help ease the groaning:

> For we know that the whole creation groaneth and travaileth in pain together until now. And not only they, but ourselves also, which have the firstfruits of the Spirit, even we ourselves groan within ourselves, waiting for the adoption, to wit, the redemption of our body. *For we are saved by hope: but hope that is seen is not hope:* for what a man seeth, why doth he yet hope for? But if we hope for that we see not, then do we *with patience wait for it* (Rom. 8:22-25).

We all need relief from the groaning, but the answer is faith, hope, and love, with patience – not experience generated by the psyche. Sin is never harmless.

The Irvingite Movement. Charismatic phenomena, with all its varied distinctives including tongues, prophecy, subjectivism, and direct revelations from God, revived in earnest in the early 19th century. Edward Irving (1792-1834) was a gifted but controversial Scottish pastor of the Presbyterian Caledonian Chapel, London. So popular was his ministry that a larger building was built (1827) at Regent Square to accommodate the congregation. At some point in his ministry, he became convinced that the apostolic office and the gift of tongues in the early church were for all time. Though he himself never spoke in tongues, he became a catalyst for a charismatic resurgence and played a prominent role in its growth and perpetuation.

---

[66] Gardiner, *The Corinthian Catastrophe*, pp. 54, 55.

This charismatic revival, however, first broke out in 1830, independent of Irving, along the Clyde River in western Scotland. The first to speak in tongues was one Mary Campbell of Fernicarry on Sunday evening March 28, 1830. Then on Friday, April 16, 1830, James and George Macdonald both spoke in tongues.[67] The Macdonald home then became a center of charismatic activity that gained wide notoriety.

MacPherson tells about prayer meetings conducted in the home of Jim and George Macdonald and their now famous sister Margaret[68] in Port Glasgow. Eyewitness to some of these meetings were both John B. Cardale and John Nelson Darby.[69] Following are statements from both of these eyewitnesses as cited by MacPherson:

> 1. Cardale: the chief speakers were "J. M'D," his brother "G. M'D," their sister "M. M'D," "the woman-servant of the M'D.'s," and "Mrs. _______ [sic], one of the ladies who had received the Spirit, but had not received the gift of tongues." (Darby: "the chief persons who spoke" were "J. M'D _______," his "brother," "their sister," their "Gaelic maid-servant," and "Mrs. J_______" who spoke only "in English.")

> 2. Cardale: "The mode of proceeding is for each person who takes a part first to read a Psalm in metre, which is sung by the meeting ... and he then prays" before "speaking in an unknown tongue." (Darby: "they read, sung psalms, and prayed" before "exercising the gifts.")

> 3. Cardale: "I have heard ... J. M'D ... . speak for twenty minutes" in tongues "with all the energy of voice and action of an orator" and with "Latin radicals." (Darby: "J. M'D_______ spoke ... for about a quarter

---

[67] Dave MacPherson, *The Incredible Cover-up* (Plainfield, NJ: Logos International, 1975), p. 54.

[68] Dave MacPherson makes the case in three books, *The Incredible Cover-up* (1975), *The Great Rapture Hoax* (Fletcher, N.C.: New Puritan Library, 1983), and *The Rapture Plot* (Simpsonville, SC: Millennium III Publishers, 1994), through thirty years of research, that the concept of a pretribulation rapture originated by this same Margaret Macdonald in early 1830 in an ecstatic vision and that this fact was covered up by later dispensational writers.

[69] John Nelson Darby, as thoroughly documented by Dave MacPherson in *The Rapture Plot*, is the person who more than anyone else popularized the pretribulation rapture theory which developed among the Irvingites.

of an hour" in tongues "with great energy and fluency, in a semi-Latin sounding speech.")[70]

Thus, we are able to sense the features of these meetings and the essence of the charismatic stirring that had broken out in the Macdonald home in Port Glasgow, and other towns in western Scotland. Since Irving, as mentioned above, had taught that the spiritual gifts of the apostolic age, apostles and all, were for all time, it is not surprising that he had a keen interest in the phenomenal activities in the Macdonald home. "Excitement filled the air," MacPherson wrote,[71] as news of this charismatic revival reached London. Consequently, a delegation from Irving's own church, and numerous others, went up to observe.

The major theme of the prophecies, visions, and ecstatic tongues of this charismatic resurgence, was the immediate return of Christ. In the words of James Macdonald, interpreting his own ecstatic tongue, "Behold he cometh – Jesus Cometh." MacPherson quotes one R. B. Lusk in a letter of April 30, 1830, that "… the burden of all they say is – that the Lord is near, near at hand."[72] Now 176 years later, many contemporary brethren who have inherited similar charismatic tongues or prophecies are still repeating the same message. In 1980-90 there was a rash of dates set for the return of the Lord. All failed and thus we have reason to conclude that these "revelations" were not of the Holy Spirit.

Yet the followers of these false prophets still wait with bated breath, for the next revised "revelation" of the time of the Lord's coming. Is there a clue here somewhere that these charismatic "gifts" – not only the Irvingites, but of many modern "prophets" as well – may, after all, be of a different spirit?

---

[70] MacPherson, *The Rapture Plot*, p. 133.

[71] MacPherson, *The Incredible Cover-up*, p. 28. Incidentally, after Margaret Macdonald had received her vision or revelation of the pretribulation rapture she sent written copies of her revelation to various ministers among whom was Irving. This new "revelation" then appeared in Irving's journal, *The Morning Watch*, and was later picked up by Darby (who had also visited the Macdonald home), then by Scofield, Dallas Theological Seminary, and today, one and three quarter centuries later, we have *Left Behind*.

[72] MacPherson, *The Incredible Cover-up*, p. 55.

> When a prophet speaketh in the name of the LORD, if the thing follow
> not, nor come to pass, that is the thing which the LORD hath not spoken,
> but the prophet hath spoken it presumptuously: thou shalt not be afraid
> of him (Deut. 18:22).

We repeat, not only is it impossible that unintelligible language or self-proclaimed prophecies could be a sign or proof of God's voice, will, or message; they prove in fact the opposite. The Scriptures neither approve nor exemplify any such activities. As we will later show, the "signs and wonders" of Scripture are wholly different and serve a broad and decisive function in the purpose of God.

It seems evident therefore that the gentle but credulous souls on the banks of the Clyde, whose sincerity we do not question, were at best responding to the stimulus of their own psyche seeking experiences. Thus, in their over-persuasion that the Lord would immediately appear, an abnormal outbreak of excitement doubtless caused a certain hysteria within the community. And that appears to be the best and most charitable explanation of these several instances.

Edward Irving was a leader around whom a growing charismatic movement coalesced, but he never spoke in tongues himself (though he "sought the gift"). Yet, he has been called "the father of modern Pentecostalism."[73] "As early as 1828 Irving had decided that the spiritual gifts of the apostolic age really belonged to the church of all ages...."[74] Though Irving's sympathies and tacit encouragement were with the growing charismatic movement, there had never been an occasion of tongues-speaking in the Regent Square assembly until 1831. Then on Sunday morning October 16 a Miss Hall:

> Finding she was unable to restrain herself, rushed into the vestry, and
> gave vent to utterance, while another ... ran down the side isle and out
> of the church, through the principal door. Then sudden, doleful, and un-
> intelligible sounds, being heard by all the congregation, produced the
> utmost confusions ...[75]

---

[73] Dave MacPherson, *The Incredible Cover-up*, p. 28.

[74] Ibid., p. 27.

[75] Margaret W. Oliphant, *The Life of Edward Irving, Minister of the National*

Irving was later defrocked by the Presbyterians, not primarily for his charismatic orientation but because of his unorthodox teaching in ascribing a sinful nature to Christ. He became a leader in the founding of the Catholic Apostolic Church.

Today, the Irvingite movement continues institutionally in the form of the Catholic Apostolic Church (CAC, about 8 million worldwide in 1994). Originally, there were twelve apostles appointed in the CAC, they were all, according to their early theology, expected to live until the return of Jesus. However, the last of them died in 1901. But when the first one died a schism occurred which resulted in a reorganization of the church in 1863, which continues until today.[76]

Hinson also cites the Irvingites as an example of a post-Reformation charismatic movement, and he says that while tongue-speaking still occurs within the CAC, it is much less frequent than at first.[77]

Though Edward Irving has been called the father of the modern charismatic movement, it is hard to trace a direct, unbroken link to him. We must remember that the excesses among the Shakers led by Mother Ann were earlier than the Irvingite movement. And there was a period when tongue-speaking was extensive among the Mormons at about the same period as the Irvingite movement. Nevertheless, the results and influences from those troubled times have never totally ceased and are alive and well today in the Pentecostal and Neo-Pentecostal movements.

Strangely enough, it was out of this same Irvingite movement within the same time frame (c. 1830) that the popular modern day pretribulation rapture doctrine originated.[78]

Again we are forced to the conclusion, that extra-biblical

Scotch Church, London (New York, 1862), pp. 426-7.

[76] *The Colombia Encyclopedia*, 2001.

[77] Hinson, *Glossolalia*, p. 61, 62.

[78] This has been thoroughly documented through thirty years of research by Dave MacPherson in *The Rapture Plot*. We should mention that MacPherson's interest in the Irvingites and Macdonalds, et al, was eschatological. However, these charismatic activities were so intertwined in the spirit of the movement, his writings offer much insight into this charismatic resurgence.

ecstatic tongues, the subjectivism, the quest for immediate and direct revelation from God, and the obsession with *experiencing* God are the result of fallen human nature. Despite the claim that such things are the work of the Holy Spirit, the contrary is true; but rather these are works which have not been brought under the control of the Holy Spirit in accordance with Scripture truth which He inspired.

The Great Awakenings. A period of great Christian revivals occurred in America, the British Isles, and to some extent in Western Europe, spanning the years from c. 1730 to the 1860s. Continuing with more or less intensity, these remarkable revival periods, the First and Second Great Awakenings, were divided by a twenty-five or thirty year lapse during which England and the American Colonies were preoccupied with the Revolutionary War.

By far the majority of these revival events bear all the marks of a genuine work of God, but it is rare in history that the most legitimate and God-centered religious awakening is not troubled by a fanatical fringe element. Even in the first century, there was Simon whom Peter encountered (Acts 8), and some among the Corinthians whom Paul encountered (1 Cor. 14). Therefore, it is not surprising that some irregular and unsettling behavior was encountered during the Great Awakening period.

The first Great Awakening was characterized generally by Christian sobriety with relatively few irregularities. It was during the second Great Awakening that the Irvingite outbreak of charismatic phenomena took place. And in addition to these, there were activities, particularly in America, that were typical of current charismatic phenomena, and some that were atypical. All these activities, however, seem to be the result of the excitement and hysteria that frequently accompanies periods of religious fervor.

When the opposing forces of light and darkness, truth and error, engage in fierce battle for the souls of men, psychic stress upon individuals is inevitable. And such stress often produces a hysteria which may result in bizarre behavior. Historian David Benedict described some of these irregularities of the second period of the Great Awakening:

> From 1799 to 1803, there were, in most parts of the United States, re-
> markable outpourings of the divine Spirit, among different denomina-
> tions.... This great work [in northern Kentucky] progressed among the
> Baptists in a much more regular manner than people abroad have gener-
> ally supposed. They were indeed zealously affected, and much engaged.
> Many of their ministers baptized in a number of neighboring churches
> from two to four hundred each. And two of them baptized about five
> hundred a-piece in the course of the work. But throughout the whole,
> they preserved a good degree of decorum and order. Those camp-meet-
> ings, those great parades, and sacramental seasons, those extraordinary
> exercises of falling down, rolling, shouting, jerking, dancing, barking,
> etc., were but little known among the Baptists in Kentucky, nor encour-
> aged by them....
>
> These jerking exercises were rather a curse than a blessing. None were
> benefited by them. They left sinners without reformation, and Christians
> without advantage. Some had periodical fits of them seven or eight years
> after they were first taken; and I know not as they have got over jerking
> yet....
>
> There was among these enthusiastick [sic] people one more exercise of a
> most degrading nature, called the barks, which frequently accompanied
> the jerks.... Some might be forced to these degrading exercises, but it
> is certain that many turned dogs in a voluntary manner. A minister in
> the lower part of Kentucky informed me, that it was common to hear
> people barking like a flock of spaniels on their way to meeting. There
> they would start up suddenly in a fit of barking, rush out, roam around,
> and in a short time come barking and foaming back. But enough has been
> said of these frantick [sic] scenes. The above accounts are not fabulous
> tales, but they are real and melancholy facts.[79]

Melancholy indeed are the facts associated with such extreme religious irregularities. Nevertheless, these phenomena
when carefully considered are of the same order as others reported
above – both pagan and Christian – falling down, jerking, ecstatic
dancing, unintelligible language, etc. It was claimed by some that
these activities were manifestations of the Holy Spirit. And apart
from the objectivity of the Bible, no one can prove them wrong
concerning either the barks or tongues.

---

[79] David Benedict, *A General History of the Baptist Denomination in America,*
II (1813; rpt. Church History Research and Archives, 1980), pp. 251-56.

Sweet also gives account[80] of some of the excesses on the western edge of the revivals in America mainly among the Presbyterians and Methodists.[81] At the peak of the Cumberland revival huge crowds assembled at camp meetings; most were sincere, but others came to see or participate in the strange activities. The largest gatherings were the joint communion services of Presbyterians and Methodists. The Baptists, Sweet said, joined with them in preaching, but would not join in the communion services.[82] The crowds were variously estimated from 10,000 to 25,000 attendees, and the meetings would last several days. Caught up in the excitement and conflicting emotions of the meetings, many attendees were seized with peculiar bodily exercises described by Sweet as:

> ... falling, jerking, rolling, running, dancing and barking.... It often happened that "sinners" were taken, cursing and swearing as they jerked. "Sometimes the head would be twisted right and left, to a half round, with [great] velocity ..."[83]

It seems obvious, since we have seen the accounts of such activities from ancient times in pagans as well as Christians, that strong emotional stresses and excitement may produce such reactions within the hysteria of an environment upon those who seek to "experience" their religions. It remains true, however, that "... the spirits of the prophets are subject to the prophets" (1 Cor. 14:32), therefore the excitement of the environment cannot overcome an individual unless he submits to it.

These reactions must not be attributed to the God of heaven; the fruit of the Spirit is "love, joy, peace," etc. Neither must we interpret the revival event itself to be somehow flawed because of the abuse of a fringe element. Neither the Holy Spirit nor the

---

[80] William Warren Sweet, *The Story of Religion in America* (New York: Harper and Brothers Publishers, 1930), pp. 228-29.

[81] However, the main body of Presbyterians, Methodists, and Baptists all denounced these practices at that time.

[82] Baptists historically have regarded communion to be an ordinance under the authority of the local congregation of those known to be in good moral and doctrinal standing.

[83] Sweet, p. 230.

Christian Gospel in and of themselves will cause such reactions, but flawed human nature may often react inappropriately to the intense influence of the power of the Gospel and presence of the Holy Spirit, as He "reproves the world of sin," bearing witness to the Gospel message.

Neither should these remarks be interpreted as an unqualified approval of the environment created by such meetings. It appears that often, with the best of intentions, true *revival* may turn to mere *revivalism*, which seems to have been the case especially in the second Great Awakening. Early leaders in the American revivals

> ... believed that a strict adherence to Scripture is the only guard against what may be wrongly claimed as the work of God's Spirit. They foresaw the danger of revivalism long before it became a respected part of evangelicalism...."[84]

A reckless abandonment to emotional and experiential activities, including tongues, was one concern of Paul when he advised the Corinthians that *all things* should be done "unto edification.... decently and in order" (1 Cor. 14:26, 40).

As Benedict noted, some of these activities are attributable to deliberate attempts on the part of some to disrupt or discredit the progress of the Gospel and the truth of God. However, the evidence indicates that most of it has been the result of psychic reactions to conflicted interests, i.e., unbelievers agitated in their resistance to the truth, and immature believers agitated in their quest to experience God in a direct experiential intimacy not accessible in this life. Moreover, it is sure that Satan himself overlooks no opportunity to exploit such weaknesses in fallen human nature.

As we consider such extra-biblical activities as the jerks, unintelligible language, or the barks, it is easy to realize that these activities are not exemplified in Scripture and therefore are not of the Holy Spirit. But there is real concern on the part of some Christians erroneously supposing that *unintelligible tongues are* a genuine gift of God. However, there is no more support in Scripture

---

[84] Iain H. Murray, *Revival and Revivalism* (The Banner of Truth Trust, 1994), p. xx.

for that notion than there is for the barks, which are also a form of unintelligible ecstatic utterance. Because intelligible communications in languages not previously learned was once a genuine gift of the Holy Spirit, exemplified in Scripture as a sign and wonder, a misguided understanding of this fact leads some to suppose that unintelligible tongues are biblical. Later we will examine biblical tongues and gifts in great detail, and note the contrast with what we have seen of extra-biblical behavior.

Concerning the cause of the phenomenon of barks, falling, tongues, etc., there are three reasonable possibilities: 1) It can be a deliberately faked act, as Benedict noted, for a sinful purpose. 2) It can be a spontaneous, but willing, psychic reaction to the hysteria of a situation, which is the most likely explanation for most of it, or 3) some of it could be satanically inspired. All three of these reasons, have probably been the source of some of these activities in one case or another, but in any individual case it is difficult or impossible to tell the cause. Yet, the one thing that cannot be the cause is the Holy Spirit. Unintelligible ecstatic tongues-speaking, falling down "slain in the spirit," and such like, have no more a part in the Christian faith than jerks, barks, or rolling. We contend, therefore, that unintelligible tongues, ancient and modern, pagan or Christian, fall into the same category as barking and other of the more obvious human abuses of Scripture truth, which we have now examined in some detail.

We make no claim to have been exhaustive in this examinaion. Others involved in tongues and other ecstatic charismatic phenomena would include the Mormons (mentioned briefly above), the followers of Swedenborg of Sweden (known as the Church of the New Jerusalem),[85] and some of the early Methodists.[86]

THE RISE OF MODERN CHARISMATA

By the end of the 19th century, the true revival power of the Great Awakenings had been eclipsed by a combination of things:

---

[85] Ibid., p. 37, 496.

[86] Timothy L. Smith. "The Cross Demands, the Spirit Enables," *Christianity Today*, Feb. 16, 1997, pp. 22-26.

First were the revivalistic manifestations and features of the second Great Awakening. Second was the double-barreled influence originating in the Irvingite movement, namely, its charismatic features (discussed in detail above) and its dispensational doctrines as popularized by J. N. Darby.[87] Third was the rise of the theory of evolution as presented by Charles Darwin in his book *On the Origin of Species* (1859) and the traction this theory gave to modernism. And finally out of the awful grief and disorientation of the Civil War, our entire nation emerged suffering, bruised, and bewildered seeking answers anywhere.

Because of these and other things, a pall of gloom fell across the country as churches "changed in remarkable lockstep"[88] from the optimistic victorious eschatology of the Great Awakenings, called the "Latter Day Glory," to the gloom of Irvingite dispensationalism preached by Darby.[89]

This was the spiritual climate in the late 19th century as the true revivals of former years gave way to revivalism, tactically planned and executed campaigns led by men like Moody and other popular revivalists. People were seeking a sign – any sign.

The Origin of Pentecostalism

Out of this spiritual black hole arose the initial phase of modern charismatic activity known as Pentecostalism. It is not far-fetched to think that a misguided human effort to regain or sustain the euphoria that had characterized the Great Awakening period may have provided fertile soil for this new wave of charismatic activity. Remember that Montanism arose in the wake of a long period of spiritual power in the 1st Century.

It is commonly supposed that Pentecostalism was a new thing sent down, as it were, from heaven; but we must remember that the early 19th century was rife with charismata. Moreover

---

[87] For a detailed documented account of this connection, see MacPherson, *The Rapture Plot*, pp. 88-120.

[88] Robert Jenson, *America's Theologian, A Recommendation of Jonathan Edwards* (New York: Oxford University Press, 1988), p. 183.

[89] For more detail see Willard A Ramsey, *The Fateful Lightning* (Simpsonville, SC: Millennium III Publishers, 2000), pp. 20-22.

our studies above show that ecstatic religious phenomena are ancient and historically persistent affecting both pagans and Christians. These intensified in the 19th century, and continued as on-going activities growing out of a weakness in human nature. The recurrence of charismata was inevitable, especially given the circumstances of the late 19th century.

Viewed in the light of this historical background, the charismatic activities that characterize Pentecostalism are nothing new or really different from the activities observed throughout history. Where Pentecostalism differs is in its doctrine and organization. As we shall see, it originated within small groups under the influence of leaders not satisfied with the status quo, but as the movement matured it coalesced around certain *doctrinal distinctives* which are now more or less common to a rather large number of organized denominations or churches.

Briefly, the principal Pentecostal beliefs are 1) sinless perfectionism or holiness as a distinctive second work of grace,[90] 2) a confirmation of this second work of grace by unintelligible tongues as a sign of the baptism of the Holy Spirit, 3) a continuation of "signs and wonders" and sensational miracles, and 4) a dispensational view of eschatology passed down from the Irvingite movement through the teachings of J. N. Darby, C. I. Scofield, et al. Other charismatic features such as, rolling, jerking, falling down in ecstatic trances (slaying in the spirit), etc., are features that have been commonly observed among Pentecostals, though not expressly claimed as a part of the doctrine.

The Holiness Movement. The soil in which Pentecostalism took root was the holiness doctrine derived from John Wesley's teaching of sanctification or Christian perfection. Though preaching a salvation message of grace, Wesley believed a Christian could reach a state of complete or "entire sanctification."

One of the most interesting questions concerning the sinless perfection theology is how Wesley's followers moved from the language of grace and atonement to a view of sanctification

---

[90] The holiness doctrine harkens back to the teachings of John Wesley and antedates the historical formation of organized Pentecostal groups.

that could be called *experience theology*. The holiness movement fashioned this transformation.

> [Wesley's followers] began about the middle of the nineteenth century to use the term "baptism of the Holy Spirit" as a synonym for the older Wesleyan phrases "perfect love," "heart purity," or "entire sanctification ..." they emphasized the cleansing power of the blood of Christ, and almost never spoke of believers being "baptized" or "filled" with the Spirit. Wesley rejected Fletcher's suggestion that Methodists employ these Pentecostal terms ... from fear that he and his preachers would be charged with mystical enthusiasm. For Wesley, nothing could be worse; Christians must hold to the moral and rational character of biblical faith."[91]

It seems evident that the holiness movement occupies a position intermediate, both historically and theologically, between Methodism and Pentecostalism. It first originated as a protest movement within Methodism, protesting what they considered a falling away from the emphasis on sanctification which Wesley originally preached. R. V. Pierard wrote,

> ... protests within the Methodist churches about the decline of discipline ... resulted in the Wesleyan Methodist secession in 1843 and the Free Methodist withdrawal in 1860. These two became the first denominations formally committed to Holiness.[92]

The Finney Factor. We are informed by Smith,[93] that Charles G. Finney was a very significant influence in the holiness development. Though Finney was not a Methodist, he made a great impression both on the Methodist church and on the general public because of his revivals in many churches and by his teaching work. He was largely responsible for the change in the American Wesleyan movement that lives on in the Wesleyan Methodist Church today.

It was Finney who began to use the term *"filled with the spirit"* and *"the baptism of the spirit."* He was concerned because

---

[91] Smith, "The Cross Demands ..." p. 22-26.

[92] R. V. Pierard, "American Holiness Movement," *The Evangelical Dictionary of Theology*, ed. Walter A. Elwell (Grand Rapids: Baker Books, 2001), pp. 564-565.

[93] Smith, "The Cross Demands ..." pp. 24-26.

he *felt* that "the responses he saw even the most earnest Christians making, and the responses he saw in his own heart and life, had not yet brought them up to the biblical standard of righteousness."

Finney taught that a man might *desire* holiness in this life, but for it to happen a person had to *will* himself to holiness and *desire* it with the whole mind, heart and soul. Just desiring is not enough, it must be *willed*, and so the achievement of this holiness is put in the hands of man and becomes a work of man and not a work of the *grace* of God.

Finney was a dispensationalist who believed that "the *baptism of the Holy Spirit* poured out initially in a dispensational way at Pentecost upon the whole of the church," pointed to the fulfillment of God's promise in the covenants – not just to Israel but to all of mankind. This, then, indicated that the *experience* would be the divine source of grace, a grace that would sanctify the hearts and souls of all believers. He was absolutely immovable that all ministers of the Gospel must have this "baptism of the Holy Spirit," this holiness, or they would never be able to lead those who professed salvation into the same experience.

For many years Finney never spoke of having *attained* the "victorious life" or "sinless perfection" experience, which was understood to be a part of the "second blessing." But there came a day, the evangelist said, when he was able to "fall back" more than ever before upon the "infinitely blessed and perfect will of God."

> The Pentecostal movement compounded these confusing tendencies, popularizing the notion, which the radical Wesleyans rejected, that the power of the Spirit's baptism was expressed chiefly in charismatic gifts, particularly the unknown tongue.[94]

From then on:

> Wesleyans, Presbyterians, Congregationalists and Friends devoted to the proclamation of Christian holiness have intermingled in preaching and in witness, the language of Pentecost, and the language of Calvary.[95]

Much of what Finney did was for the express purpose of

---

[94] Ibid., p. 26
[95] Ibid.

resisting the Calvinist doctrine of election which he believed was of the Devil and was there to undermine God's call to Christian perfection – or "sinless perfection" in this lifetime.

From Holiness to Pentecostalism. Numerous independent schismatic holiness bodies formed in the last half of the 19th century, but the holiness movement has survived in modern times in denominations like the Church of the Nazarene and the Church of God (Anderson, Indiana).

From the emphasis on sanctification of these earlier holiness bodies, it was only one short step to add the Pentecostal doctrine of the Baptism of the Holy Spirit as evidenced by *speaking in tongues*. It seems safe to say, then, that Pentecostalism is a hybrid. It simply added to Finney's teachings on holiness a misconception of the Holy Spirit's actions on Pentecost saying that perfectionism is fine but that it must be achieved or confirmed by the gifts of the Spirit.

Tracing Pentecostal Origins. One of the holiness bodies that arose in the late 19th century was the East Tennessee Holiness Association (ETHA), c. 1880. This organization was short lived, but it illustrates some basic characteristics of the times, and shows a link to early Pentecostalism. Though some among the holiness bodies spoke in ecstatic tongues, they were rarely troubled with tongues or other charismatic features. This, however, was not the case with the ETHA which was plagued with charismatic excesses:

> Some said they had "the baptism of fire" while others had received "dynamite" or "lyddite," the latter of which allowed, or permitted them to walk the top of the benches without criticism (for no one wanted to question the Lord). Some got what they called a "Wheel-In-A-Wheel" experience which they claimed delivered them from certain foods ...[96]

Davidson further notes that "there was no government among them," and that many sold their homes, farms, and worldly possessions and moved to Zion City, Illinois,[97] to await the "soon-com-

---

[96] C. T. Davidson, *Upon This Rock* (Cleveland, TN: White Wing Publishing House and Press, 1973), Vol. 1, p. 290.

[97] Zion City, Illinois was founded in 1901 by John Alexander Dowie, who

ing of the Lord that was expected within the next year or two." So the ETHA dissolved within a decade or two. One of the members of the disillusioned ETHA was Andrew J. Lawson who became a member and later treasurer (1923-1948) of the Church of God (Cleveland, Tennessee).

To trace the actual development of the Pentecostal churches, we must look back to c. 1886 to those events which led to the formation of the Church of God (Cleveland, Tennessee). Davidson tells us that in Monroe County (East Tennessee) a licensed Missionary Baptist minister, Richard G. Spurling, Sr., "seized with a spirit of unrest and dissatisfaction," called a special meeting at Barney Creek Meeting House on Thursday, August 19, 1886. A small group assembled to which Spurling, Sr., made the following proposition:

> As many Christians as are here present that are desirous to be free from all men-made creeds and traditions, and are willing to take the New Testament, or law of Christ, for your only rule of faith and practice; giving each other equal rights and privileges to read and interpret for yourselves as your conscience may dictate, and are willing to sit together as the Church of God to transact business as the same, come forward.[98]

Eight souls came forward, and the new organization was called *The Christian Union*. Subsequently Richard G. Spurling, Jr., son of the elder Spurling and also a licensed Baptist minister, joined the group and was chosen as pastor.

As noted above, the purpose was to "...sit together as the Church of God to transact business as the same..." It might be noted that such an act presumes that "the church of God" had not been perpetuated throughout the centuries, intact and doing

---

also founded The Christian Catholic Church in 1906. He ruled the church as "Elijah the Restorer" and the city as a dictator until he was deposed in 1906. Zion City, now called Zion, Illinois (north of Chicago) remained a theocracy until 1936 (*Encarta*, 1999).

[98] Davidson, p. 292. As we read the proposition proposed by Spurling, it is difficult to see anything that had not been treasured by Missionary Baptists long before this date. What was not stated here, however, was the underlying affinity for the second work of grace and speaking in tongues, which were foreign to the Baptists.

business, from the days of Christ and that it had no identifiable existence. Such an act is presumptuous indeed in view of the words of Christ that the "gates of hell shall not prevail against [His church]."

Pentecostal Development. The Christian Union had slow growth in the early years. But in 1896 three concerned individuals from Monroe County, William Martin, Joe Tipton, and Milton McNabb, went over into Cherokee County North Carolina to conduct a series of meetings at Schearer Schoolhouse. According to Davidson:

> They preached a real "born again" experience with God, and sanctification as the second definite work of grace, subsequent to justification, the eradication of the Adamic nature by the blood of Jesus Christ.[99]

This was an instance, Davidson continued, where the widespread preaching of "the Wesleyan doctrine of sanctification – sanctification as a second definite work of grace – was brought to life, more vividly than ever."[100]

The activities in Cherokee County were opposed by the people of the community, and over one hundred of them, along with the Justice of the Peace and the Sheriff, barred them from the schoolhouse. This act only "served to fan the revival fires now blazing almost out of control," and the meetings continued in a nearby log building. It was here that the now familiar Pentecostal activities reached full expression for the first time, or very nearly so. Davidson records:

> ... a rushing of "mighty wind," the Holy Ghost and fire swept down among them and several were baptized and spoke with other tongues as the Spirit gave them utterance. It was the same kind of Holy Ghost that fell on the disciples on the day of Pentecost.... . many fell prostrate at times, others staggered like drunk men, and all over the house people shouted, praised God and danced in the spirit, while others trembled, yelled and jerked, swaying to and fro in peculiar antics, as wave after wave of God's power swept among them.[101]

---

[99] Davidson, p. 294.
[100] Davidson, p. 295-6.
[101] Davidson, p. 297.

In these 1896 meetings over one hundred persons were "baptized with the Holy Ghost and fire and spoke in other tongues...." Davidson says that baptism with the Holy Ghost was "with the evidence of other tongues...."[102] If that was a conscious doctrine in that group, we have pure Pentecostalism in 1896.

Local opposition also destroyed the log meeting house, and the revival group began to meet in the home of W. F. Bryant. Richard G. Spurling, Jr. of the Christian Union had been a frequent visitor to the Cherokee County revival, and he had urged the group to organize. Finally they consented, and on May 15, 1902 they organized as The Holiness Church at Camp Creek. Spurling, Jr. was chosen as pastor.

Approximately a year later A. J. Tomlinson became associated with the Camp Creek Church, and on Saturday, June 13, 1903 at 8:00 A.M., it is said that God gave him "the light and true vision of the church of God of the Bible." The Christian Union, though claiming to be a recovery of the Church of God in 1886, had been tenuous in its claim to this distinction. But Tomlinson told his vision to the Camp Creek Church making this proposal:

> I then asked if they were willing to take me in with the understanding that it [the Holiness Church at Camp Creek] IS (sic) the Church of God – not going to be, but IS the Church of God? They were willing....

> Tomlinson became the first member of the Church of God by covenant this side of the Dark Ages... [103]

They changed the name to Church of God, and Tomlinson was chosen as the pastor. Today there are markers on the site where the Bryant home stood at the base of Burger Mountain in Cherokee County, North Carolina, commonly known as *Fields of the Wood,* designating the place where it is supposed that the Church of God was recovered in 1903 for the first time since the Dark Ages began in 325. Yet in the historical sketch on the church's current web

---

[102] Ibid. The doctrine that tongues is the evidence of being baptized with the Holy Ghost is typically attributed to Charles Parham in 1901, but if Davidson is accurate, that would not be true.

[103] Davidson, pp. 314, 315.

site, the origin of the church is counted from the Christian Union on Barney Creek, Monroe County, Tennessee.

Davidson considered this movement the true origin of the Pentecostal groups. He wrote: "This seems to have been the first revival series in which one hundred or more people had been filled with the Holy Ghost in the Western World in the last days."[104]

He acknowledges, however, that other individuals had spoken in tongues earlier. One woman he knew spoke in tongues about 1892. Earlier yet, a personal friend of Davidson was the powerful Methodist preacher Robert S. Sheffey of Virginia. Davidson said he was told by attendants at Sheffey's meetings that they personally heard him speak in tongues "when the power of God would seize him and slay him prostrate in the pulpit."

Though Davidson says nothing of the Irvingites, Quakers, Mormons, or other tongues-speaking movements, throughout history long before the Pentecostal period, he did acknowledge other Pentecostal activity near the turn of the 20th century:

> Holiness was being preached and lived in many areas, and "fire-baptized" groups were now springing up nearly everywhere, especially in the Mid-West, the South, Texas and elsewhere. Here and there an occasional one could be heard to *"speak in tongues" a strange experience that appeared to lift him out of the mediocre to a kind of exalted plane with God* [emphasis added].

There is ample evidence that the Pentecostal phenomenon was being exhibited by numerous independent groups about the turn of the 20th century. However, the dubious honor of chronological priority as an organization, holding as its primary distinguishing factor sanctification as a second work of grace with the baptism of the Holy Spirit evidenced by speaking in tongues, appears to belong to the Spurling/Tomlinson movement. This group became a large, stable denomination as the Church of God (Cleveland, Tennessee).

Pentecostalism Explodes

Meanwhile, other persons in other places were being affect

---

[104] Ibid.

ed by the impulse of the times. The 19th century spawned innumerable and diverse "winds of doctrine." Accordingly, as the core feature of the holiness movement (entire sanctification) converged with the core features of the Irvingite movement (tongues and dispensationalism), Pentecostalism was born. In hindsight now, given the historical quest in human nature for a peer relationship with God, sinless perfection in holiness, confirmed by subjective experience, Pentecostalism it seems was inevitable.

The convergence of the holiness doctrine with tongues-speaking as confirmation was present in the Spurling group, but the activities of that group did not have a high visibility in the media. It remained for another place and time to give Pentecostalism the high profile visibility needed for a world-wide explosion. The time and place for this explosion came in 1906 at the Azusa Street revival in Los Angeles; and because of its high visibility, most people believe it to be the origin of Pentecostalism.

Three ingredients were needed for this explosion: 1) *sensational doctrine* with some semblance of a biblical foundation, 2) *sensational articulation* – some firey messenger to deliver the message, and 3) *sensational publicity* – a means to tell the story abroad. These three ingredients were provided respectively by three different men: Charles Parham, William J. Seymour, and Frank Bartleman.

Charles F. Parham. In 1901, as the march of this phenomenon continued, Parham started a small teaching ministry called Bethel Bible College in a farmhouse near Topeka, Kansas. He encouraged the student body to seek the gifts of the Holy Spirit, and on New Years Eve 1901, a student, Miss Agnes N. Ozman, claimed that she had received the baptism of the Holy Spirit and had spoken in tongues. Then on January 3, Parham himself received the "baptism." Before long practically the whole student body had the same experience.

After a time of study, Parham put forth his theory that tongues were the biblical evidence of being baptized in the Holy Spirit.[105]

---

[105] It is not clear whether or not Parham derived this doctrine independently. The North Carolina group seems to have preceded him.

For the next four years, Parham preached this doctrine, and then in 1905 he opened a Bible School in Houston, Texas.[106]

William J. Seymour. In Houston, a black Nazarene evangelist named William Seymour enrolled in the classes taught by Parham. Seymour soon embraced Parham's teachings which now included five points: 1) Justification, 2) Sanctification (i.e., perfectionism), 3) Baptism in the Holy Spirit with the "initial evidence" of speaking in other tongues, 4) Divine healing, and 5) The premillennial second coming of Christ.[107]

Armed with these new doctrines, Seymour went to Los Angeles and about 1906 is said to have spoken in tongues. He went to a Nazarene Church on Bonnie Brae Street and gave his testimony of the "baptism." But the elders of the church would not accept his testimony; whereupon Seymour found an abandoned Methodist Church on Azusa Street and began to hold meetings. Most of the Nazarene congregation followed him, and in 1906 there broke out the famed "Azusa Street Revival" under the preaching of Seymour.

The *Los Angeles Times* gave sensational though negative coverage to the meetings, calling Seymour's followers a "sect of fanatics" who worked themselves into a state of frenzy, calling their tongues "weird babble." But this coverage brought out spectators in large numbers, and these proceedings grew and continued for over three years.

Frank Bartleman. Born in Pennsylvania (1871), Bartleman (through a circuitous path from Baptist, to holiness, to Wesleyan, to the Pillar of Fire church and other religious bodies), arrived in California in 1904. He was 33. Already he had been subject to many mystical experiences: shouting, jumping, electric shocks, slain in the spirit, and an attack by Satan "to destroy" him. Having been ordained by a "Pentecostal connection," he was an itinerant

---

[106] Hinson, *Glossolalia*, pp. 68-9.

[107] These five points are cited in "Azusa Street and Frank Bartleman," an article introducing a musical drama, *The Fire Still Falls*, reprinted from *Azusa Street* by Frank Bartleman. See www.firestillfalls.org for additional details of Parham, Seymour, Bartleman and other Pentecostal features.

preacher, but his greatest contribution to the Pentecostal explosion was through journalistic writing.

By 1906, Bartleman had established a reputation with the holiness press as a reporter. He was on hand at the Azusa Street revivals from the beginning, and he provided favorable press for the revival:

> ... it became apparent that Bartleman's role would be that of reporter to the religious world about the Los Angeles Pentecost. His articles gained a wide audience across America and in other lands. Stories about Azusa Street ... passed from hand to hand.[108]

The wide publicity given to Azusa Street brought holiness and Pentecostal leaders from across the nation and around the world, from Canada, Europe, Russia, South America, and virtually every continent. There many of them experienced the Baptism and tongues for the first time. They liked it and took it back to their own people, and Pentecostalism exploded around the world.

Parham, however, saw much Scriptural abuse in the movement, and an irreparable breach developed between him and Seymour, his famous student.

A careful reading of Bartleman's later book,[109] taken mostly from his diary, will reveal friction between Bartleman and Seymour also, which eventually led to a full breach. It is generally considered that the Azusa revival lasted from 1906 to 1909. Bartleman's account of its demise is as follows:

> [By 1909] ... The work had gotten into a bad condition generally ... the missions had fought each other almost to a standstill. Little love remained. There was considerable rejoicing, but in the "flesh." A cold, hardhearted zeal, and human enthusiasm, had taken the place of divine

> love.... The Lord continued to bless my ministry at Eighth and Maple, and at Azusa Street.... I met with persistent opposition, especially from the leaders [i.e., from Seymour, et al.].... The old Azusa mission became more and more in bondage.[110]

---

[108] Ibid.

[109] Frank Bartleman, *How Pentecost Came to Los Angeles* (Los Angles: Self-published by Bartleman, 1925).

[110] Bartleman, pp. 139, 140.

In 1910, Bartleman left Los Angeles and took a trip, preaching his way around the world. He returned in February, 1911. After his return, Bartleman joined with a Brother Durham who had begun preaching at Azusa while Seymour was back east on an evangelistic trip. And "the fire began to fall as at the beginning." But Seymour "hastened back" and locked Durham and Bartleman out of the Azusa Street mission, whereupon:

> Durham rented a large building at the corner of Seventh and Los Angeles Streets ... Here the "cloud" rested. God's glory filled the place. Azusa became deserted.[111]

The Azusa Street phenomenon finally passed into history but not before the seeds of Pentecostalism were scattered around the world.

The Rest of the Story. Meanwhile back in Cherokee County, North Carolina, the Spurling holiness group had reached a somewhat definitive doctrinal platform. Under the leadership of A. J. Tomlinson, in 1904, two years before the Azusa Street phenomenon, the Church of God was settled in Cleveland, Tennessee. Despite subsequent divisions, it is now a denomination with a world-wide membership of about 6 million.

It is commonly believed that the Azusa Street group was first in the tongues movement; it seems apparent, however, that the North Carolina group has the distinction of priority. The Tomlinson group further claimed that they are the biblical Church of God restored in 1903 for the first time since 325 A.D. C. T. Davidson, Church of God historian, wrote:

> Therefore, the Dark Age period is from 325 A.D. to June 13, 1903, when the Church of God was uncovered in what is now Fields of the Wood, Cherokee County, North Carolina, United States of America.[112]

It is a most remarkable leap to ignore the numerous churches of the baptistic faith throughout the pre-Reformation centuries that rejected the Catholic apostasy in their amalgamation with Rome and stood true to the faith – the Donatists, Waldensians, and cer-

---

[111] Bartleman, p. 146.
[112] Davidson, *Upon this Rock*, p. 281.

tain Anabaptists who finally emerged as Baptists. But such is the rationale of this early Pentecostal group, though not shared by all Pentecostals.

Following World War II, Pentecostalism saw its greatest growth:

> In 1943 the Assemblies of God, the Church of God (Cleveland, Tennessee), The International Church of the Foursquare Gospel, and the Pentecostal Holiness Church became charter members of the National Associations of Evangelicals ... disassociating themselves from the organized fundamentalist groups which had disfellowshipped the Pentecostals in 1928.... In 1947 the first World Pentecostal Conference met in Zurich.... The next year the Pentecostal Fellowship of North America was formed in Des Moines, Iowa.... By 1980 the classical Pentecostals had grown to be the largest family of Protestants in the world ...[113]

In view of the historical record, it is now clear that the *subjective religious experience*, in various forms, strikes a responsive chord in the fallen human psyche, whether pagan or Christian. The mushroom growth of Pentecostalism implies, however, that Christians need to feel that there is a biblical basis for such experiences before they can embrace them. Pentecostalism has provided that "need" in its quasi-biblical doctrinal rationale; and having gained a measure of venerability and cultural approbation, the Pentecostal phenomenon was embraced with reckless abandon.

Now, a century later, elements of Pentecostalism have penetrated virtually all the traditional mainline denominations as the modern *Neo-Pentecostal* movement.

Rise of Modern Charismata

Until about 1950, Pentecostalism was regarded by most of Christendom as a low-prestige, somewhat fanatical movement. The religious establishment viewed it with condescension or even contempt, not realizing that within a generation or so all the traditional denominations were to be infiltrated with the same excesses. And now, with a pseudo-doctrinal foundation, Pentecostal

---

[113] V. Synan, "Pentecostalism," *The Evangelical Dictionary of Theology*, ed. Walter A. Elwell, pp. 899-902. Synan estimated the number of classical Pentecostals in 1980 at 51 million.

influence has expanded throughout all Christendom – both fundamentalist and liberal, Bible believers and modernist cynics, from low church to high church, from snake handlers in southern Appalachia to the Canterbury Cathedral to St. Peters in Rome – all have embraced the *subjectivist Pentecostal experience,* with only slight variations in doctrine. How did this happen?

Oral Roberts. In the 1950s a very charismatic faith healer came along named Oral Roberts. At first he worked among the traditional Pentecostal churches until he and his setup man decided they would bypass the churches and go directly to the people using an 18,000-seat tent and simultaneous broadcasts on 63 stations:

> Within two years, his radio and television programs were being broadcast on 400 stations in the United States, Canada, Alaska and Hawaii and by short-wave to listeners around the world.[114]

By these means, claiming at one time to reach nearly 1 billion persons, Roberts gave massive publicity to his message. But the most effective tool for planting the Pentecostal experience into the high church venue was the Full Gospel Business Men's Fellowship International (FGBMFI):

> The Full Gospel Business Men's Fellowship International proved to be an extraordinarily effective tool for spreading the Pentecostal message to the American middle class. By 1975 it had 1,650 chapters, in every state and in fifty-two foreign countries …[115]

Full Gospel Business Men's Fellowship International. The FGBMFI was founded in 1951 by California millionaire Demos Shakarian.[116] But Oral Roberts, says David Harrell, "was the organization's high priest and most coveted friend." After the FGBMFI held its first meeting in Los Angeles, neo-Pentecostalism began a rapid growth; it grew in size, prestige, wealth, and influence. Many prestigious businessmen got the "baptism," but

[114] *St. Petersburg Times*, September 7, 1985

[115] A review of *Oral Roberts: An American Life,* by David E. Harrell, Jr., *Christian News*, December 9, 1985.

[116] David W. Kling, *The Bible in History* (New York: Oxford University Press, 2004), p. 265.

rather than join the lowly-esteemed Pentecostal churches, they remained in their own traditional churches. They formed charismatic sub-units within the old-line denominations, many of which were decaying into liberalism. Thus the religious establishment did not join Pentecostalism, but rather Pentecostalism joined the establishment, and the FGBMFI became the bridge by which Pentecostalism passed over into the modern, prestigious *charismatic movement.*

> In order to distinguish these newer Pentecostals from the older Pentecostal denominations, the word "charismatic" began to be used widely around 1973 to designate the movement in the mainline churches. The older Pentecostals were called "classical Pentecostals." By 1980 the term "neo–Pentecostal" had been universally abandoned in favor of "charismatic renewal."[117]

The High Churches Get the Baptism. It was around 1960 that this tongues-speaking movement began to break out of its old confines and make its way into the main-line denominations.

> The first well known person to openly experience glossolalia and remain within his church was Dennis Bennett, an Episcopal priest in Van Nuys, California. Although forced to leave his parish in Van Nuys because of controversy over his experience, Bennett was invited to pastor an inner-city Episcopal parish in Seattle, Wash. The church in Seattle experienced rapid growth after the introduction of Pentecostal worship, becoming a center of Neo-Pentecostalism in the northwestern United States.[118]

Soon charismatic phenomena broke out among the Episcopalians, Presbyterians, Lutherans, Methodists, Baptists, the Anglican high-church, and practically every other denominational movement. When it began to break out in the old liberal denominations, the major television networks and other news media decided this was a news-worthy story. It was not much news-worthy as long as it was confined to the Pentecostal groups that lacked wealth and sophistication. But when Pentecostalism spread into the prestigious high-church people, this was news.

And so a wave of publicity began, and the more publicity it

---

[117] V. Synan, "Pentecostalism," *Evangelical Dictionary of Theology*, ed. Walter A. Elwell.

[118] Ibid.

got, the more the upper class of the social strata was drawn to it. Neo-Pentecostalism soon became "respectable" in all of the mainline denominations. And when they found that it satisfied a "need" in the human psyche, it caught on like wildfire and the new wave moved rapidly throughout the world.

By 1967, the Charismatic Movement had made its way into the Catholic church. Then the Catholics also began to experience the "baptism" and to speak in tongues.

Even the liberals, unbelievers, and skeptics became involved; some saw it as a golden opportunity to promote ecumenism. George Gardiner, a reclaimed charismatic, said this of the modern charismatic movement:

> … often includes those who do not meet biblical standards as "born again" believers. It is admitted by leaders of the movement that there are those who do not believe in such essential doctrines as the Trinity, the Virgin Birth and Deity of Christ. Yet these people speak in "tongues."[119]

They claim the baptism of the Holy Spirit, the third person of the Trinity, even though they deny the deity of Christ, the second person of the Trinity. This movement is a great boon for ecumenism, liberalism, modernism, and postmodernism; for when they speak in tongues, it implies that God honors them even in their unbelief.

Conclusion. So now a huge charismatic influence pervades much of Christendom, and it has drawn many together around *the experience* – not around the Word of God – but around *the experience*. They believe that God is pouring out His Spirit upon them, confirming, and validating the movement by the phenomenon of tongues. Are we then to believe that God has now approved every church and "wind of doctrine," ranging from the pedophile scandal-ridden Catholic Church leadership to the practicing homosexual Bishop of the Episcopal Church? Behind it all we can easily see the deceitful and crafty hand of Satan attempting to validate the divided and empty shell of "Christian" discord, attempting to forge the signature of God.

---

[119] Gardiner, pp. 49, 50.

III.
The Relentless Ascent of
Subjectivism in Recent History

The ancient human passion to know God through subjective personal experience, including presumed direct revelation from God and/or ecstatic phenomena, has invaded contemporary Christendom on a broad basis. Subtlety has been the craft of our common enemy from the beginning (Gen. 3:1). And what could be a more subtle influence upon the human mind than the claim that truth is drawn from within – that what we *feel* is somehow the truth. How convincing it is. How effortless. How comfortable. How self-exalting.

When Bishop George Ridding (1885) said in a sermon: "I feel a feeling which I feel you all feel," it is likely that he appealed to every soul in the audience; and yet there may have been dozens of differing feelings and emotions, some based on truth and some upon error. Our subjective feelings and experiences are no reliable guide to truth. They must be tested by Scripture. As previously explained, valid feeling is *created* only as the Holy Spirit applies the objective Word of Scripture – God's revealed, confirmed, and changeless standard of truth – to our understanding.

INFLUENCING FACTORS

For over two centuries now, many religious movements and theological theories have developed which seem to have been motivated by a need for direct personal experience and knowledge of God. In the late 18th century there were the Quakers, then the ecstatic phenomena of the Great Awakening; then with the Irvingites the charismatic phenomenon began its relentless march to the current notoriety of the 20th and 21st century. Thus the Pentecostal, charismatic, and subjectivist features of today did not develop in a vacuum. Developing contemporaneously with them, subjectivist theologians of the 19th and early 20th centuries, quite independently, were busy publishing new theories which helped to pave the way for modern charismata and other forms of subjectivism.

Subjectivism and the Theologians

A valuable survey of some developing theologies is provided by Hugh Ross Mackintosh in his book, *Types of Modern Theologies.*[120] Of the six influential theologians discussed by Mackintosh, three are of particular interest concerning the preparation of the world for the explosive growth of subjectivism and the more destructive philosophies of existentialism and postmodernism. They are Schleiermacher, Kierkegaard, and Barth.

Friedrich Schleiermacher (1768-1834). Of the three men named above, all of whom were enormously influen-

---

[120] Hugh Ross Mackintosh, *Types of Modern Theologies: Schleiermacher to Barth* (London: Nisbet and Company, Ltd., 1937).

tial, Schleiermacher's influence may have been the greatest. Mackintosh wrote:

> Next to the *Institutes* of Calvin [Schleiermacher's *The Christian Faith*], is the most influential dogmatic work to which evangelical Protestantism can point ... [121]

A similar statement appears in the Editors' Preface to the English translation of Schleiermacher's dogmatic work, *The Christian Faith:*

> In the opinion of competent thinkers *The Christian Faith* of Schleiermacher is, with the exception of Calvin's *Institutes*, the most important work covering the whole field of doctrine to which Protestant theology can point.[122]

Accordingly Mackintosh devotes two chapters in his *Types of Modern Theologies* to the discussion of Schleiermacher, which he calls "The Theology of Feelings (A)" and "... (B)." He says:

> ... there exists a general harmony between the conclusions of [Schleiermacher's] the *Dialectic* ... and some positions taken in Schleiermacher's great dogmatic work, *The Christian Faith*. In both books equally it is taught that *God is originally presented in feelings;* that we possess *no strictly objective* cognition of Him ... [123] [emphasis added].

Schleiermacher does not argue from feelings generated by objectively discovered truth. All Christians acknowledge that feelings and emotions consistently and appropriately arise as a response to God's objective revelation whether in Scripture or nature.

AUTHENTIC SUBJECTIVITY. As previously discussed, God Himself created human emotions with the normal capability of subjective *responses* to truth, but feelings are not a *source* of truth. God created feelings and emotion for the joy and motivation of His people, just as He created the ability for humanity to engage accurately and profitably in the reasoning process when guided by objective revelation. These are valuable gifts from God.

---

[121] Mackintosh, p. 60.

[122] Friedrich Schleiermacher, *The Christian Faith*, ed. H. R. Mackintosh and J. S. Stewart (Edinburgh: T. & T. Clark, 1928), p. v.

[123] Mackintosh, p. 40.

Therefore, subjective responses such as *love, joy,* and *peace* are valid only if derived from objective truth. This truth comes only as the Holy Spirit illuminates our understanding as we read or hear the objective Word. This is orthodox subjectivity in action.

The Schleiermacher Difference. But the Schleiermacher doctrine is different. It bypasses objective Scripture and its confirmation by the Holy Spirit. He argues that in "feeling itself we grasp God directly as the 'Whence' of all things."[124] Schleiermacher contends that all theology is simply the acting out of experience and the understanding of a pious feeling, and this strictly reflects man's dependence on God. For example, he asserts and defends at length this proposition:

> The piety which forms the basis of all ecclesiastical communions is ... neither a Knowing nor a Doing, but a *modification of Feeling* [emphasis added], or of immediate self-consciousness.[125]

His work does not take the form of a systematic delineation of objective truth revealed from God in Scripture, but rather a generalization of the piety of all Protestant communions as derived from their feelings. Concerning the attributes of God, for example, he says:

> All attributes which we ascribe to God are to be taken as denoting *not something special in God*, but only *something special in the manner in which the feeling* [emphasis added] of absolute dependence is to be related to Him.[126]

Objectivity toward the biblical revelation of God does not show up as a characteristic of Schleiermacher's theology; thus it is fair to say that if, according to his contention, the basis of all Christian communions is feelings, then his own 700 page tome reflects only *his* feelings, and as such is essentially worthless. Nevertheless, the extreme obscurity and abstractness of his theology has so fascinated certain academicians that they have made it widely influential – further aggravating the serious human propensity toward *subjectivity*.

---

[124] Mackintosh, p. 65.

[125] Schleiermacher, p. 5.

[126] Schleiermacher, p. 194.

Schleiermacher was a young German whose parents followed the Moravian religious concepts. This young man had deep longing to have the peace in himself that he saw in the community of the Moravians. He had a great love for what he called the "beauty and dignity" of the services that were held every day. He was struck to his very soul with the ideas of human corruption and forgiveness.

With all of this there was a personal struggle being fought within him that soon led to his break with the community. Even though he believed in things supernatural, and the peace that forgiveness can bring, the experience of these things eluded him. He wrote that the certainty that he *sought* always seemed ever to "flee."

That personal struggle continued for several years and then, finally, he wrote to his father that what he was going to say pained him very much and would cause his father's hope in his son to waver. It has been said that he could not believe that the One Who called Himself the Son of Man was the same as the true and eternal God and that he rejected the death of Jesus on the cross as a vicarious atonement.

> The impression is all but unavoidable that eventually Schleiermacher puts "archetypal humanity" rather than the personal Incarnation of God at the center of his view of Christ.[127]

Though much could be, and has been, said about the broader theology of Schleiermacher, we must limit our discussion to the influence he may have had on our immediate subject, the rapid growth of subjectivism, existentialism, and postmodernism in the late 20th century and continuing into the 21st century. His doctrine that truth is apprehended subjectively through human *feelings*, is certain to have influenced young theologians from the 19th century to the present.

This is not to say that good folks like the grass-roots early charismatic tongues-speakers on the banks of the Clyde, or the Pentecostals in Fields of the Wood, North Carolina, or on Azusa Street, knew much if anything about Schleiermacher; but for

---

[127] Mackintosh, p. 90.

countless young pastoral students and their professors in many seminaries throughout the twentieth century, the authority of Scripture has been steadily undermined or weakened by exposure to Schleiermacher and other such theologians in the name of Christian scholarship.

Soren Kierkegaard (1813-1855). Kierkegaard has been called the father of existentialism[128] even though existentialism has had many variations over long ranges of time. Speir tells us: "Existentialism is not isolated, it reaches all the way back to the Stoics and Plotinus; but some of its main roots are to be found in modern Humanism."[129]

Our main interest in the existentialism of Kierkegaard is its influence on the growing subjectivism of modern Evangelicalism and the charismatic movement, and its influence on the 20th century as a forerunner of postmodernism. It has contributed appreciably to the trend toward reliance upon personal experience and subjectivism as a source of religious knowledge. "Subjectivity," says Frederick Sontag, "is the concept most often associated with Kierkegaard."[130] To him, the individual was the only concern. He considered that the only truth was individual subjectivity,[131] i.e., the only knowledge is to know a subject internally in personal experience as one encounters life.

Mackintosh gives the leading principle of Kierkegaard's point of view:

> ... the principle of spiritual inwardness, or, as it is often called, subjectivity, has a determinative influence on all his thinking. By inwardness is meant the personal appropriation of Divinely presented truth ... Truth, Kierkegaard declares, is subjectivity, as subjectivity is truth.... . His point rather is that the coldly objective counts for nothing by itself; or, as he

---

[128] Frederick Sontag, "Soren Kierkegaard," *Great Thinkers of the Western World*, ed. Ian P. McGreal (New York: HarperCollins Publishers, 1992), p. 369.

[129] J. M. Speir, *Christianity and Existentialism*. Trans. with notes by David Hugh Freeman. (Presbyterian and Reformed Publishing Company, 1953), p. 5.

[130] Sontag, "Soren Kierkegaard," p. 369.

[131] Speir, pp. 7-8.

expresses it in familiar words, "only the truth that edifies is truth for thee."[132]

Karl Barth (1886-1968). Barth is the final example of theological influence we will consider as it relates to the rapid rise of subjectivism and modern charismata. Again we are interested, not in his whole theology checkered with many problems, including what Carson suggests is a cautious universalism,[133] but in his subjectivist view of divine revelation. Mackintosh describes Barth's position as follows:

> ... revelation is revelation only when by the Spirit it "gets through" to man... . Holy Scripture, comprising documents derived from prophets who looked forward to the great event of Jesus Christ, or from apostles who looked back, is not as such the revelation; it is ... revelation, if and when He speaks to us through the prophetic or apostolic witness.[134]

This view clearly abandons Scripture truth to human subjectivity. In other words, the objective propositional declarations of Scripture must first be passed through the filter of human acceptance before they become revelation from God to man.

The influence of Barth on the 20th century was great enough and swift enough that Barth himself felt the need to joke about it:

> "It is a real question," he has suggested, "whether there is as much joy in heaven as there is on earth over the growth of the Barthian school."[135]

The great joy on earth over Barthianism is doubtless the response of the human propensity toward subjectivism; what sinner would not rejoice upon finding that he need not worry about such things as the "lake of fire" unless it really "spoke" to him.

It is not typical that a theologian or philosopher lives to see a "school" of followers within his own lifetime, but Barth did. This fact may have been due to the preconditioning influence of both existentialism and the rising charismatic trend. Barth, at first, seemed to reflect Kierkegaard's existentialism, but he later

---

[132] Mackintosh, p. 224.

[133] See D. A. Carson, *The Gagging of God* (Grand Rapids: Zondervan Publishing House, 1996), p. 143-4.

[134] Mackintosh, pp. 281-2

[135] Macintosh, p. 265.

renounced it.[136] With the one hand, he seems to pull his followers toward the Scripture, and with the other he pushes them back to the ambiguity of subjectivism. At the end of the day, Barth does not acknowledge the Scriptures themselves as God's infallible revelation wholly independent of the human subjective response.

What is relevant to our discussion is that men like Schleiermacher, Kierkegaard, Barth, et al., have seriously muddied the waters; they have managed to make obscure what God has made clear. Though these men have all gone to meet their Maker, they, and many following them, have contributed to the contemporary retreat from strong personal biblical convictions and to the halfhearted regard many Christians have for objective, infallible Scripture truth. This includes many within Christian academia, modern charismatics, the existentialists, postmodernists, and now the general subjectivism of a large portion of evangelicals.

Existentialism Reaches the Grass Roots.

The long-range influence of the theologians, however, was not made directly by their own writings nearly so much as by 20th-century writers such as Jean-Paul Sartre and Albert Camus reflecting the essence of existentialism in novels, plays, and other works. It has been a theme in movies and musicals to look within, follow your heart, be true to yourself.

Trickle-Down Subjectivism. By this and other means, the influence of Kierkegaard and other subjectivists has been delivered namelessly and subconsciously to the inner self of multitudes of college students who have become teachers, writers, journalists, entertainers, and even pastors. Thus the whole of our culture has become virtually saturated with a subjectivist worldview. Millions of persons at the street level who know little or nothing of Kierkegaard or existentialism are subjectively oriented.

Just as fish in an aquarium do not know they are wet, the crowds on the street, including many Christians, are unaware of their subjectivist orientation in this postmodern culture. Eventually, the pervasiveness of these philosophies so thoroughly altered the

---

[136] Mackintosh, p. 263-4

atmosphere of the culture in which we all live that millions have been dyed or tinctured with existentialism and postmodernism and have never even known it.

Although orthodox Christian voices have been raised in protest to this trend, they are either too few or too timid to have a serious impact upon the august and venerable oracles of academia, or to gain the ear of the man on the street or Christians in the pew.

It "Eats as Doth a Canker." Reinforcing the existential trend is the naïve notion of certain Christian leadership – pastors, writers, publishers – that we must avoid troubling the persons in the pew with the "heavy" doctrinal or theological principles which God gave to anchor the souls of His people and fortify them against destructive philosophies. Since the early 20th century denominational publications such as Sunday school and training literature have very weakly protested, if at all, the dangers facing Christian people, deliberately avoiding the weighty doctrinal and theological content that defines the Christian faith.

The pulpit has followed suit lest, God forbid, a preacher should utter a word now and then that would require a listener to consult a dictionary. This trend of biblical shallowness continues today in the form of "contemporary worship" in the no-name[137] or stealth churches, where it is not considered good marketing strategy to openly proclaim, or even to disclose, a historical or doctrinal position, if any. From such churches the great doctrines of Scripture have virtually vanished, and the typical worshipper does not have a clue as to the nature of apostolic Christianity.

Because of fallen human nature, it is to be expected that unbelievers and immature Christians would flock to these vacuous but euphoric churches. Not wanting to be troubled with objective truth or the effort required to understand, identify, and avoid destructive doctrines and morals, many have resisted, or at least neglected, sound doctrine (2 Tim. 4:3).

---

[137] That is, churches that no longer include the denominational identity in the name of the church. Thus its orientation toward Scripture or its historic or theological position within the broad spectrum of Christian ideas, if any, remains unknown as the subjectivist wants it.

Then many Christians mature enough to know better have been proselytized by these euphoric churches. In fact many who are well grounded in the unchangeable objective truth are somehow intimidated by the euphoric exuberance of their subjectivist friends. And being taken by surprise, they are often too intimidated to urge their friends to attend a church where they will be exposed to substantive biblical teachings – teachings that can convict the unsaved and fortify the souls of believers with God's objective, unchangeable revelation of absolute truth. Thus the bold subjectivists seem to be winning the day.[138]

These and other factors have left the population wide open to a blind subjectivism. The false philosophies incubated in and perpetuated by academia, including many seminaries and the decaying culture around us, are being ignored by the passivity of otherwise sound leaders who, rationalizing the status quo, remain undisturbed, sounding no convincing warnings, joining no battles, putting down no strong holds. Thus the lure of the stealth churches and modern charismata has been virtually irresistible. Worse yet thousands of young people – having been ripped apart by the pull of humanism in their culture and school systems on the one hand and the pull of Scripture truth in their churches on the other hand – finally decide with postmodernism (though they don't even know what it is) that there is no absolute standard of truth. Many abandon all hope, turning to lawlessness, and despair – the inevitable consequence of existentialism, postmodernism, and a passive orthodoxy.

CHARACTERISTIC WEAKNESSES
OF SUBJECTIVISM

The human passion to know God directly from within, subjectively, has been reinforced by the further development of the existential seeds planted by these older theologians. In this section

---

[138] We have known individuals trained in the objective truths of Scripture who, when surprised by the bold exuberance of subjectivism, feel that they must leave their own church and go shopping around to all the feelings-oriented churches, thinking "What have I been missing?" And the progress of the weak is thus inhibited or reversed.

we will examine the broader effects of subjectivism as it continues its relentless march into the modern world of evangelicalism. First we will consider the charismatics.

Traditional Pentecostalism

The traditional Pentecostal movement has finally found at least a modicum of doctrinal rationale in the doctrine borrowed from the holiness movement. This doctrine, while unable to bear the scrutiny of Scripture, has brought enough creedal stability to traditional Pentecostalism to maintain a more or less permanent position as stand-alone churches and denominations.

However, many of the older Pentecostals are now morphing into the anonymity of the no-name, or stealth, church growth movement. This practice is common to other historical denominations as well, as various churches lose their historic identity. Designed to attract the multitudes who will not "endure sound doctrine," or any doctrine, churches hide or abandon their historic doctrinal identity behind generic names like *Community Church, Shady Brook Church*, etc. – names which have no historic doctrinal legacy and tell the public nothing of their belief system, if any.

Nevertheless, there are still traditional Pentecostals, holding to their traditional convictions, who would not go where their younger sister, Neo-Pentecostalism, has gone.

Neo-Pentecostalism: Doctrinal Ambiguity Indispensable

Neo-Pentecostalism, on the other hand, having no definitive doctrinal position of its own, is parasitic by nature.[139] Like any parasite, it is not possible for it to live and grow on its own apart from a host life-form. Doctrinal ambiguity is therefore indispensable to its survival. It must by necessity remain vague enough to adapt itself to any host ranging from fundamentalism to ultra-liberalism. This doctrinal ambiguity reflects an opportunistic theolo-

---

[139] The historic manifestations of charismata, as observed in the previous chapter, have never been self-sustaining. Like all parasitic forms, its quintessential character is remarkably at home with any host; e.g., it has thrived in numerous pagan religions, and in Montanism, the Shakers, Irvingites, Mormons, and today in virtually every Christian denomination, liberal or conservative.

gy which has been spontaneously cobbled together, or improvised off-the-cuff, by various individuals for almost two centuries.

Even Pentecostals acknowledge a weakness in doctrinal justification for their claims: "The charismatic movement as a whole is doctrinally unpredictable, at the time marked and marred by a Corinthian elitism,"[140] lamented Russell Spittler, Assembly of God minister, and currently Provost and Vice President of Academic Affairs, Fuller Theological Seminary. But he also noted, "Moral convictions often lag behind religious conversion."[141] And again: "The fact that people did not immediately understand all doctrine and did not adopt a biblical lifestyle did not mean their experience was not genuine."[142]

Neo-Pentecostalism, however, promotes no uniform creed or theology. Its strongest feature or doctrine (if doctrine it may be called) is experience, the baptism of the Holy Spirit, accompanied by speaking in tongues. Thus the only firm doctrine by which Neo-Pentecostalism is uniquely identified is a doctrine which allows continuous adaptation to any church, denomination, or creed which will permit tongues-speaking and the like.

Accordingly, God may now "speak" directly and personally to one person, saying, "Go join yourself to that liberal Episcopal Church" (perchance with an openly practicing homosexual Bishop). To another He may say, "Go join yourself to that fundamentalist Bible church"; and to a third He may say, "Join that liberal Methodist church," or that "charismatic Presbyterian Church." And to others, "Go join the Catholic Church." Thus Neo-Pentecostalism, far from being a movement with a single benign error, as some suppose, may now be seen, even if well-meaning, as embracing any doctrine across the spectrum of denominational discord clearly contrary to the prayer of Christ for unity in truth (John 17:17-21). We must admit that if God has bestowed direct revelation and the baptism of the Holy Spirit upon all Christian

---

[140] See Kenneth S. Kantzer, "The Charismatics Among Us," *Christianity Today* 22 February 1979: 29.

[141] Ibid.

[142] Ibid.

discord, this would imply God's approval upon "every wind of doctrine."

God's goal is unity in truth only. But Neo-Pentecostals represent, or rather misrepresent, the Triune God as One who endorses, with His highest order of approval, the present ecumenical conglomeration of splintered and divided churches as being the fulfillment of His vision for the church on earth. It is one level of sin for *men* to endorse the sin at the roots of Christian discord; it is another level of sin to implicate *God* in the same error.

Neo-Pentecostalism: Ecumenical and Existential

As we probe deeper into the features of Neo-Pentecostalism, there is a growing awareness that it is both *ecumenical* and *existential* in character.

Neo-Pentecostal Ecumenism. Modernism, which questions the central truths that make Christianity unique including the infallibility of Scripture, the deity of Christ, the vicarious atonement, the bodily resurrection, etc., reached its zenith early in the 20th century.

Many within the old-line liberal denominations, having been robbed by unbelief of the glorious hope in their basic doctrines, felt a sense of shallowness, emptiness, deadness, or "dryness" both in the pulpit and in the pew. They recognized the deadness, and they longed to have something that was alive; they sought something to vindicate their profession of faith: Neo-Pentecostalism rose to the occasion. Dead in the hopelessness of liberalism or "existential 'nothingness,'"[143] many grasped for the opiate of subjective experience.

Episcopal Neo-Pentecostal rector, Dennis Bennett, was among the first in the mainline churches who "sought the Baptism of the Holy Spirit," Mook said, because of *"his 'dryness.'"* Another example, in 1966, was a group of faculty members at Duquesne University who sought the baptism for a similar reason.[144] Neo-Pentecostalism may now be seen as a doctrine of ecu-

---

[143] James Richard Mook, "Basis of Neo-Pentecostal Ecumenicity," thesis, Dallas Theological Seminary, 1980. p. 70.

[144] Ibid.

menical *pseudo-unity* built upon the carcasses of *discordant*, dry, empty, denominations, churches, and individuals. The normative work of the Holy Spirit in regeneration allows for no "dryness," but rather brings "joy unspeakable and full of glory" (1 Peter 1:8). So where is the new emphasis on regeneration?

Dr. George Gardiner, having once been deeply involved with charismatics but who turned from it, said that there are liberals who deny the deity of Christ but who still have received the charismatic "baptism" and have spoken in tongues.[145] Christians in many churches sensed the deadness that liberalism created, but they turned to Neo-Pentecostalism rather than to the objective Word of God to fill the void.

Mook confirms that:

"... the emergence [of Neo-Pentecostalism] was prepared by three principal factors: 1) the formation and growth of the Full Gospel Business Men's Fellowship International (FGBMFI); 2) the life and work of David du Plessis; 3) the emphasis of Vatican II ecumenism, the Holy Spirit, and renewal."[146]

David du Plessis was probably the most influential of the three factors above as Neo-Pentecostalism became a unifying force in ecumenicalism. Since about 1918 when he received the "Baptism of the Spirit," du Plessis had been a traditional Pentecostal. Mook informs us that in 1952, he was introduced and "warmly received" at the meeting of the International Missionary Council by Dr. John S. Mackay, President of Princeton Seminary and President of the International Missionary Council of the World Council of Churches.[147] Finally:

... in 1959 du Plessis lectured on Pentecostalism at several mainline educational institutions: Princeton Seminary, the Evangelical Congregational School of Theology, Yale Divinity School, Union Theological Seminary in New York, the Ecumenical Institute of the WCC at Chateau de Bossey in Switzerland, and Perkins School of Theology in Southern Methodist

---

[145] Gardiner, p. 50.
[146] Mook, p. 16.
[147] Mook, p. 19.

University in Dallas.... [He also] participated in the eighteenth Council of the Presbyterian World Alliance in Sao Paulo, Brazil.[148]

As the list of institutions above demonstrates, the liberal, ecumenical wing of Christendom seemed to have received the Neo-Pentecostal message "anon with joy." Was this change because these institutions – having long exerted their august influence on the side of modernism, never having been admirers of fundamentalist Pentecostalism, and being no friend of the doctrine of the infallibility and inerrancy of Scripture – then suddenly fell under the conviction that the Word of God requires them to embrace the central doctrine of Pentecostalism? Or did they see that here was a powerful issue which could be exploited to strengthen ecumenical bonds across otherwise irreconcilable denominational boundaries? Could this be the cement that would bind Catholic and Protestant once again into a manageable ecumenical union?

The final factor which made Neo-Pentecostalism fully ecumenical, involving both the mainline Protestant denominations and the Catholic Church, was the Second Vatican Council (October 1962 – December 1965). Vatican II was called by Pope John XXIII, who set the initial tone and agenda. But after the death of John XXIII, his successor, Pope Paul, continued the spirit of the Council. Mook describes the council:

> A significant part of [the] tone was an emphasis on the Holy Spirit, renewal, unity, ecumenism, charisms, lay involvement, and a "new Pentecost." ... the emphasis [was] on the work of the Holy Spirit in drawing the "separated brethren" (Protestants) back to the "faith in its entirety" and ecumenical union with the Roman Catholic Church.[149]

Thus Vatican II opened the door for full Neo-Pentecostalism to enter, which it did in 1967:

> In 1966 some faculty members of Duquesne University prayed that the Holy Spirit would renew the graces given to them in their sacramental baptism and confirmation.... . they developed a desire to receive the Baptism of the Holy Spirit. On January 13, 1967 at a prayer group organized by a Presbyterian woman, Ralph Keifer, a Theology instruc-

---

[148] Mook, p. 20.
[149] Mook, p. 21-23.

tor at Duquesne University, experienced the Baptism of the Spirit and spoke in tongues. These occurrences at Duquesne marked the origin of the Catholic Pentecostal movement.[150]

From this 1967 beginning, the Catholic Pentecostal movement has spread; and in 1975 at the 9th annual Pentecostal Council held in Rome, the movement was given the official blessing of the Pope himself.

Neo-Pentecostalism thus became the tie that would bind together an extensive ecumenical movement over the quarter century to follow. If this show of unity were unity in *truth, for which Jesus prayed* (John 17:17-21) and as defined by Paul (1 Cor. 1:10), it would be a blessing to the world beyond measure. But that was not the case; this was unity *despite* the truth. It was a pseudo-unity around a single issue, an erroneous and sinful abuse of one doctrine of Scripture, the Baptism of the Holy Spirit, now used in the hope of restoring the broken Reformation bond in the Roman Catholic Church. Yet, it seems to be working:

> In July of 1977 the 1977 Conference on Charismatic Renewal in the Christian Churches was held in Kansas City. Approximately 50,000 people participated in this conference. These represented various traditions: Baptist, Catholic, Episcopal, Lutheran, Mennonite, Messianic Judaism, Pentecostal, Presbyterian, United Methodists, and nondenominational... [bringing together] Christians as diverse as erudite Roman Catholic university professors and unlettered Pentecostals only a generation removed from snake-handling.[151]

Neo-Pentecostal Existentialism. On the heels of the void left by liberalism, popular existentialist subjectivism swooped in on the wings of Neo-Pentecostalism. This seems to have sounded the death knell to any ray of hope for a return to the biblical objectivity of the older mainline Protestant churches. The premise of Mook's judicious thesis is that Neo-Pentecostalism is and will continue as an "impetus to modern ecumenism for three reasons: 1) the ecumenical history of Neo-Pentecostalism; 2) the *existential epistemological center* of Neo-Pentecostalism – the 'Baptism of the Holy Spirit'; 3) the group dynamics of Neo-Pentecostalism."

---

[150] Mook, pp. 26, 27.

[151] Mook, p. 28.

In defining the existential character of the Neo-Pentecostal understanding of the baptism of the Holy Spirit, Mook includes these features:

> ... 3) There is a stress on transfer from "inauthentic" to "authentic" essence by means of "extreme and exceptional" experiences.... 4) There is a stress on subjective truth as opposed to objective truth. That is, truth is only meaningful when it is internally experienced and not just intellectually perceived. 5) There is a stress on the internal locus of objects of faith, emotion, and will ... The experience is one in which one internally experiences spiritual truth and focuses his faith, emotion, and will on this internally experienced truth.... Put more simply, existential epistemology will mean certain knowledge of spiritual truth, which certain knowledge is gained by an irrational experience of authentication.[152]

In other words, the ecumenical Neo-Pentecostal emphasis is that *authenticity* is realized only by *extreme and exceptional experiences*; i.e., certainty in the knowledge of truth is only perceived *internally* (subjectively), not objectively, which confirms our earlier observation that, for the charismatic, experience trumps Scripture truth. This new epistemology means that knowledge of spiritual truth is gained by *irrational experience*, not objectively. Mook's work positively identifies the *existential* characteristics of the charismatic version of the baptism of the Holy Spirit. It reveals a very real affinity between the subjectivism of Neo-Pentecostalism and the more generic subjectivism of the existentialist concepts of Schleiermacher, Kierkegaard, and even Barth.

This affinity is clearly discernable in the words of Donal Dorr, a Catholic Pentecostal theologian:

> ... baptism in the Holy Spirit may mean something rather different to a classic Pentecostalist, to a strict Evangelical Protestant, to a Catholic in the Ignatian tradition of spirituality, to a Catholic involved in the Charismatic Renewal, and to any Christian who has been taught to distrust deep feelings, at least in religious matters.[153]

We must conclude from this statement, considered in the light of Scripture, that the Neo-Pentecostal understanding of the

---

[152] Mook, pp. 39, 40.

[153] Donal Dorr, *Remove the Heart of Stone: Charismatic Renewal and the Experience of Grace*, pp. 55-56, as quoted by Mook, p. 41.

baptism of the Holy Spirit is both existential and grossly in error. It is contrary both in experience and purpose to the biblical baptism of the Holy Spirit (which we will discuss thoroughly in the next chapter) that came at Pentecost. This baptism came upon a single gathered assembly of one hundred and twenty people who were all in "one accord in one place," not upon an ecumenical conglomeration of differing denominational and theological factions.

It does seem dubious that so many differing factions or divisions of the historic schisms in Christendom would all experience the baptism of the Holy Spirit and each gather a *different meaning* from it.

If the experiences to which Dorr referred are valid works of the Holy Spirit, there would have to be a biblical rationale behind them. But apparently there is not; there is no unity growing around a common body of objective Scripture truth in the ecumenical movement. We must therefore agree with Mook's evaluation of Dorr's statement:

> So Dorr is saying the objective doctrinal context of the experience is meaningless. What is meaningful is the *experience itself.* In other words, the *experience* stands as valid apart from any specific doctrinal context.... the Baptism of the Holy Spirit is central to Neo-Pentecostalism and that this Baptism is existential in nature... [The baptism] is the *basis of certainty of knowledge of spiritual truth....* Thus, through the existential experience of the Baptism of the Holy Spirit Neo-Pentecostalism finds its *basis for knowing and being certain of spiritual truth....* Thus knowledge ... is not gained on the basis of rational processes but on the *basis of existential experience*[154] [emphases added].

The Neo-Pentecostal "baptism" is, therefore, ecumenical, epistemological,[155] and existential. This stands in stark contradistinction to the *unity in Scripture truth* for which Christ prayed: *"Sanctify them through thy truth: thy word is truth"* (John 17:17-23); and again, *"Thy will be done in earth, as it is in heaven"* (Matt. 6:10).

No Epistemological Value at All. As with the pagan experi-

---

[154] Mook, p. 51.

[155] We have previously discussed the epistemological worthlessness of subjectivity.

ences discussed earlier, we do not doubt the reality of the experiences; what we doubt is that the experiences were indeed baptisms of the Holy Spirit! With each person holding tenaciously to his or her own traditional denominational doctrines, this does not sound like the unity in Scripture truth for which Christ prayed (John 17:17-21). This, we believe, is proof enough that the experience is not of the Holy Spirit. We must conclude the experience springs out of the common subjectivism of the human psyche, independent of biblical doctrine. Thus such experiences could have no epistemological value at all.

Unity in Truth. The implications of this new ecumenical template or paradigm, which has been pressed down over Christianity, ignores the biblical doctrine of the immutable unity in truth of the Trinity (John 17:21). It disregards the righteousness and beauty of the *holy divisiveness* which the character of Christ brings to the human scene:

> Think not that I am come to send peace on earth: I came not to send peace, but a sword. For I am come to set a man at variance against his father, and the daughter against her mother, and the daughter in law against her mother in law. And a man's foes shall be they of his own household (Matt. 10:34-36).

This passage does not imply that the prayer of Christ for peace and unity, noted above, will never be answered; it will be (Isa. 2:1-5). Rather it asserts that the unity and peace He brings will be genuine, dividing truth and error, with His people *agreeing in Scripture truth and practice* (1 Cor. 1:10).

Unity in truth will not be a cheap compromise or a white wash, ignoring the current discord between conservative and liberal views of the infallibility of Scripture, the virgin birth, the deity, the vicarious atonement, and bodily resurrection of Christ. Nor can the Holy Spirit forever forebear the long standing doctrinal errors between churches, denominations, and Christians. The ecumenical movement is not God's answer to "peace on earth, good will toward men" (Luke 2:14); the answer to that is Christian unity around a full orbed body of objective biblical truth (1 Cor. 1:10).

This false paradigm of existential subjectivism has created

a changing attitude within evangelicalism that the Scriptures no longer represent fully and exclusively the divine will of God. It implies that one can no longer pick up his or her Bible and read it and hear it say in crystal clear words, *"This is My Will, this is My Way, walk ye in it"* (Isa. 30:21, author's expanded paraphrase).

The Progression and Impact of Subjectivism

In the heyday of modernism, human reason reigned autonomously and sat in judgment over Scripture. Truth was what human reason said it was, and the rest was myth. Ironically, however, the trend toward subjectivism was already on the rise. At the grass roots, it took the form of charismata and Pentecostalism. In academia it took the form of existentialism and eventually postmodernism. Later, we will discuss more fully how these two categories of subjectivism are related.

As the expectations of autonomous human reason in modernism failed to vindicate its optimism in the early 20th century, the pendulum began to swing rapidly to the opposite extreme into the burgeoning subjectivism of the late 20th century. Gary L. W. Johnson expressed it well:

> We are sadly experiencing, on a rather large scale, a subjectivism that betrays its weakened hold on the objective truth and reality of Christianity by its neglect or even renunciation of its distinctive objective character.[156]

The pendulum swing of human trends and fads, rarely comes to rest on the dead center of revealed Scripture truth.

How did we come to this? There are many factors, but the one-two-three impact of Schleiermacher, Kierkegaard, and Barth, et al., on 20th century evangelicalism is immense. The influences of these men were largely embraced by the world of the academic elite. Their existentialist doctrines were launched more or less concurrently with the *spontaneous* rise of early charismata and Pentecostalism at opposite ends of the social spectrum. But now the two subjectivist strains have merged and have effectually undercut the objective authority of Scripture truth across the evan-

---

[156] Gary L. W. Johnson, "Does Theology Still Matter," *The Coming Evangelical Crisis*, p. 66.

gelical landscape. Both these movements found fertile ground in the ancient and ever-present sinful human proclivity toward subjectivity, direct revelation, and ecstatic experience; and these have been reinforced by factors in the late 20th century.

The *academic subjectivism* of Schleiermacher, Kierkegaard, and Barth began in academia and trickled down to the pew, while the *spontaneous subjectivism* of the early charismatics and Pentecostals began in the pew and percolated up to academia. The two strains of subjectivism have thus reinforced each other and opened the door for the mushroom growth of Pentecostalism, Neo-Pentecostalism, existentialism, postmodernism, and other manifestations of subjectivism within the evangelical churches.

Additional Categories of Subjectivism. However, the problem of subjectivism and extra-biblical revelation has now grown beyond the traditional movements of Pentecostalism, existentialism, and Neo-Pentecostalism. Some aspects are rather benign and some more serious, but all tend to subvert the authority of Scripture.

There is a large and growing segment of evangelicals, who do not necessarily embrace existentialism, speak with tongues, or engage in other charismatic behavior, but who nevertheless affirm that God *speaks directly* to men today just as He did in the days prior to the close of the canon of Scripture. The traditional Christian position is that the Bible is the supreme and final authority in all matters of faith and practice, a *complete and closed body of divine revelation.* Yet there are those who think otherwise. R. Fowler White informs us:

> Certain evangelicals, however, have begun to add an additional proposition.... This new proposition states that God also speaks to His people today apart from the Bible, though He never speaks in contradiction to it.[157]

But before commenting on this problem, let's take a quick glance at something less serious, but nevertheless it can lead to a problem.

---

[157] R. Fowler White, "Does God Speak Today Apart from the Bible?" *The Coming Evangelical Crisis*, p. 77.

THE GOD-SPOKE-TO-ME SYNDROME. It is common knowledge today that many evangelical Christians habitually use a popular manner of speaking of how they receive knowledge of the will of God. They say for example "God really *spoke to me* in my devotions today about...." Or, "*God said to me*" do this, or that, meaning only that they were led to some insight or behavior as the Holy Spirit illuminated some biblical truth to them. Most of the time it is apparent that they are speaking of the revealed Word through Scripture as it is made clear to the heart by the Holy Spirit. Most Christians understand this.

It is certainly a blessed work of the Holy Spirit in His role of Comforter or Paraclete. There is an intimacy through prayer and worship – a personal communion wherein His Spirit "bears witness with our spirits" sharing Himself and opening to us many truths of Scruipture. But that is not new revelation. He often prompts or directs us, bringing things to our remembrance or understanding (John 14:26), but always drawn from the objective Word.

This Word, however, must be first learned; we must read, be taught, or remember the Word having previously hidden it in our hearts. But since the close of the canon of Scripture, God never "speaks" directly to us or gives new revelation.

This way of speaking is, on the surface, harmless; but it can become an unfortunate and misleading habit which may add fuel to the present subjectivist environment, further undermining the authority of Scripture. Some loose-thinking pastors, radio and television personalities, careless and misguided Christians, have created a "God-spoke-to-me" order of spiritually elite Christians. This would be a relatively benign matter except that it is not the exact truth, and in this environment it can mislead the immature and subvert the motivation for more careful and consistent Bible study.

We have known some wonderful Christians who have taken this subjective "God-spoke-to-me" point of view and have made some really serious mistakes, when a more objective approach to the written revealed truth would have spared them much trouble and the Lord much reproach.

We know a person who said, "God told me I would marry" such-and-such a person. But when it became apparent it would never happen, there was shame to the person and to the Lord's name.

Moreover, we have known young people who have floundered around for years seeking "God's will for their lives," waiting for some "word" or sign from God, which He will never send independent of truth which has formerly been revealed. Of course the Holy Spirit leads or gives *subjective assurances* based on revealed truth, but that is not a *word, sign,* or *direct revelation* and we should not speak of it as such.

When we are faced with decisions concerning *things not written in Scripture* – which car to buy, which job to take, etc. – we would do well to invoke the principle in 2 Timothy 1:7: "For God hath not given us the spirit of fear; but of power, and of love, and of a sound mind." This assumes 1) we have a *fearless* trust in what the Holy Spirit has revealed in Scripture to guide us, 2) we *love* Him and the study of His Word, 3) that He has given us *power* (Acts 1:8) as our Paraclete, and 4) that He has created us with a rational, functional, *sound mind,* which, when informed with objective principles from Scripture the Paraclete will enable us to make *sound-mind decisions* based on these objective principles. We must do our homework, and be bold enough to trust His leadership according to finished revelation, not seeking for a sign.

The psalmist's practice, "Thy word have I hid in mine heart, that I might not sin against thee" (Psa. 119:11) will work wonders for making sound-mind decisions concerning things not categorically expressed in Scripture. Then we can certainly expect the Holy Spirit to confirm them to us subjectively, but that is not direct revelation.

The benign God-spoke-to-me syndrome, being itself an exaggeration of reality and only a step away from the Pentecostals, should be abandoned; for it will eventually lead to further mischief.

DOES GOD STILL GIVE DIRECT REVELATION? But White, in the quotation above, is referring to a deeper problem. He continues:

> Some present-day evangelicals ... believe and teach that God speaks to-
> day apart from the Bible.... using all the same means that He used in
> the past.... In my judgment, what these teachers and their disciples fail
> to appreciate is that, in the Bible, God's activity of speaking apart from
> the Scriptures occurred at a time when those documents were still being
> written.... now, with centuries of Christian orthodoxy, we confess that
> *the writing of Scripture is finished, that the canon is actually closed*[158]
> [Emphasis added].

Thus we can distinguish several categories of subjectivism:

1. A thoughtless, habitual way of speaking (e.g., "God spoke to
    me last night") suggesting a more subjective way of speaking
    or thinking but not claiming to receive extra-biblical divine
    revelation.

2. The claim of traditional Pentecostals and Neo-Pentecostals to
    direct revelation.

3. The claim of subjectively oriented non-Pentecostals, men-
    tioned by White above, that any individual may indeed re-
    ceive divine revelation apart from Scripture.

4. And finally the extreme subjectivism of existentialists and
    postmodernists, not Christian at all, who believe there is no
    absolute objective truth at all.

A Clear and Present Danger. The new doctrine of *universal
direct individual revelation from God*, discussed by White, is anything but benign.[159] Like its charismatic counterpart, it is certain
to add another serious layer of discord and confusion to what we
already have.

Think on the scenario of millions of individual Christians in
daily study, devotion, worship, meditation, with strong subjective
impressions, emotions, thoughts, insights, interpretations, and
misinterpretations surging through their minds. Then suppose we
were to accept the new proposition of *universal direct revelation*

---

[158] White, "Does God Speak ..." p. 86.

[159] For a valuable in-depth scholarly treatment of the contemporary problem
of continuation of revelation see O. Palmer Robertson, *The Final Word*, pp.
85ff.

(UDR); we would be obliged to accept the thousands of claims to new doctrine on a par with Scripture. The subjective notions of any Christian may then become the Word of God! To accept this doctrine at any time, especially into the loose and shifting sands of this present diverse, subjectivist environment, would create a theological quagmire with no hope of escape. It would destroy forever any hope of true Christian unity around the objective truth for which Jesus prayed (John 17:17-21). UDR is definitely no part of God's plan for revealing His will to man.

Consider now the claims of certain brethren: that God directly reveals infallible[160] truth to them that is not found in Scripture. Although they acknowledge the authority of Scripture, are we to suppose that any claim of revelation which does not directly contradict Scripture is therefore the absolute Word of God? Are we free to add to Scripture any word or doctrine we *subjectively feel* to be God's Word as long as it doesn't contradict?

Then how can such revelation be tested? Should we simply take the word of every brother without question, that God has spoken to him? Should we, along with Pentecostals, charismatics, and other subjectivists, stop fretting about such matters as objectivity, confirmation, validation, final ultimate standards, and absolute truth?

Au contraire! God commands us: "Beloved, believe not every spirit, but try the spirits whether they are of God ... Every spirit that confesseth that Jesus Christ is come in the flesh is of God" (1 John 4:1, 2). Yet, John's test is not satisfied by the simple utterance of a verbal confession that "Jesus Christ is come in the flesh." John knew that verbal confession alone is not a sufficient test. "For Satan himself transforms himself into an angel of light" (2 Cor. 11:14). John takes us further:

> We are of God. *He who knows God hears us;* he who is not of God does not hear us. *By this we know the spirit of truth and the spirit of error* (1 John 4:6).

"He who knows God *hears* [the apostles]" and other con-

---

[160] Every revelation of God is *necessarily infallible*. God cannot utter a *fallible* word.

firmed inspired writers. And how do we hear them? We hear them today *only through the Scripture*. Thus the final standard for truth that is presently accessible to us is *Scripture*. It is, and has been regarded by Christian orthodoxy since the first century, the final word over any individual claim to revelation. We will discuss at length the matter of Scripture as God's final standard of truth on earth in the final chapter of this book.

But now, confronted as we are with the claim that every Christian may be a recipient of God's direct revelation, we must examine the implications of this claim more closely. If this claim is correct, we then must treat each such claim as having the same authority as Scripture, as the infallible Word of God. God's Word is authoritative regardless of the medium through which it is presented, whether a donkey (Num. 22:28-30), or a man.

Now, in light of our duty to "try" the spirits by the Word of God, if we accept the UDR claim we have a dilemma, which renders the examination of the claim impossible. If the word which the claimant speaks is a revelation from God, it is now a part of the body of revelation. Whereas traditionally there has been only *one standard,* there are now thousands. How shall we test the validity of each claim? Do we try the claimant by the Word of Scripture, or do we try the Scripture by the word of the claimant, since both present themselves as infallible truth? Has God now made us subject to the *unconfirmed* word of every religious movement, cult, or individual who claims to have a direct revelation from God with no clearly validated standard?

"Every word of God is pure" (Prov. 30:5). "Your word is very pure; Therefore your servant loves it" (Psa. 119:140, NKJV). It is a shame that these modern revelations, so pure and so loved by the servants of God, are not all preserved. This author would walk a hundred miles to hear one new sentence on any subject that was known to be uttered by God. Should we not preserve them in an ever-growing collection and publish them in a multivolume set of special books? We could call it: *The Holy Word of God Revealed through UDR*; or perhaps, *New Light from God not in the Bible*; or how about, *The Supplemental Bible: the Rest of the Story*? We are not trying to be facetious, but the proposition of UDR itself evokes these questions and demands serious answers.

What great things we could learn about God by reading the things He had spoken to others. What great lessons we learned from the past by reading the words He has spoken to others, e.g., Joshua (Josh. 1:1f), or even through Balaam's donkey (Num. 22:28). The Word of God could never be a bad thing; if such claims are real revelation, they should be preserved.

But God has not, in fact, placed us on the horns of this dilemma; *"We have also a more sure word of prophecy; whereunto ye do well that ye take heed"* (I Pet. 1:19). The very idea of UDR contradicts the very idea of divine revelation as one unique, complete, authenticated Standard. The argument need not go much further than that.

Many, perhaps the majority of evangelical Christians, think the claims of direct individual revelation by Pentecostals, charismatics, and now the modern revelationists (discussed by R. Fowler White and O. Palmer Robertson) are only harmless, if mistaken, claims. But think again. These claims have the effect of robbing the Scripture of the lofty *uniqueness* with which God has, at great pains, endowed it. They strip the Scripture of its status as having, uniquely, the signature of God, as being confirmed by God Himself, of being the final and only fixed, infallible, objective standard of absolute truth accessible to men on earth.

The claims to direct individual revelation today are no harmless and benign claims. Like postmodernism, they would leave mankind with *no uniquely confirmed and absolute standard of truth,* and if followed to their logical conclusion will eventually lead to the same state of hopelessness and despair as existentialism and postmodernism: that we are all alone in the universe with no certain authenticated light.

Fallout from Academia. The long drift of secular universities toward naturalism and of seminaries and other pastoral training institutions away from the objective biblical landmarks is a serious factor. The very institutions that have presumed to give us guidance have, in some cases, let us down. With the rise of modernism early in the 20th century, many seminaries abandoned the traditional view of Scripture as objective truth. And in the latter part of the 20th century, there has been serious erosion of Scripture authority within evangelicalism as subjectivism has taken root. More recently the trend is hardening into postmodernism and truth becomes increasingly obscure. One college president said:

> I've told several seminary presidents that I think most of the graduates from seminary that I know do not have a well-integrated biblical world and life view.[161]

A Truism: "As go the seminaries, so go the churches." This is much too obviously true for debate, which highlights the immense responsibility of those who direct the seminaries. Many a young pastoral student, brought up in the traditional Christian worldview centering upon the uniqueness, objective authority, and inerrancy of Scripture, has been spoiled. As they are exposed to naturalistic and humanistic issues percolating down through academia, their biblical convictions are weakened, if not in some cases destroyed.

The result is weak pastoral preaching and teaching. Thus the full stabilizing power of Scripture as an infallible source of objective truth has been denied to thousands of mainline churches in virtually every denomination. Because of this, many have turned inwardly to subjectivism, and almost every denomination has become fertile grounds for personal charismatic experience or other subjectivist postures, while the growth rate of churches remaining true to scriptural objectivity has declined.

Pure subjectivism is self-revelation, and the fruit of self-revelation is inevitably self-interest or self-esteem. The self turns to a feelings orientation rather than a commandment orientation, to personal revelation rather than Scripture truth, to subjective experience rather than a walk by objectively informed faith (Heb. 11:1, 3; Rom. 10:17), to instant personal gratification rather than self-sacrificial obedience.

---

[161] John Seel, *The Evangelical Forfeit* (Grand Rapids: Baker Book House, 1993), p. 65.

Marketing "One-O-One." Having thus created a self-oriented population, an opportunistic church growth movement arose. If the individual is about self, the mega-church movement is about numerical growth. Growth means marketing, and marketing "one-o-one" is *consumer satisfaction.* The evangelical mega-church trend, therefore, is to indulge the subjective passions, the "felt-needs" and personal desires of the individual. Thus we are witnessing a shift in what is called Christian leadership, as these following verbal comments show:

> Evangelicalism is focused on how can (sic) man's needs be met and how God can make you a happy camper. American Evangelicalism is based on a self-serving theology... .

> The market-driven movement within the evangelical church has a dynamic of its own. The evangelical church is characterized by the self-fulfillment ethic and the reign of the therapeutic to a larger degree than the secular culture. And it's lost a sense of guilt about this... .

> The [evangelical] leaders frequently mentioned the apparent shift in the qualifications considered necessary for leadership within evangelical organizations – from truth-centered to market-responsive criteria. This change adds to the devaluation of theological thinking and traditional seminary education within evangelicalism.

> The tendency today in the evangelical world is to do whatever it takes to see growth. And I think they are tickling themselves with fantasies of grandeur through a compromise of truth.[162]

Market-driven "evangelism" is as diametrically opposite to biblical evangelism as anything could be. Subjective passions, "felt-needs," or personal desires originating from within the individual are *self-centered*; objective evangelistic truth from Scripture is *God-centered*. Basic marketing practice displays a product that the consumer wants, but the consumer of evangelism (fallen human nature) does not *want* the Gospel:

> As it is written, There is none righteous, no, not one: There is *none that understandeth, there is none that seeketh after God.* They are all gone out of the way, they are together become unprofitable; there is none that doeth good, no, not one... . There is no fear of God before their eyes. Now we know that what things soever the law saith, it saith to them who

---

[162] Seel, pp. 62-63.

are under the law: *that every mouth may be stopped, and all the world may become guilty before God* (Rom. 3:10-19).

By the nature of the case the "consumers" of evangelism, unconverted sinners, do not *want* what they *need*. They are desperately searching for their subjective passions, "felt-needs," or personal desires to be met, but biblical evangelism focuses upon their real objective needs. They have a real objective problem, and that is real objective guilt before the law of God. Their real need is to be pardoned, forgiven. It is impossible, by marketing techniques, to draw unconverted sinners to acknowledge their guilt and to seek forgiveness. To the extent that biblical evangelism is inserted into the process, marketing techniques fail and crowds typically diminish. Therefore for marketing techniques to work, biblical evangelism must be eliminated and vice-versa. Biblical evangelism requires supernatural intervention by the Holy Spirit in conjunction with the proclamation of the Gospel which is "the power of God unto Salvation" (Rom. 1:16).

The evangelists of Scripture focused their preaching on *personal repentance:*

> In those days came John the Baptist, preaching in the wilderness of Judaea, And saying, *Repent ye: for the kingdom of heaven is at hand. - John* (Matt. 3:1, 2).

> … Jesus came into Galilee, preaching the gospel of the kingdom of God, And saying, The time is fulfilled, and the kingdom of God is at hand: *repent ye, and believe the gospel. - Jesus* (Mark 1:14, 15).

> *Repent ye therefore, and be converted*, that your sins may be blotted out… *- Peter* (Acts 3:19).

> Testifying both to the Jews, and also to the Greeks, *repentance toward God, and faith toward our Lord Jesus Christ. - Paul* (Acts 20:21).

Marketing techniques work to obscure the true solution to the sinner's problem by lulling him into a false satisfaction; and that, whether intended or not, deceives them, blinding them further to the objective evangelistic truth of Scripture.

> The widespread devaluing of truth, theology, and theological education illustrates the move away from traditional confessional evangelicalism and from those institutions concerned with its preservation. While mar-

ket-driven evangelicalism thrives in the short-term, the factors contributing to its success may simultaneously corrupt its spiritual vitality. And so evangelicalism may be responsible for digging its own grave.[163]

The Great Evangelical Divide. Pastors and other Christians who have continued in the traditional objective view of Scripture truth, have marveled at the difficulty to engage subjectively oriented Christians, whether charismatic or not, in a friendly but earnest discussion of *biblical doctrine*. In a doctrinal discussion between an objectively-oriented Christian and a subjectively-oriented Christian, the typical response of the latter is not to engage in a serious exchange of propositional points of view. There appears to be no concept of dialogue aimed at a real knowledge of truth. There seems to be no awareness that a part of every Christian's duty is a mutual, charitable concern to help one another find and walk in the unity of God's absolute truth as revealed in Scripture (see 1 Cor. 1:10; John 17:17-21).

Paul observed of the Romans that they were "... filled with all *knowledge*, able also to *admonish* one another" (15:14). This is a charitable Christian duty. Yet it seems to have escaped the subjectivist that mutual Christian admonition and dialogue in pursuit of the knowledge of truth is even possible, let alone a virtuous, good, and loving thing to do.

Attempts at dialogue with subjectivist Christians on matters of doctrinal truth usually produce nothing – not even an angry response or disagreement. The response is typically a complete lack of concern, total boredom, torpid disinterest, and a vacuous oblivion that there exists an objective source of inerrant, authoritative, absolute truth.

The worldview of today's subjectivist Christian did not develop in a vacuum. It has developed under the impact of our mixed cultural environment – under the blended progression of subjectivity in charismatic, existential, and finally postmodern stimulus:

> In postmodernism, all viewpoints, all lifestyles, all beliefs and behaviors are regarded as equally valid. Institutions of higher learning have em-

---

[163] Seel, p. 65.

braced this philosophy so aggressively that they have adopted campus codes enforcing political correctness. Tolerance has become so important that no exception is tolerated.

But if all ideas are equally valid, as postmodernism insists, *then no idea is really worth our allegiance; nothing is worth living or dying for – or even arguing about* [emphasis added]. And this climate of apathy can actually make it harder than ever to witness to the truth of Christianity.[164]

The effect of these developments has been to create two distinctive, but not well-defined or widely-realized, classes of Christians, which we have called *objectively*-oriented Christians and *subjectively*-oriented Christians. This distinction is similar to a distinction drawn by Albert Mohler in *The Coming Evangelical Crisis*. He distinguishes a "Doctrinal Party" and an "Experience Party." We could call our distinction the "Objectivist Party"[165] and the "Subjectivist Party."

Mohler presents his two parties as antagonists in an on-going debate to define evangelical Christianity. He wrote:

> The collision of the two parties is taking place at virtually every level of evangelical life. The Doctrinal Party claims the mantle of the apostolic Fathers, the Reformers, and the Puritans to define and limit evangelical identity to those who hold to the core doctrines of Protestant orthodoxy... . the inerrancy and authority of Scripture ... [including] doctrines such as justification by faith alone and the eternal punishment of the impenitent.

> The Experience Party has vigorously resisted such doctrinal preoccupation and has attempted to broaden the definition of evangelicalism to include a pluralistic notion of doctrine. This party includes the progressivist evangelicals, who advocate liberal positions on issues such as

---

[164] Charles Colson and Nancy Pearcey, *How Now Shall we Live* (Wheaton: Tyndale House Publishers, Inc., 1999), p. 23.

[165] We want to acknowledge, again, that objectivist Christians do indeed respond subjectively and often emotionally to God's objective revealed truth; they are guided by it and emotionally rejoice in it. God's revealed truth is more than rote factuality. "The words that I speak unto you," Jesus said, "they are spirit and they are life" (John 6:63). "The statutes of the Lord are right, rejoicing the heart ..." (Psa. 19:8). But this rejoicing is a response to the objective truth, not to feelings, beliefs, or desires generated subjectively by the psyche.

abortion and homosexuality, and ... to recast evangelicalism in a mode more attractive to late-twentieth-century secular culture and the dominant academic elites.[166]

Mohler's use of the Doctrinal Party vs. Experience Party seems to be restricted more specifically to the evangelical definition debate, which goes to the core of the rift in evangelicalism. Mohler seems to have in mind a distinction further advanced toward the logical conclusion to which the division inevitably leads. Yet, the terms *doctrine* and *experience* represent a fair correspondence to *objective* and *subjective,* which we have applied more generally in the Christian population to two differing postures toward God's revelation, but which, we believe, are but a less advanced progression finally leading to the hard-core moral issues such as abortion and homosexuality and/or core doctrinal issues involving the Person and purpose of God Himself.

The Doctrinal or Objective Party regards revelation as a rigorous, unchanging, complete, and final body of truth that stands true, independent of human acceptance or rejection. The Experience or Subjective Party treats revelation as a soft and flexible awareness received through feelings, moods, experiences, or ecstasy within the individual psyche. Both parties acknowledge the subjective influences of the Holy Spirit, but the objective party contends that since the close of the canon of Scripture, The Holy Spirit works always and only by or through objective Scripture truth which He Himself inspired, never apart from it. And these two postures yield very different results.

It is true that most Pentecostal and Neo-Pentecostal Christians, unlike the Experience Party mentioned by Mohler, stand clearly against such issues as abortion and homosexuality, though clearly oriented toward feelings and direct revelation. Nevertheless, we believe that the more benign subjectivist road leads finally to these grosser elements of immorality and to a stance that can in no way be classed as evangelical. And some have already arrived.

Any view of revelation that does not try every subjective notion by the objective Word of God makes itself vulnerable to ev-

---

[166] R. Albert Mohler, Jr., "'Evangelicalism': What's in a Name?" in *The Coming Evangelical Crisis*, p. 32.

ery sort of sin or wind of doctrine. The subjectivist view of truth, carried to its logical conclusion, will eventually descend into the same morass of sin and error that eventually engulfs all who disregard the authority, uniqueness, and finality of Scripture as God's full and only revelation.

The Low Road to Ruin. In the last few pages, as we have considered the progression and impact of subjectivism, a dim picture has emerged. The general problem of a low view of Scripture and a serious erosion of the authority of Scripture has brought us to a critical point in the process of evangelical surrender of time-honored truths.

A mystifying indicator of this evangelical surrender is the alarming number of professing Christians who are being deceived by unbelieving scientists, teachers, philosophers, and advocates of naturalistic evolution.

This trend is being opposed by a significant number of scientists and advocates of biblical scientific creationism, among whom is Dr. Henry Morris III of the Institute for Creation Research. Morris places the blame squarely on the erosion of the authority of Scripture:

> The authority of God's Word has been replaced by the authority of human opinion. In many churches, Christian Colleges, and seminaries, the diluting down of biblical authority has been led by those who want to hybridize Scripture with the "more scientifically acceptable" view of long ages of death and struggle.

> The National Center for Science Education (NCSE) was formed to ban creation from our public classrooms. Should students ask about creation, the NCSE recommended that teachers simply tell the students to ask their pastors or clergymen – knowing that, in most cases, their pastors will tell students it is okay to accept evolution. The sad part about that strategy is that it works very well![167]

A surprising number of Christians are turning away from the most foundational truth of Scripture, direct creation, in favor of so-called theistic or other nuanced evolutionary positions, all wholly contrary to Scripture. But our public schools are teaching

---

[167] Henry M. Morris III, *After Eden: Understanding Creation, the Curse, and the Cross* (Green Forrest, AR: Master Books, 2003), p. 11.

naturalistic evolution with the survival of the fittest as its driving principle and only moral guideline. Confused Christian children read Genesis 1 on Sunday with the loving God as our moral standard; and on Monday in the public school the god Chance is creator with Self-survival the moral standard.

> At the center of the survival motive is the *self.* When our venerable institutions of learning teach that the driving force of life is self survival at the expense of the less fit, the whole social order suffers decadence. Inordinate self-esteem, self-centeredness, violence, crime, immorality, dysfunctional families, and the non-Christian educational and cultural philosophies that feed all of these, are to a great extent the result of over a century of evolutionary indoctrination.[168]

How remarkable that survival of the fittest and pure psychic subjectivism both produce self-orientation and self-interest (see above). What chance does a child have when subjectivism pervades his church and evolution pervades his public school?

What are churches and Christian parents thinking – or not thinking? For a century we have looked the other way allowing the forces of darkness to get the advantage of us! Many Christians have denied their birthright of direct creation and most others do not seem seriously alarmed. True Christian education is running a deep deficit, which will take decades to make up – and more if we do not start now.

Many do not seem to realize what we have done to our children and to ourselves. We have not shot ourselves in the foot, but in the heart.

A Philosophy of Despair. Subjective experience has become for some the supreme oracle, an authority for truth equal to or above the objective written Word of Scripture. The rejoinder, "I *experienced* it; I *know*," is more and more common today when charismatic Christians are challenged by Scripture. But little do subjectivist Christians realize that as the objectivity and finality of Scripture fades in their worldview, if finally our faith has little or no objective undergirding (Rom. 10:17), the next stop is the

---

[168] Willard A. Ramsey, *Facing Eternity* (Simpsonville, SC: Millennium III Publishers, 1999), p. 9.

existentialism of Kierkegaard, Camus, or Sartre; and all that is left is "a philosophy of despair":

> "There are no divine judges or controllers," proclaimed French philosopher Jean-Paul Sartre. "The world is all there is, our existence is all we have." Thus was born the word *existentialism*. In Sartre's play *No Exit,* one character distills the existentialist creed to a catch phrase: "You are your life, and that's all you are." There is no higher purpose or goal or meaning to life.[169]

Hope comes only from One who is self-existent, independently outside ourselves – the transcendent God. There is a higher meaning! But nothing good can come from within us that He did not put within us.

By late in the 20th century, subjectivism had paved the way for an even more menacing development: the advance of postmodernism. And yet, just how modern is postmodernism? Albert Mohler suggests: "Postmodernism is, in reality, modernity in its updated costume, a hypermodernity made all the more seductive by its sophisticated dress."[170] While Kierkegaard, et al., introduced confusion, obscuring the clear, direct objectivity of Scripture truth, postmodernism denies the existence of any absolute truth at all.

> ... the shift to this new philosophy has been breathtakingly rapid. In the 1960s the percentage of young people going to college suddenly surged, and attitudes once held only by the intellectual elite suddenly became common coinage. The philosophy of *existentialism,* a precursor of postmodernism, swept the campuses, proclaiming that life is absurd, meaningless, and that the individual self must create his own meaning by his own choices.... It was a small step from existentialism to postmodernism ...[171]

At the street level, not only unbelievers but many professing Christians have been profoundly influenced by existential and postmodern conditioning without realizing it. And if the subtle influence of the culture were not enough, there is the aggressive "evangelistic" zeal of the Emergent Village, the "emerging church," an international movement which has actually embraced

---

[169] Colson and Pearcey, p. 254.
[170] Mohler, "Evangelicalism ..." p. 39.
[171] Colson and Pearcey, p. 23.

postmodernism, thus surrendering all hope of finding absolute truth. Moreover, the marshy sands of subjectivism, charismata, and the doctrinally ambiguous "praise and worship" of the "church-growth" movements are, unwittingly, reinforcing the effects of postmodernism by neglecting to ground their patrons in the objective truths and doctrines of Scripture, which alone lead to the "city which hath foundations" (Heb. 11:10).

Brilliant Strategist. If the two-century sequence of events (from Schleiermacher to postmodernism – from Edward Irving to Neo-Pentecostalism) was planned and executed by Satan, it was brilliant strategy. He attacked where fallen humanity has demonstrated an ancient and persistent weakness, where the innate embers of subjectivism were fanned into flame both in academia and at the grass roots of the population. And what a price we have paid because of this one human weakness which Satan has exploited so cunningly.

IV.
The Baptism of the Holy Spirit

In the first three chapters of this book, we have been concerned exclusively with three related historical issues. They are the historic manifestations of 1) the human quest for experience in religion, 2) the epistemological sterility of subjective experiences including speaking in unintelligible tongues and other charismatic activities and ecstatic phenomena, and 3) the ascent of subjectivism, including some background on existentialism and existential features of modern charismata. We have found all of these activities among diverse pagan religions ancient and modrn, among numerous historic Christian sects and denominations, and among modern contemporary Christian movements and categories. These experiences continue among Christians as widely divergent as the snake-handling sects of Appalachia, traditional churches both liberal and fundamentalist, high church bishops both Protestant and Catholic, and erudite professors in academia both within seminaries and the great secular universities.

The common thread running throughout all these categories is this: fallen human nature seeking a direct experiential contact with, or revelation from, a god or God Himself.

From the data and arguments presented in the first three chapters of this book, though not exhaustive, we believe the case has been made that none of these subjective phenomena have any true epistemological value. Moreover, it is evident from the features, claims, and practices of those who pursue these phenomena, that the energy behind them is not from the *gods* (in the case of pagans), or from the *Holy Spirit* (in the case of Christians). That leaves either the *fallen human psyche*, which probably accounts for most of the Christian claims, or *fallen angelic influences* (i.e., demonic influences) probably accounting for most of the pagan claims.

Our primary concern here is not with pagan claims,[172] but that 1) the name of God and the body of Christian truth and doctrine might be cleansed and purged of these exceedingly adverse claims and practices once and for all, and 2) that millions of our Christian brothers and sisters might be delivered from these deceitful claims and captivating experiences, and 3) that a deep conviction may be restored among all Christians of the unique, objective authority of Scripture which could lead to a high-profile, actual unity in truth (John 17:17-21; 1 Cor. 1:10).

Undergirding most of the Christian subjectivism is a grossly misunderstood doctrine of Scripture, the baptism of the Holy Spirit. This doctrine is relatively simple to understand except for the obscurities introduced by both charismatic and non-charismatic evangelicals. In this chapter we will undertake to sort out the truth concerning the baptism of the Holy Spirit and develop a

---

[172] Not that we are indifferent to the needs of the pagan population of the world, but that is a wholly different problem and must be addressed by evangelistic efforts.

concise biblical definition for it. Moreover, we trust that a greater objectivity toward Scripture will, in time, open the door for a greater unity in truth among all Christians.

A BRIEF LOOK
AT THE NORMATIVE WORK OF THE HOLY SPIRIT

Since the expression *baptism in the Holy Spirit* describes a feature of Christian doctrine unique to the New Covenant era, it will simplify our analysis to first consider briefly the ancient normative work of the Holy Spirit.

Within the charismatic movements are doubtless many sincere Christians who misunderstand the completeness and sufficiency of spiritual regeneration or the new birth, as well as other aspects of the personal ministry of the Holy Spirit to all regenerate individuals. Thus they may seek an additional experience with God, not realizing the wonder of the relationship that all believers already have in regeneration, which has been the primary normative work of the Holy Spirit ever since the need first arose in Eden. But this normative work has nothing to do with the baptism of the Holy Spirit which was initiated 4000 years later; which, in turn, as we will see later, has nothing directly to do with God's unchangeable work of salvation.

Ever since sin entered into the world, men and women have been "dead in trespasses and sins," and, if dead, then regeneration by the Holy Spirit is essential and sufficient for a new life with God. Jesus chided Nicodemus for not knowing this elementary doctrine: "Art thou a master of Israel, and knowest not these things?" (John 3:10).

Regeneration

Regeneration is the primary and normative work of the Holy Spirit as related to fallen humanity: He comes to those chosen of God, "dead in trespasses and sins," gives life (Eph. 2:5), and they are "born ... of God" (John 1:13). Thus they become *"partakers of the divine nature"* (2 Pet. 1:4) as the Holy Spirit Himself takes up permanent residence within every believer. This is both a miracle of God and a great mystery, but "... greater is he that is in you, than he that is in the world" (1 John 4:4). With such a Spirit dwelling within, why should we seek a second work of grace by the same Spirit?

> But ye are not in the flesh, but in the Spirit, if so be that the Spirit of God dwell in you. *Now if any man have not the Spirit of Christ, he is none of his*... . But if the Spirit of him that raised up Jesus from the dead dwell in you, he that raised up Christ from the dead shall also quicken your mortal bodies *by his Spirit that dwelleth in you* (Rom. 8:9-12).

Regeneration or the new birth is absolutely essential to salvation (John 3:3; 1:12, 13), and it is also an *actual experience* having a strong subjective element. The work of the Holy Spirit within the believer produces intense *subjective* feelings of love, joy, and peace, relief from the guilt of sin and assurances of eternal salvation; but these are always associated with and produced by the *objective promises and truths of the Word* of Scripture as applied by the Holy Spirit (review chart, p. 10). In the new birth, "the objective authority of Scripture and the subjective encounter of the believer with the Holy Spirit, Who is the Author of Scripture, are focused in one event."[173] This basic principle is also true in all our other interactions with God subsequent to regeneration. All valid experiences or reliable feelings and assurances must grow out of objective truth only:

> Wherein God, willing more abundantly to *show unto the heirs of promise the immutability of his counsel, confirmed it by an oath:* That by two immutable things, in which it was impossible for God to lie, *we might have a strong consolation,* who have fled for refuge to lay hold upon the hope set before us (Heb. 6:17-18).

This consolation is certainly experienced subjectively, but it is objectively created, fortified, and confirmed by two immutable things as expressed by God's authenticated Word of Promise. Why should we seek more? It is a normative work of the indwelling Holy Spirit to bless the believer in many ways, especially in the assurance of salvation: "The Spirit Himself bears witness with our spirit that we are children of God" (Rom. 8:16, NKJV).

---

[173] This quotation is by an esteemed Brother, R. Charles Blair, D. D., from personal correspondence.

Sanctification

Once regeneration has taken place in a person and the life principle has been imparted by the Holy Spirit, He then indwells that life. Having delivered us by justification and forgiveness from the *penalty* of sin, He continues His normative life-long work toward personal sanctification. That is, He ministers within the new life for spiritual maturity and growth for a lifetime of progress toward separation from the *practice* of sin.

> But the *fruit of the Spirit* is love, joy, peace, longsuffering, gentleness, goodness, faith, Meekness, temperance: against such there is no law. And they that are Christ's have crucified the flesh with the affections and lusts. *If we live in the Spirit, let us also walk in the Spirit* (Gal 5:22-25).

The nourishment on which the new life thrives is knowledge of Jesus Christ the Savior. The ministry of the Holy Spirit in personal, progressive sanctification is to unveil the person of Jesus Christ and His commandments to the new-born soul *through the Scriptures.* This Word of objective truth is the completed and wholly sufficient work of the same Holy Spirit that indwells each individual believer, so that there is no need for either a new operation beyond regeneration or a new revelation beyond Scripture. But the need is for growth in the Word:

> Wherefore laying aside all malice, and all guile, and hypocrisies, and envies, and all evil speakings, *As newborn babes, desire the sincere milk of the word, that ye may grow thereby:* If so be ye have tasted that the Lord is gracious (1 Pet. 2:1-3).

In His normative work, the Holy Spirit, in conjunction with the revealed Word, is the great revealer of the glories of our Lord and Savior. By the Holy Spirit's witness, assurance is given of Christ's deity and that He is the very image of the all-wise God, the creator of heaven and earth, who holds the universe together. It is the Holy Spirit who, in conjunction with objective Scripture truth, testifies of the incarnation of God in Jesus Christ, that God the Son became incarnate so that the divine and human nature were united in one perfect union. It is the Holy Spirit who, again in conjunction with the objective Word, testifies to our spirit of His sinless, guileless life and substitutionary propitiatory death and literal resurrection, by which He redeems those chosen of God. For these are some of the glories of our Lord and Savior that nourishes believers in growth:

> But we all, with open face beholding as in a glass the glory of the Lord, are changed into the same image from glory to glory, *even as by the Spirit of the Lord* (2 Cor. 3:18).

As the glory of the Lord is presented to the believer in these ways, there is both a subjective experience of the Holy Spirit producing the "fruit of the Spirit ... love, joy, peace, longsuffering, gentleness, goodness, faith...," but always in conjunction with the objective ministry and sanctifying truth of the written Word. So what subjective experience does the individual believer yet lack that is not available through the normative ministry of the Holy Spirit in conjunction with Scripture? What is missing that must be sought through a "second blessing" of which the Scriptures speak not a word?

The Word inspired by the Holy Spirit, when normatively illuminated to the believer by that same Holy Spirit, is a sufficient blessing for anyone. The objective Word is here; believe it, and the Holy Spirit is ready to make it live in our hearts.

In the normative ministry of the Holy Spirit and the Scriptures which He inspired, we have the best of all possible worlds (short of being with the Lord in glorified bodies). We have, objectively, the immutability and infallibility of the Word. We have, subjectively, the witness of the Holy Spirit (Rom. 8:16; 1 John 5:10). Both objectively and subjectively we thus know Christ by faith: "Whom having not seen, ye love, though now ye see him not, yet believing, *ye rejoice with joy unspeakable and full of glory*" (1 Peter 1:8). Why should we seek a blessing beyond that? "The Lord is my shepherd, I shall not want."

Teaching

The third phase to be discussed here is the work of the Holy Spirit as a teacher. He makes plain the teachings of our Lord. The teaching work of the Holy Spirit is of great importance, for it is by His teaching or illuminating work, when we read and study His Word, that we begin to understand the deep things of God.

> ... for the Spirit searcheth all things, yea, the deep things of God. For what man knoweth the things of a man, save the spirit of man which is in him? even so the things of God knoweth no man, but the Spirit of God. Now we have received, not the spirit of the world, but the spirit which is of God; *that we might know the things that are freely given to us of God.* Which things also we speak, not in the words which man's wisdom teacheth, *but which the Holy Ghost teacheth; comparing spiritual things with spiritual* (1 Cor. 2:10-13).

It is with the gentle and unobtrusive guidance of the Holy Spirit that we begin to partake of the meat of the Word. We grow in grace and knowledge for we should always remember that He is called in Scripture the *Spirit of Wisdom, of understanding, knowledge, and truth* (see Isa. 11:2; John 14:17). He was the One who inspired the Scriptures; and, having done so, He then enables us to understand them. From the Holy Spirit's application of Scripture we learn the things that pertain to God.

It is not at all amazing that a person needs the influence of the Holy Spirit to comprehend the written Word of God. Just as physical light makes it possible to read the printed page, so also, the constant illumination of the indwelling Holy Spirit opens the meanings of Scripture to the believer. But He will not tell us what it says; we must read it or otherwise hear it. And since we cannot always carry a copy of the Scriptures for instantaneous reference, the Psalmist gives us the solution: "Thy word have I hid in mine heart, that I might not sin against thee" (Psa. 119:11).

Unbelievers are often confused and confounded by Scripture, but Christians are enlightened. It is the Holy Spirit that makes the Bible live to a believer; while it remains confusing to unbelievers (see Isa. 28:9-13). And it is through the Bible, not directly, that God teaches His people today: *"Sanctify them through thy truth: thy word is truth"* (John 17:17). There is no other way we can learn the doctrines of God other than in the Word of God, inspired and illuminated by the Holy Spirit, and that is sufficient.

Thus charismatics, misunderstanding the completeness of the believer in Christ (Col. 2:10), seek a shortcut to revelation. When the Holy Spirit of God takes up permanent residence in the believer through regeneration, a great initial work of grace is performed in a believer, then other works of God's grace follow without number – from the clothing on our backs to the sun in the sky – yet there is no special "second" work of grace distinguished in the Bible.

Since most of the serious charismatic errors stem from a misunderstanding of the biblical teaching concerning the baptism of the Holy Spirit, we turn now to a study of Scripture to determine the truth about that great doctrine. And we hope to disabuse many of our Christian brethren of the errors that have been developed and spread abroad in recent centuries.

BAPTISM IN THE HOLY SPIRIT: UNRAVELING A SERIOUS DOCTRINAL PROBLEM

The work of God in the "baptism of the Holy Spirit" is different from His normative work in regeneration from ancient times. No doubt there is some overlap in these respective ministries; after all, the Holy Spirit is always the Holy Spirit. But whatever else we may find, the *baptism of the Holy Spirit* is a special initiative of Jesus Christ on behalf of the New Covenant church. Regeneration is old, universal among believers, essential to salvation and personal sanctification. The baptism of the Holy Spirit came later in history as a ministry in the New Covenant era, or the church age, and its purpose is to *empower* the New Covenant church as an institution (Acts 1:8), God's official agency for the great commission (Matt. 28:19-20). Although individuals within the church are affected and gifted by the Holy Spirit in this new role, the baptism of the Holy Spirit is not directed toward the individual; it is not a universal work of the Holy Spirit normative to every believer, as is regeneration.

The biblical concept of the baptism of the Holy Spirit was prophesied by Joel (2:28-32) in the Old Testament, though not by that name, and by John the Baptist who first used the phrase *baptize with (in) the Holy Spirit.* It is thus a major doctrine of the New Testament which is seriously misunderstood, not only by charismatics but also by many non-charismatic evangelical Christians.

To the Law and to the Testimony

If anyone would know the truth of a biblical doctrine, there can be no substitute for going straight to the Scripture to analyze the words and sentences God has revealed about it. Though we seek the help of all, we must not rely on any historic hermeneutic, whether "charismatic leaders," the "church fathers," the "Westminster divines," or any other preferences one may have as to the outcome of a study, especially in one as controversial as this one.

There is one legitimate motive which is essential to learning and knowing any doctrine of Scripture: that is the *willingness*[174] to do the will of God with respect to that doctrine. Jesus said: "My doctrine is not mine, but his that sent me. If any man will [i.e., is willing to] do his will, he shall know of the doctrine, whether it be of God, or whether I speak of myself" (John 7:17).

Scripture is the only standard against which any doctrine may be tested. We all have equal opportunity before that standard.

Baptism with [in] the Holy Spirit: Usage of the Phrase in Scripture

We begin this study by a review of all the occasions in Scripture where the phrase itself is used. What may be known about this doctrine must be learned primarily from these occasions. Then we can extend our study to other relevant principles and passages, where the phrase itself may not be used.

References. The phrase "baptized with [in] the Holy Ghost," with slight variations, is mentioned six times under that peculiar terminology in the New Testament Scriptures. One of those refer-

---

[174] The opposite is also true: if a person is *unwilling* or *reluctant* to do God's will concerning any doctrine of Scripture, he will never be able to learn that doctrine. The principle of a *reluctance* to hear is applicable to individual truths even in the lives of believers. Jesus taught that even some who are "in the kingdom of heaven" will resist certain of His commandments and will even "teach men so" (Matt. 5:19). If one is reluctant to obey, then the only recourse is to rationalize; and in rationalization one modifies the meaning of a doctrine. Therefore, he *cannot* learn the real truth. Jesus called this class "least in the kingdom of heaven," and the writer of Hebrews called them "... dull of hearing" (Heb. 5:12).

ences is from the preaching of John the Baptist, and recorded in each of the four Gospels. This accounts for four of the six usages. One of these six is repeated by Jesus, and the other is repeated by Peter. Only these three persons, therefore, ever used the phrase in Scripture, and all three used it to refer to a single event. Following are the six references:

> I indeed baptize you with water unto repentance: but he that cometh after me is mightier than I, whose shoes I am not worthy to bear: he shall *baptize you with the Holy Ghost*, and with fire. - *John the Baptist* (Matt. 3:11)

> I indeed have baptized you with water: but he shall *baptize you with the Holy Ghost. - John the Baptist* (Mark 1:8).

> John answered, saying unto them all, I indeed baptize you with water; but one mightier than I cometh, the latchet of whose shoes I am not worthy to unloose: he shall *baptize you with the Holy Ghost and with fire. - John the Baptist* (Luke 3:16).

> And I knew him not: but he that sent me to baptize with water, the same said unto me, Upon whom thou shalt see the Spirit descending, and remaining on him, the same is he which *baptizeth with the Holy Ghost. - John the Baptist* (John 1:33).

> And, being assembled together with them, [Jesus] commanded them that they should not depart from Jerusalem, but wait for the promise of the Father, which, saith he, ye have heard of me. For *John truly baptized with water; but ye shall be baptized with the Holy Ghost not many days hence...* . But ye shall *receive power*, after that the *Holy Ghost is come upon you:* and ye shall be witnesses unto me both in Jerusalem, and in all Judaea, and in Samaria, and unto the uttermost part of the earth. - *Jesus* (Acts 1:4-5, 8).

> Then remembered I the word of the Lord, how that he said, John indeed baptized with water; but ye shall be *baptized with the Holy Ghost. - Peter* (Acts 11:16).

Since John introduced Christ to Israel as the One who would baptize in the Holy Spirit, and since both Jesus and Peter repeated it; this work must be accounted as one of the important doctrines of the New Testament. But unfortunately, the great value of it has not been realized by most Christians because most Christians, both charismatic and non-charismatic, have so distorted or misunderstood its meaning that they have been unable to appreciate the immense value and power available to them through the ministry of the Holy Spirit called a baptism.

Elementary Observations. From these six direct references we learn certain characteristics of the baptism of the Holy Spirit which must be regarded as objective, consistent features. These features will help us understand the nature of the doctrine. On the face of John's description, we notice the following factors:

1. "Christ" is the *administrator* of the baptism. He does the baptizing.
2. The "Holy Spirit" is the *medium* into which Christ baptizes the subject.
3. And "you" (a plural pronoun, the audience, at least part of it, before John) were the *subjects* to be baptized.

It is clear that whatever the baptism in the Holy Spirit is, Christ is the *administrator* and the Holy Spirit is the *medium* into whom the *subjects* are baptized. These elementary facts will help us to interpret accurately certain disputed passages when the issue arises.

There is within some of the primary references, another medium of baptism mentioned, that of *"fire."* Matthew and Luke are the only ones who mention the fire; it is ignored in all other references. The immediate context of these two references strongly implies that the fire is a reference to the fire of judgment:[175] "Whose fan is in his hand, and he will thoroughly purge his floor, and gather his wheat into the garner; but he will burn up the chaff with unquenchable fire" (Matt. 3:12). If the fire refers to judgment, that means John, by the plural pronoun "you," was addressing a mixed audience: 1) some believers, who would later be gathered with the 120 as the church (to be baptized in the Spirit at Pentecost) and 2) the unbelievers [to be baptized in the fires of judgment, the "lake of fire" (Rev. 20:15)].

Since nothing further is mentioned of the "fire," it would seem irrelevant to the current subject except that there are those

---

[175] Some have regarded it as a reference to the "tongues of fire" which were sent as a visual manifestation of the advent of the Holy Spirit, of which the sound filling the room was an audible manifestation (Acts 2:2-3).

who believe it refers to the "tongues of fire" that sat upon the 120 members of the church at the Pentecost event (Acts 2:3). Moreover, for those who defend the proposition that the Pentecostal event is a gift to be repeated and anticipated by all believers of all time, it might be a little embarrassing to mention, but we have yet to hear the sound of a "mighty rushing wind" or to see "tongues of fire" accompanying those claiming to be experiencing the "baptism." Yet we must admit we have heard some say that they had heard others say it has happened. Yet most "baptisms," by the claimant's own admission, are missing these audible and visual manifestations.

Distinguishing Terminology from Substance. The terminology, *baptism with (or in) the Holy Spirit,* has very limited usage[176] in Scripture. The use of baptism to describe this special work of Christ was coined by John to highlight or underscore a correlation between his work of water baptism and the greater work Christ would do for the same people. John said:

> I indeed *baptize you* (a plural pronoun) *with [or in] water* unto repentance: but he that cometh after me is mightier than I, whose shoes I am not worthy to bear: *he shall baptize you (plural) with [or in] the Holy Ghost* ... (Matt. 3:11).

In other words, John was saying that those whom he baptized in *water* Jesus would later baptize in the *Holy Spirit,* namely, those who would be in the institutional church which Jesus would build.[177] The full mission of John the Baptist was to identify those who had repented by baptizing them in water, and thus *"to make ready a people prepared for the Lord"* (Luke 1:17). These, at least some of them, became followers of Jesus, and some of them were assembled with the 120 souls on the day of Pentecost; others

---

[176] It is remarkable that a phrase with such limited usage has been seized upon by modern charismatics to make it the centerpiece within their view of Christianity.

[177] This statement, we believe, expresses the general rule intended by the Lord and exemplified in all events to follow except one, i.e., the gentiles at the home of Cornelius (Acts 10) which we will consider later. Thus we do not mean to deny the sovereignty of the Holy Spirit in His gifts and choices.

among them were doubtless baptized by Jesus' disciples who also baptized in water (John 4:1, 2).

John's term, *baptize with the Holy Spirit,* is a figure of speech, a metaphor. No visible submergence occurs. It was drawn from his literal baptism in water. As mentioned, so far as is recorded in the Scripture, only three persons ever uttered the term: 1) John the Baptist (recorded in each of the four Gospels), 2) Jesus (in Acts 1:4), and 3) Peter (in Acts 11:16). In each of these cases the reference is to a single event: *the descent of the Holy Spirit upon the water-baptized and assembled church waiting at Jerusalem on the day of Pentecost:*

> And when the day of Pentecost was fully come, *they were all with one accord in one place.* And suddenly there came a *sound from heaven as of a rushing mighty wind,* and it *filled all the house* where they were sitting. And there appeared unto them *cloven tongues like as of fire, and it sat upon each of them* (Acts 2:1-3).

Thus the Holy Spirit came and submerged the church as an institution, and so it has been ever since. He came *once* in this special role and has never gone away nor left an obedient church. It is the advent itself which John called a *baptism* and which Joel called a *pouring out.* John does not elaborate upon the work the Holy Spirit is to do in this special role, but Joel does. Joel goes beyond the *pouring out* – the advent – and comments also about the work.

We must, therefore, recognize the difference between the advent and presence of the Holy Spirit, i.e., the *event* itself, called a *baptism* or *outpouring,* and the countless multifaceted *works* He has done. The works He has done in this special paracletic role are the results of His coming, or of the baptism of the Holy Spirit, but the works themselves are not the baptism. His advent was a baptism; His works are, and continue to be, as numerous as the tasks to be accomplished.

This leads us then to a broader discussion: Why did He come? What is this special role or the purpose and work for which He came? What did He do when He came? And what has He been doing over the centuries ever since He came? There was *one* advent or baptism in the Holy Spirit upon the churches, but the works of the Holy Spirit are innumerable, and these works we now must examine.

Background: Old Covenant Roles of the Holy Spirit

To understand the essence of the biblical doctrine of the baptism of the Holy Spirit requires some background from the Old Testament, for those roles were similar to the New Covenant role. As these roles relate to our subject of baptism of the Holy Spirit, B. H. Carroll[178] mentions two typical occasions which we may now consider with great profit[179] (Ex. 40:33-38, 2 Chr. 5:11-14, 1 Kings 8:10, 11).

The Old Covenant. With the establishment of the Mosaic Covenant, God *institutionalized* the representation of His name to the world. With that covenant, God would establish an *institution*, a "kingdom of priests, and an holy nation," to represent His name on earth.

> Now therefore, if ye will obey my voice indeed, and keep my covenant, then ye shall be *a peculiar treasure* unto me above all people: for all the earth is mine: *And ye shall be unto me a kingdom of priests, and an holy nation.* These are the words which thou shalt speak unto the children of Israel (Ex. 19:5-6).

This institutional representation is officially distinguished from individual representation and categorically expressed in these words:

> But unto the place which the LORD your *God shall choose* out of all your tribes *to put his name there*, even unto *his habitation* shall ye seek, and thither thou shalt come ... Ye shall *not* do after all the things that we do here this day, *every [individual] man* whatsoever is right in his own eyes.... Then there shall be a place which *the LORD your God shall choose to cause his name to dwell there;* thither shall ye bring all that I command you; your burnt offerings, and your sacrifices, your tithes, and

---

[178] B. H. Carroll, *An Interpretation of the English Bible*, XII [Acts], (Nashville: Broadman Press, 1947), pp. 31, 32.

[179] For a more complete discussion of the significance of those events to the nature of the church, see William C. Hawkins and Willard A. Ramsey, *The House of God,* 2nd ed. (Simpsonville, SC: Hallmark Baptist Church, 1980), pp. 14-28.

> the heave offering of your hand, and all your choice vows which ye vow unto the LORD (Deut. 12:5, 8, 11).

Moreover, this Old Covenant is clearly an institutional *type*, of which the New Covenant church is the institutional *antitype*. Thus Peter uses the same terms for the church in the following words:

> But ye are a *chosen generation, a royal priesthood, an holy nation, a peculiar people;* that ye should *show forth* the praises of him who hath called you out of darkness into his marvellous light (1 Peter 2:9).

Along with these similarities, we notice also that there are distinctions between the Old and New Covenant institutions: The visual centerpiece or agency of the New Covenant is an *ecclesia*, an *assembly*: "Ye also, as *lively stones, are built up a spiritual house*, an holy priesthood, to offer up spiritual sacrifices, acceptable to God by Jesus Christ" (1 Peter 2:5); whereas the visual centerpiece or focus of the Old Covenant was a *building*: "And let them make me a sanctuary; that I may dwell among them. According to all that I show thee, after the pattern of the *tabernacle*."

The Tabernacle. Since a structure with its associated ceremonies would represent God on earth, He gave specific details to Moses to build a tabernacle which would be identified as the place where the name of the Lord would dwell. Moses therefore led the people to build a tabernacle. After it was finished – every post and socket, the furnishings, the coverings, with everything in place – it stood there complete but empty. If this humble badger-skin tent was to be taken seriously by the people and the nations as the representation of the name of the most high God, the transcendent Creator of heaven and earth, it would need something more to commend it than the word of Moses.

Was God's name in the Tabernacle?

How were the people to know that this was the place chosen by God to "dwell"? How was the world to know? How were all the children of Israel to know that God really told Moses to do this? Moses *said* this was God's house. The people had Moses' word for it. But how are ordinary people to know that God has put His name in a certain place or institution as opposed to all others?

Were there not great and impressive religious temples in Egypt, with solemn ceremonies and a very "spiritual" atmosphere? There were other so-called gods in many more impressive religious surroundings. Some said, "Here is where God lives." Others said, "in Egypt is where God lives." Everywhere today, as well as then, people are saying "here" or "there" is the house of God.

This is a universal question; and most people, despite the self-revelation of God, still cannot seem to learn the answer.

Who will settle the matter?

Only God Himself can settle this question, and at that time He began the process of authenticating His representative institution on earth. God Himself attested to the fact that this tabernacle was the place He would, at least for the time then present, "dwell":

> ... So Moses finished the work. *Then a cloud covered the tent of the congregation, and the glory of the Lord filled the tabernacle.* And Moses was not able to enter into the tent of the congregation, because the cloud abode thereon, and the *glory of the Lord filled the tabernacle* (Ex. 40:33-35).

When the cloud covered the tent, prefiguring the coming of the Holy Spirit on the New Covenant house of God – the church, one thing it certainly proved: the Tabernacle was *God's* house. This institution of religion, mediated through Moses, was a work of God. The Covenant people were now objectively and authentically linked to the God of creation, the flood, and to Abraham, Isaac, and Jacob. God took over; and not even Moses was able to abide in the Tabernacle.

After the Tabernacle was finished, the *glory of the Lord overshadowed it.* Was this "glory" a manifestation of the Holy Spirit? It seems self-evident to us that it was,[180] but the relevant principle of the authentication and empowerment of God's Old Covenant institution hardly turns upon a rigorous proof of which person of the trinity was active. Some have called it the Shekinah Glory or

---

[180] We will not argue the point. However, it was not uniquely a manifestation of the Son or of the Father.

the glory which dwells. It is the role of the Holy Spirit to *dwell* with His covenant people, to accompany them and lead them; and the manifestation of His presence was the pillar of cloud and fire.

In His normative role of regeneration, the Holy Spirit would operate the same everywhere and always. But in His role of superintending, assisting, and giving gifts to His Old Covenant people – a paracletic type of action – He would come and go according to the needs of the people and the occasion. So also it is said of the Holy Spirit when He *came upon* His New Testament people as Paraclete[181] (Acts 1:8). Thus the Old Testament work of the Holy Spirit is not so different from the New Testament work. They did not have power to speak in tongues all the time, or raise the dead and heal the sick every day. The Paraclete empowered them as it pleased Him.

But undeniably the presence of God upon the Tabernacle confirmed *miraculously* and *visibly* before possibly over a million witnesses: "This is my house." This was God's validation of the fact that He had chosen and accepted this tabernacle as the place to put His name. Without this miraculous corroboration, the people would have had nothing but Moses' word as evidence that this was God's house. The house of God, in any age, is the institution *God chooses* to represent Himself through human agencies. It is the institution *chosen* and *confirmed* by God to interpret His truth to the people of earth, where He meets with men and works through them for the extension of His purpose.

The Tabernacle was designed and built for the specific purpose it needed to serve: a portable building for an unsettled people. It served its limited purpose, and the purpose of God moved on to greater things.

---

[181] Many dispensationalists teach that the normative work of the Holy Spirit in the Old Testament is to "come upon" His people as he chooses, whereas in the New Testament He permanently indwells them. This is a misunderstanding, even a misreading, of the Holy Spirit's work. The distinction between to "come upon" and to "indwell" is not an OT vs. NT distinction, it is a *paracletic* vs. *regeneration* distinction. In His NT paracletic work, the terminology of "coming upon," "falling upon," or "poured out," etc., is used just as in the OT (see Acts 1:8; 8:16; 10:44, 45; 19:6; cf. Luke 1:35).

The Temple. Just as God had commanded Moses to build the Tabernacle, He in like manner commissioned Solomon to build Him a permanent house. And Solomon, as Moses had done, built the Temple exactly as God had commanded:

> *So was ended all the work that King Solomon made for the house of the Lord.* And Solomon brought in the things which David his father had dedicated; even the silver, and the gold, and the vessels, did he put among the treasures of the house of the Lord (I Kings 7:51).

The Temple was finished but empty. They reestablished the Ark of the Covenant in the house of God, and when this Temple that Solomon had built in all its beauty and all its glory was completely finished and everything was totally in its place, the same issue would arise: Was this a work of God, or merely a work of Solomon? If the question did not arise at that time, it would surely arise later; and it is with us to this day.

Was this new house the house of God? Was His name there? Was there evidence to the people that God had accepted this place for His name? Most of the academic world today regards it as merely the work of a brilliant and ambitious king. So God anticipated the world's skepticism and was careful to authenticate the work by a visual, objective wonder which only God could produce, and the account of this event was firmly embedded in the memory of the nation and in the record of the event. Thus He answered the question before it was asked. The same record that tells about the brilliant king also says that when the house was finished God again authenticated and validated this work, witnessed by a million or more people:

> And it came to pass, when the priests were come out of the holy place, that *the cloud filled the house of the Lord,* so that the priests could not stand to minister because of the cloud: for *the glory of the Lord had filled the house of the Lord.* Then spake Solomon, the Lord said that he would dwell in the thick darkness. I have surely built thee an house to dwell in, a settled place for thee to abide in for ever (I Kings 8:10-13).

The old portable tent was now obsolete, but the "house of God" continued, and God authenticated the work and placed in the record an indisputable account, acknowledged by the many thousands of the children of Israel who witnessed the event. Then the purpose of God moved on to greater things; One greater than Solomon came on the scene, who also built a "house."

The Church. Just as Moses prophesied (Deut. 12:10-11) that the Temple itself would be built and supersede the Tabernacle, so a new institution, the church, would supersede the Temple. In the book of Joel we find the prophecy of this event:

> And it shall come to pass afterward, that *I will pour out my spirit upon all flesh* ... And it shall come to pass, that whosoever shall call on the name of the Lord shall be delivered: *for in mount Zion and in Jerusalem shall be deliverance,* as the Lord hath said, and in the remnant whom the Lord shall call (Joel 2:28, 29, 32; cf. Acts 2:16-21).

This passage is recognized immediately as the prophecy of the special work of Christ in sending the Holy Spirit which occurred at Pentecost. That God would establish a new format for His house was no strange thing by now. It was no strange thing at all to a Jew that the Holy Spirit of God would come to assist them. He had been with them in the Tabernacle and Temple era long before Pentecost. In the days of both the Tabernacle and the Temple, He had *empowered* His Old Covenant people to do mighty works. But then Joel prophesied that God would pour out His spirit upon *all flesh* – not merely Israel but all flesh – both Jew and Gentile. This would be the church, the antitype of the Tabernacle and Temple.

Now this was a strange new thing to a Jew. Never before had the Gentiles as such (without circumcision, becoming Jewish proselytes) been included among the Covenant people as representatives of the name of God to the world. The Gentile had always had direct access to God's salvation by grace, e.g., the Ninevites, but not to His covenant people. There is a difference.

But now God would bring forth another format, a new configuration of the institutional house of God. This would be neither a tent nor a stone building but an assembly, including not Jews only but Gentiles also:

> So then ye [Gentiles] are no more strangers and sojourners, but ye are *fellow-citizens with the saints, and of the household of God,* being built upon the foundation of the apostles and prophets, Christ Jesus himself

being the chief corner stone; in whom *each several building, fitly framed together,* groweth into a holy temple in the Lord; in whom ye [Ephesians] also are *builded together for a habitation of God in the Spirit* (Eph. 2:19-22, ASV).

This institution would be "… the house of God, which is the church of the living God, the pillar and ground of the truth" (1 Tim 3:15).

Jesus had said concerning the former house, the Temple, just prior to His death, "Behold your house is left unto you desolate" (Matt. 23:38), and when Christ died the veil was rent leaving the Temple (having served its purpose) standing obsolete and "desolate." But the house of God would continue serving the purpose of God, in a new and functional format, as He moved on to greater things.

In keeping with God's declaration to Moses, the name of God would be kept in memorial to "all generations" (Ex. 3:15). God's name would be represented on earth by this final and most functional design ever to come from the wisdom of God. When Jesus came to the earth, He came to die, but He also came to establish a new kind of house, *His church*, to continue as the pillar and ground of truth. As Moses had built a physical tabernacle and Solomon a physical temple, both of which the Holy Spirit had filled with His glory, so Christ built an assembly.

The church, contrary to most contemporary interpreters, was not born on Pentecost. The church existed in its infancy before Pentecost; created by and tutored under the personal direction of Christ Himself, not the Holy Spirit. He ordained and set His apostles first in the church (cf. Mark 3:13, 14; 1 Cor. 12:28). He continued the ordinance of baptism instituted through John the Baptist (John 2:1). He conferred upon the church, by His own personal authority, the custodianship of the kingdom of heaven and the discipline of the church on earth (Matt. 16:18-19; 18:17-18). He personally instituted the Lord's supper (Matt. 26:26-29). He commissioned His church for the long range work of world evangelism (Matt. 28:19, 20). On the last day He was with them He led them out as far as Bethany, and they watched the Lord

Jesus ascend bodily up into the heavens. Then an angel instructed them *to not go immediately out* to fulfill the great commission; they would need special power. But rather, they were to wait just a few days for the "promise of the Father" (Acts 1:5), which Joel and John had foretold.

Jesus, personally, then left them. But He had prepared them for this hour by the same promise which Joel and John had foretold, though in different words:

> It is expedient for you that I go away: for if I go not away, the *Comforter* (Paraclete, παράκλετος) will not come unto you; but if I depart, *I will send him unto you* (John 16:7).

This little church was about to launch out into a hostile world which hated their Lord. The world was not just disagreeable; it was deadly. They needed *power*. But Jesus had assured them:

> Ye shall *receive power*, after that the Holy Ghost is *come upon you*: and ye shall be witnesses unto me both in Jerusalem, and in all Judaea, and in Samaria, and unto the uttermost part of the earth" (Acts 1:8).

Thus they waited – one hundred and twenty of them – in an upper room. Christ had said, "I will build my church (ecclesia)." And there it was – baptized, obedient, trained, assembled, organized, commissioned, unified, waiting. This assembly had ordinances, officers, and members in particular. The apostles knew who and how many there were; if all the saved of earth were to receive this power and authentication, it would be pointless and misleading to designate these hundred and twenty gathered saints. The assembly elected an officer to fulfill the place of Judas (Acts 1:26). It was a new "house," finished and ready. But was it God's house?

The Advent of the Paraclete

Thousands of foreign-born Jews had arrived in Jerusalem from many countries for the feast of Pentecost. They found Jerusalem in confusion. A mysterious power, only weeks before, had rent the temple veil, and some had told of a strange unexplainable darkness followed by earthquakes, and people came out of their graves. A vague sense of dread gripped the city; things were not right. There had been rumors that a great prophet had risen from the dead. Some claimed the Messiah had come and the Jewish and Roman leaders had killed Him. Instigating a horrible crucifixion, they had put him to death.

How could this be?

The Messiah? Dead?

Could anyone be trusted anymore?

To whom could one turn? How are men to know, once and for all, who speaks in the name of God? Where has *God chosen* to place His name?

The Waiting Church. Jesus had left His church, but He would not send them out into a hostile world all alone. God had placed His name in the Tabernacle and His presence went with them. Likewise, in the Temple, His glory and power was with them. Jesus had said, "I will build *My assembly*," and now it was ready. About 120 of Jesus' disciples had been mysteriously secluded in an upper room for several days, praying. Could this be the new house of God? Could this be the New Covenant people?

God would not leave this great question to the subjective speculations of every self-appointed mystic. This issue would be settled in God's usual objective way. If Jesus of Nazareth was the Messiah and His 120 disciples were His assembly, then God alone could authenticate this astounding truth once and for all.

He must do something that would link the huddled disciples of Jesus to the God of Abraham, Isaac, and Jacob. There must be continuity. Thus in an unequivocal way, just as He miraculously and visibly authenticated the Tabernacle and the Temple, God likewise miraculously and visibly authenticated His church:

> And when the day of Pentecost was fully come, they were all *with one accord in one place.* And suddenly there came a *sound from heaven* as of a rushing mighty wind, and it filled all the house where they were sitting. And *there appeared unto them cloven tongues like as of fire, and it sat upon each of them* (Acts 2:1-3).

You Shall Receive Power. Here, in one stroke, the Holy Spirit came to His waiting church. Jesus had promised, "I will be with you." Then in one electrifying moment He came both to *em-*

power and to *authenticate* His church, the new format of God's house. On that day He poured out His Spirit upon that specific assembly localized at Jerusalem in contradistinction to all others; each person had been water-baptized in the name of the Holy Trinity. Multitudes of people had been saved throughout Israel, but where were they? This unified, obedient assembly of 120 was *His choice* of a new house – the place where He would place His name. It would be called *"... the house of God, which is the church of the living God, the pillar and ground of the truth"* (1 Tim. 3:15).

With this miraculous, audible, and visible demonstration, God again put the world on notice, just as He had done concerning the Tabernacle and the Temple, and said in effect, "This is the place *I have chosen* to put my name" (see Deut. 12).

What God desired now was not a stone building but an institution filled with a *regenerate* and *obedient* people who were now authenticated and empowered, ready to launch out upon the commission which Jesus had already given:

> Go therefore and *make disciples* of all the nations, *baptizing them* in the name of the Father and of the Son and of the Holy Spirit, *teaching them* to observe all things that I have commanded you; and lo, I am with you always, even to the end of the age" (Matt. 28:19, 20 NKJV).

Jesus from now on, faithful to His promise, would be with them through the Holy Spirit, the *Comforter*, the *Paraclete*. It is now apparent that Joel's *outpouring* of the Holy Spirit is the same as John's *baptism* of the Holy Spirit and refers only to the *advent* and continued *presence* of the Holy Spirit in His broad and long-range role of Paraclete [παράκλετος: one called to one's side, an advocate (John 16:7)]. A paraclete, Thayer says, is "in the widest sense, a helper, succorer, aider, assistant." The Holy Spirit was sent by Christ to assist His New Covenant people, in the churches, to do the difficult work of the great commission, to go with them and enable, facilitate, strengthen, comfort, to give gifts and power, to assist in ten thousand ways on their long journey to the end of the age.

This baptism did not come in the form of many individual baptisms of selected individuals, it was a baptism of everyone in the assembly simultaneously. They were all baptized and had immediate access to the Holy Spirit's paracletic sovereignly-distributed gifts and empowerment by virtue of their relationship to the Spirit-baptized church.

John the Baptist meant nothing more by His use of the phrase *baptize in the Holy Spirit* than that Christ would pour out, or send, the Holy Spirit upon the same subjects whom John had prepared for the Lord (Luke 1:17) by baptizing them in water. John had given some of these saved and baptized prepared ones to Christ (John 1:33-37; 3:29, 30); these water-baptized disciples would eventually be baptized in the Spirit. Then He would assist them in their work within the churches. Had John not been baptizing in water, the term *baptize* would, doubtless, never have been applied to the Holy Spirit's advent: "I indeed baptize you with water; but … he shall baptize you.…" He used it as a metaphor, a simile, to call attention to the fact that those he had baptized in water, Christ would later baptize in the Holy Spirit.

Neither John, Jesus, nor Peter, the only persons to ever use the term in Scripture, displayed any intent or purpose to make it a technical term describing *an individual experience verified by unintelligible or any other tongues.* Nor did they intend to catalog under this term all, or any, of the multifaceted gifts the Holy Spirit would give or the works He would do on behalf of the churches in His special role of Paraclete. It simply refers to the Holy Spirit's advent and continued presence in this role, in the absence of Jesus, nothing more.

This will no doubt seem over-simplistic in today's theological atmosphere where John's prophecy has been loaded with theological implications that it is unable to bear – from a second work of grace to a late modification of the ancient doctrines of salvation and the creation of a mystical body of Christ. When we examine the contemporary doctrines that have been identified by John's terminology, alas, we find a theological quagmire.

SORTING OUT A THEOLOGICAL QUAGMIRE

It may sound presumptious to suggest that we can make coherent theological sense out of an issue that has troubled many of the giants of the faith for centuries. But judging from the many differing, discordant, and nuanced opinions, it seems clear to us that conventional evangelical wisdom has so far failed to produce a coherent, satisfying conclusion as to the meaning of the baptism of the Holy Spirit.

There are two theological positions today that dominate evangelical thinking on this issue, and neither of them is supported by a substantive body of objective propositional truth from Scripture:

- The first is the second-work-of-grace doctrine created by the charismatics in the late 19th century.

- The second, held today by non-charismatic evangelicals, could be called the first-work-of-grace doctrine: that "Spirit baptism is actually an integral part of every Christian's salvation experience.... thereby giving us a common life principle."[182]

In this second doctrine the believer is thought to be placed into a mystical body of Christ through some undefined process in regeneration or some aspect of salvation. This mystical-body doctrine is older than the charismatic doctrine, older than the Westminster divines who regarded the mystical body or invisible church to be comprised of all believers of all time.[183]

Dispensationalists, however, consider the mystical body to be comprised merely of those saved since Pentecost, those who "in this dispensation, have been born of the Spirit of God and have by that same Spirit been baptized into the body of Christ."[184] This unfortunate view presumes to change the ancient work of God in

---

[182] John F. MacArthur, Jr., *Charismatic Chaos* (Grand Rapids: Zondervan Publishing House, 1992), p. 230-231.

[183] The Westminster divines, however, do not categorically connect the mystical body doctrine with the baptism of the Holy Spirit in either the *Confession* or the *Catechism.*

[184] Henry C. Thiessen, *Lectures in Systematic Theology* (Grand Rapids: Wm. B. Eerdmans Publishing Co., 1949), p. 407.

which the life principle had for four thousand years been imparted to the elect in regeneration. This is an imprudent approach to the theology of salvation, not supported by any propositional statement of Scripture. The only passage that seems to have a scrap of support for this view is 1 Corinthians 12:13, and therefore this tortured passage is forced to support a load it just cannot bear.

Oh, What a Tangled Web!

D. A. Carson, in discussing 1 Corinthians 12:13 at some length,[185] made a not-so-surprising statement. He said, "Almost every word and syntactical unit in this verse is disputed...."[186] But there are long-standing reasons why the issue of the baptism of the Holy Spirit, and 1 Corinthians 12:13 in particular, are in such confusion. The difficulties experienced in discovering Paul's exact meaning have arisen because most evangelicals, we propose, come to the verse with a mistaken presupposition.

This presupposition is that the "body" into which Paul said they were "all baptized" (1 Cor. 12:13) is a *mystical body* comprised of all the saved.[187] We suggest that the idea of *the church as mystical body* is first a contradiction in terms, and second that neither in the mind of Paul, nor Christ, nor in Scripture is there any such concept. This problem resolves to an ecclesiological issue.

To bring a coherent solution to the interpretation of 1 Corinthians 12:13, and solve other problems at the same time, we must first briefly survey the core issues in an ancient ecclesiological rift and review the rudimentary elements of New Testament ecclesiology.

Invisible, Universal, Mystical Body of Christ. The concept of an *invisible church* vs. a *visible assembly of baptized believers in a particular location* was at the core of the ancient rift

---

[185] Carson, *Showing the Spirit*, pp. 42-49.

[186] Carson, *Showing*, p. 43.

[187] That all the saved exist somewhere on earth or in heaven no one denies, but we contend that neither Paul nor Christ ever thought of the sum total of the saved as a *"mystical body"* or as an *"invisible church,"* as designated in the Westminster Standards (*Confession* XXV; *Catechism* 64, 65) and perpetuated in evangelicalism today.

between the Catholics and the Donatists. Augustine first originated the idea of an "invisible church" (though he didn't call it that) within the developing Catholic state-church to have somewhat to answer the Donatists. As the Catholics moved away from the original concept of the church toward a merger with the state, they abandoned the apostolic concept of the church as local, disciplined assemblies each answerable to Christ as head. The Donatists regarded the church as a local body of baptized, disciplined believers, independent of the state, answering only to Christ as head.[188] This view continued in apostolic churches throughout the dark ages. Verduin wrote, "This 'Donatism' was never absent from the medieval scene."[189]

After the Reformation it became necessary for Protestants to retain the concept of the "invisible church" and infant baptism, for the reformed denominations were also initially state churches wherein all citizens of the state were in the church. In time a theology of the *invisible universal church, or mystical body of Christ* comprising all the saved, evolved and coalesced largely around 1 Corinthians 12:13 and a misinterpretation of the doctrine of the baptism of the Holy Spirit. This was reinforced when dispensationalism arose in the 19th century when Darby and Scofield embraced the "invisible church" theory for both eschatological and ecclesiological reasons. Summarizing his "true church" doctrine, Scofield wrote:

> ... composed of the whole number of regenerate persons from Pentecost to the first resurrection (1 Cor. 15:52), united together and to Christ by the baptism with the Holy Spirit (1 Cor. 12:12, 13), is the body of Christ of which He is Head (Eph. 1:22, 23).[190]

Finally, the above views became entrenched in virtually all seminaries, both reformed and dispensational; and young pastoral students by the thousands, having no time or inclination to chal-

---

[188] Thomas M. Strouse, *I Will Build My Church* (Virginia Beach: Tabernacle Baptist Theological Press, 1995), p. 57.

[189] Leonard Verduin, *The Reformers and their Stepchildren* (Grand Rapids: Baker Book House, 1980), p. 35.

[190] C.I. Scofield, *Scofield Reference Bible*, Note on Hebrews 12:23.

lenge the doctrine, carry it back to their churches where it is typically accepted without question.

As we can see in the views above, there are ecclesiological and soteriological principles involved, and the non-charismatic evangelical view (the first-work-of-grace theory) violates both these doctrines.

A New Salvation at Pentecost? The baptism of the Holy Spirit was unknown in the history of the world until John the Baptist coined the term; but regeneration, justification, and salvation by grace through faith is as old as the human race: "By faith Abel offered unto God a more excellent sacrifice than Cain, by which he obtained witness that he was righteous" (Heb. 11:4).

This statement is consistent with Paul's treatment of the nature of salvation in the book of Romans which is based on the ancient principles of an unchanging salvation as reflected in the Old Testament:

> For what saith the scripture? Abraham believed God, and it was counted unto him for righteousness (Rom. 4:3, Gen. 15:6).

> Therefore it is of faith, that it might be by grace; to the end the promise might be sure to all the seed (Rom. 4:16).

The creation of a new class of believers or altering the work of God in regeneration or salvation based on the late-in-history baptism of the Holy Spirit – which refers simply to the coming of the Paraclete to accompany the churches on their commission and to empower their people – is poor theology, tampering with the eternal plan of God. There has never been and never will be but one theology of salvation. Paul has nailed the features and principles of salvation to the sovereignty of God in eternity past:

> According as he hath chosen us in him *before the foundation of the world,* that we should be holy and without blame before him in love: Having predestinated us unto the adoption of children by Jesus Christ to himself, according to the good pleasure of his will, To the praise of the glory of his grace, wherein he hath made us accepted in the beloved. In whom we have redemption through his blood, the forgiveness of sins, according to the riches of his grace (Eph. 1:4-7).

Moreover, since the human race has had a common problem,

spiritual death; God has provided for the elect in regeneration a common solution, *spiritual life:*

> *And you hath he quickened, who were dead in trespasses and sins;* Wherein in time past ye walked according to the course of this world, according to the prince of the power of the air, the spirit that now worketh in the children of disobedience: Among whom also we all had our conversation in times past in the lusts of our flesh, fulfilling the desires of the flesh and of the mind; and *were by nature the children of wrath, even as others.* But God, who is rich in mercy, for his great love wherewith he loved us, *Even when we were dead in sins, hath quickened us together* with Christ (by grace ye are saved) ... (Eph. 2:1-5).

If this applies to us, it applied to Abel and Abraham; they too were *dead* and were *quickened*, given the life principle by regeneration. Since all sinners have the same problem, all who will be saved require the same remedy. We must keep the doctrines of salvation free from unfounded, injudicious theological speculation. As important as the advent of the Paraclete (the baptism of the Holy Spirit) is to the New Covenant churches, it has nothing directly to do with salvation. B. H. Carroll wrote:

> In no way, then, could the baptism in the Spirit be counted as regeneration. In regeneration the Holy Spirit is the agent, a sinner is the subject and the purpose is to make him a Christian; but here Jesus is the agent, the subject is a Christian, and the purpose is to increase his efficiency as a Christian ... It is evident that in Acts 2 the members of the church, converted people, received the baptism ... .
>
> Paul asked, "have ye received the Holy Spirit since ye believed?" [Acts 19:2].... Showing that they had to have faith before receiving the miraculous gift of the Spirit. In every age of the world, through all its preceding dispensations, the plan of salvation was one; that is, by regeneration on its divine side and by contrition, repentance and faith on its human side.[191]

The baptism of the Holy Spirit is strictly a New Covenant phenomenon to empower the churches in Christ's absence; but the way, the features, and doctrines of salvation were fixed from before the foundation of the world. In every example of Scripture, the gifts of the Holy Spirit fell upon *believers*; the basis of reliable

---

[191] Carroll, *An Interpretation ...*, XII [Acts], pp. 38-40.

and careful theology is to base conclusions on what is revealed, not on what is obscure.

The weighty doctrines of salvation are too voluminous, too ancient, too sharply defined and immutable to be altered by any event late in history, or by any imprecise and difficult verse such as 1 Corinthians 12:13, especially when the alternative is simply to accept the meaning and implications of a relatively simple doctrine, namely, baptism in the Holy Spirit.

Any valid conclusion must preserve these three clear and rigorous propositions intact:

- There is only one kind of individual salvation recognized in Scripture.

- There is only one kind of individual New Covenant baptism recognized in the Scripture.

- There is only one kind of New Covenant church recognized on earth in the Scripture.

With all due respect to our esteemed brethren, the hour is late in history, and we have had more than adequate time for these issues to be resolved and for all believers to reach a unity in truth – not in diversity – "that the world may believe" (John 17:17-23). It just will not do to continue the proliferation of theories which have little or no biblical support at the expense of the dominant pattern and usage of Scripture.

A Coherent Solution

The baptism of the Holy Spirit is an ecclesiological issue. It has to do with the church. We will therefore examine it on an ecclesiological basis, and we believe it will yield a conclusion coherent with broad New Covenant theology, with the grammar and syntax of the disputed passage (1 Cor. 12:13), and especially with the context of that passage.

The Apostolic Concept of the Church. These issues will remain obscure until we understand the nature of the church as the apostles and writers of Scripture understood it, and that is discernable primarily by their usage of the word *ecclesia* in the New Testament:

1. *Ecclesia* is used in the *singular* to designate a particular, specific, local church: **56 times**.

2. *Ecclesia* is used in the *plural* to designate two or more specific local churches: **36 times**.

3. *Ecclesia* is sometimes used in the *singular* to refer to all churches or members as an aggregate[192]; and sometimes it is used in the abstract, generically,[193] as a kind or class: **18 times.**

4. *Ecclesia* is used to refer to an assembly of silver tradesmen: **2 times.**

5. *Ecclesia* is used to refer to an assembly of the tribes of Israel in the wilderness: **1 time.**

6. *Ecclesia* is used to refer to a legal assembly (the historic meaning) of the governing body of a city, in this case Ephesus: **1 time.**

7. *Ecclesia* is used to refer to a *future* assembly in heaven comprised of all the angels, all the redeemed from among men of all time, and the Lord Himself: **1 time**.

8. The total of all these usages: **115 times.**

Therefore, from the inspired record we can gain an immense insight into the thinking of Paul and the other writers of Scripture as to how they thought of the church. Of the usages above, numbers 1 and 2 (80%) are the most enlightening because these reveal their normative understanding: They considered any local assembly of apostolic Christians to be a church, a whole church, not part of a larger single entity called "the church."

---

[192] *Aggregate*: A group of distinct things considered as a whole.

[193] Generic usage is a very common occurrence in conversation. One may say, "*The horse* is a beautiful animal." This use of the word horse is *generic* usage. It refers to *horses as a class*, in an abstract sense, but no one contends there exists somewhere a numerically single big *universal horse*. Why? It is because we all understand the nature of a horse from childhood; we know *it has no existence except as specific observable, local horses*. A ten-year-old Greek would have known the same about *ecclesia*. Other biblical examples of generic usage are: "... *the husband* is the head of *the wife* ..." (Eph. 5:23). "... *the church* ..." is *the* "*house of God* ..." (1 Tim. 3:15).

If there were two such assemblies, they were *churches*. Each was individual and complete. Christ (not Peter, Paul or any central hierarchy) was the Head of each church, just as He is the head of "every man."

We are not at liberty, when reading the Scriptures, to impose the contemporary concept of a mystical church upon the writers.

Numbers 4, 5, 6, and 7 above refer to other kinds of assemblies, not to the New Covenant assemblies on earth. There are 5 such usages and they are not relevant to the issue under discussion except that they consistently demonstrate the concrete localized, character of any *ecclesia*.

Now there remain 18 usages (15%, see number 3), over against the 97 already accounted for as being unequivocally individual, localized assemblies. The immediate and most reasonable conclusion, in view of what we know so far, is that these 18 singular, non-specific references would also prove to be simply references to the other localized assemblies as an aggregate, or generically as a class – as already established by the majority usage. *Upon, careful examination of the contexts of these 18 references, they all are easily classified as simple aggregate or generic usage referring to all local churches as a whole or as a class.*[194]

None of these usages establish or require the concept of a numerically single, mystical church. Moreover, if the concept of the invisible, mystical church had not been created by Augustine as a *theological necessity* to support what Verduin referred to as a "Hybrid"[195] church (the union of church and state which was continued by the reformers), the mystical presupposition, now deeply planted in the mindset of contemporary evangelicalism, would not have been brought to 1 Corinthians 12:13 or elsewhere.

Therefore, we conclude that the apostolic concept of the New Covenant church is that of a localized assembly wherever it is found. We know this is a minority view, but we trust enough

[194] For more on this see William C. Hawkins and Willard A. Ramsey, *The House of God*, pp. 33-54, also, Willard A. Ramsey, *The Nature of the New Testament Church on Earth*, pp. 4-6.

[195] Leonard Verduin, *The Anatomy of a Hybrid* (Grand Rapids: Wm. B. Eerdmans Publishing Co., 1976), pp. 91ff.

biblical evidence is presented here to be taken seriously. Then in time, through further dialogue, it is our Christian duty to try to reach one accord – an observable unity around Scripture truth (see Acts 15).

Jesus' Usage of Ecclesia. Jesus used the word *church(es)* only about nineteen times (counting those spoken after He was glorified in Revelation chapters 1-3, and 22). In *eighteen* of these nineteen times (95%) Jesus refers unequivocally to individual localized assemblies. The remaining one therefore, the first mention of *church* in the Scripture (Matt. 16:18), must for consistency be understood in the same way, or as a generic reference to future churches as a class. We would need to have strong, unequivocal proof to suppose Jesus had a mystical church in mind in this *one first* mention, and then never referred to it again. And since no such strong proof exists, let us give the Lord credit for consistency. In fact, on the very next page in Matthew, without any explanation, Jesus uses ecclesia twice in the context of a local, actual church setting (Matt. 18:17).

THINKING REALISTICALLY. Now, let us think realistically about the aggregate of all the saved of earth. There is a special affinity for fellow believers, brothers and sisters in Christ, regardless of their church or denominational affiliation, or lack thereof, that has no parallel in any other relationship on earth. This is inevitable by the nature of the case and derives primarily from our mutual love of Christ. "Beloved, if God so loved us, we ought also to love one another" (1 John 4:11).

But this has a flip side: Anyone who loves desires the best for the object of his love, and the best is to walk in the truth, righteousness, and commandments of Christ. John said, "I have no greater joy than to hear that my children walk in truth" (3 John 4). For this reason we are commanded to "… exhort one another daily …" (Heb 3:13). And Christ prayed "Sanctify them through thy truth: thy word is truth" (John 17:17).

All of this means that Christ sees problems and desires one accord, doctrinal and moral unity in truth among the saved. All the saved are within the "kingdom of Heaven" (Matt. 5:19), kingdom of God (Luke 17:20, 21), "kingdom of his dear Son" (Col. 1:13), or "heirs of the kingdom" (James 2:5). But the kingdom is not the same as the church. Sadly, many of them are not careful to obey Him:

> Whosoever therefore shall *break one of these least commandments*, and shall *teach men so*, he shall be called the least in the *kingdom of heaven:* but whosoever shall *do and teach them*, the same shall be called great in the kingdom of heaven (Matt. 5:19).

Christ wants us all to be corrected by Scripture truth. Therefore He wants all His saints baptized and gathered into *obedient* churches, each exercising righteous formative and corrective discipline over its members in particular. But many have substituted an emotional, subjective mental image that all the saved of earth comprise an idyllic "body" of unified, virtuous, obedient, doctrinally blameless believers out there somewhere called *the church*. But that idea has no propositional support in Scripture. The unity for which Christ prayed is not fulfilled in salvation alone.

Thinking realistically, we must ask where are the saved on earth today?

Actually they are distributed throughout the various denominations – some Catholic, Lutheran, Presbyterian, Baptist, Methodist, Pentecostal, charismatic, and various other groups ranging from high-church to the Jesus People. Alas, that is the melancholy truth, and this open recognition and discussion of it is a long-overdue act of love. If we face this reality and make a deliberate choice to lay our specific differences before one another in love, detail by detail, we can resolve them objectively before the Scriptures, just as they did in the counsel of Jerusalem (Acts 15).

But unfortunately the search for objective doctrinal truth is in low demand. Millions today are flocking to the no-name community churches. A sad but trendy expression today goes something like this: "I'm in the body of Christ, but I have no use for the 'institutional church.'" Little do they realize that when Jesus built His church, He built an institution. Thus, refusing biblical baptism, they refuse to live under the church-administered moral and doctrinal discipline as prescribed by Jesus (Matt. 18:15-18; 1 Cor. 5).

The aggregate of the saved of earth embrace virtually "every wind of doctrine," and is in fact about as far from Jesus' ideal unity (John 17:17-23; 1 Cor. 1:10) as Christians can be. Is this the ideal church Jesus had in mind when he said, "I will build *My* church" (Matt. 16:18, 19)?

Far from satisfying the analogy of a human "body," as in 1 Corinthians 12, it is an amorphous, scattered, invisible, divided entity comprised of every wind of doctrine, whether they are baptized or not, whether obedient or not. Sadly enough, not every saved person is an exemplary Christian. Peter mentions "just Lot," grieved with the sin of Sodom and Gomorrah; and who today could not empathize with him? Nevertheless, he hung in there until dragged out of Sodom by angels. Yes, grace delivers; and we rejoice for the Lots of earth, but what a poor example of a Christian and a father Lot was.

But even so, many of the individual units of the amorphous aggregate of Christendom are our beloved brethren. Therefore, we each are duty bound to make an effort to direct one another to one of Jesus' ideal baptized, disciplined, assemblies walking blamelessly before Him – as for example the churches of Smyrna and Philadelphia (Rev. 2:8-11, 3:7-13). If we love one another, we must recognize this present diversity for what it is, a sin of discord. We must call each other to something better: the real body of Christ, "the church of the living God, the pillar and ground of the truth" (1 Tim. 3:15), as identified in Scripture.

A REPRESENTATIVE BODY. The church is a *representative body* – a pillar supporting the truth (1 Tim 3:15); a city set on a hill (Matt. 5:14); a candlestick upholding the light (5:15; Rev. 1:20); a morally and doctrinally disciplined body (Matt. 18:15-18; 1 Cor. 5; Titus 3:10); it has definition, a "within" (inside) and a "without" (outside) (1 Cor. 5:12, 13). Not all Christians are "within."

The church is the New Covenant body representing the name of Christ to the world, and *representation* requires more than salvation (Matt. 28:19, 20; Acts 2:41, 42; Heb. 10:16-25). Salvation is by grace, but *representation* is by *grace plus faithful obedience to, and the accurate teaching of, Scripture truth*. Anything less is *misrepresentation*.

Jesus envisioned each church as an institution to which He could entrust the "keys of the kingdom" and the custodianship of the great commission (Matt.16:19; 28:19, 20). He would build a kind of institution to which he could bind Himself by promise that "Whatsoever ye shall bind on earth shall be bound in heaven: and whatsoever ye shall loose on earth shall be loosed in heaven" (16:19; 18:18). This requires obedience, purity, and objective biblical doctrine – not a mystical body or an invisible church.

The Pauline Analogy of the Church as a Body. One, and only one, writer of New Testament Scripture draws for us the beautiful, highly accurate, and effectual analogy of the church as a *human body*. The Apostle Paul developed this extremely enriching picture to help us understand and perform effectually within a well coordinated church as Jesus conceived, designed, organized, trained, launched, and named it. In the long-standing misapplication of this analogy to the so-called mystical body, we not only have lost the great value of this biblical lesson, but the result is a discord and confusion as witnessed by the many "winds of doctrine" in differing movements and denominations. This can be resolved by actual, obedient churches, seeking unity in truth within and between themselves, each representing the name of Christ as the pillar and ground of truth.

But Paul's beautiful inspired and inspiring picture of the true unified and coordinated church body is conveyed more clearly in the context following 1 Corinthians 12:13 than in any other place in Scripture. If we distort the picture of the church in that context – which portrays a specific, localized, baptized, obedient, organized, functional, coordinated, unified living organism answerable to Christ alone as its head – we miss the main point in New Covenant ecclesiology.

The Pauline analogy of the term *body* as applied to the church occurs in the following places: Rom. 12:4, 5; 1 Cor. 10:16,17; 12:12-31; in Ephesians (several times); and finally in Colossians.

It is in Colossians 1:18 that Paul makes a categorical equation: "And he is the head of *the body, the church:*" i.e., *the body = the church.* Whatever the church is, the body is. Since the church is created to be a localized, unified, functional body, so the human "body of Christ" is the perfect analogy for the church. All functional human bodies are assembled, local, and visible; but there are no mystical, disassembled, and invisible functional human bodies; therefore the beautiful Pauline analogy breaks down for a mystical body. Thus there are not two *kinds* of churches. Body, therefore, in 1 Corinthians 12:13 is understood by Paul and his readers to refer to any local church. The facts discussed above provide reasonable objective evidence that Paul fully expected his readers to clearly understand his meaning: unified obedience of baptism in water into the church, a localized body.

Paul uses the term *one body* to emphasize the *unity* of a church. If a church qualifies as a *unified body* per Paul's definition (1 Cor 1:10), only then does it suit the analogy to Christ's body:

> For as the body is one, and hath many members ... so also is Christ" (1 Cor. 12:12).

Christ Himself is unified and coordinated; and if a body does not have these features, it is no "body of Christ." The so-called mystical body just cannot qualify as an appropriate analogy of the body of Christ.

The function of the church of Jesus Christ is threefold: to evangelize, baptize, and teach (Matt. 28:19, 20). This requires that its many members be baptized, gathered, organized, unified, coordinated, and functional, for "so also is Christ" (1 Cor. 12:12). Therefore, the body of 1 Corinthians 12:13 refers to any one of the several local, unified apostolic churches expected to meet the conditions of coordinated unity set forth in the context (vs. 14-28).

In the context of 1 Corinthians 12:13, each distinctive member is to be consciously coordinated with the others. It seems that each detail of the passage leads farther away from the mystical body theory, while strengthening the dominant pattern that the apostolic thought was of the church as local unified assemblies. Today the dominant pattern of thought is just the opposite.

Moreover, the biblical church body is to be unified within and obediently related to its Head in practice and doctrine. Therefore, if Church A is righteously related to its Head and Church B is righteously related to its Head; then, they are righteously related to each other – unified, in one accord. They are of the same essence. Thus Paul's statement, "we all," is perfectly valid considering all churches as an aggrigate. When Paul uses the editorial "we," as he does throughout his writings, he does not mean that he is including himself as a member of each specific church to which he is writing.

The principle of *conscious coordination* between known members is at the heart of the doctrine of the church as a body. As the context (of 1 Cor. 12:13) makes clear, the ideal church is beautifully illustrated by the normal features of a human body having attached feet, hands, eyes, ears, and other body parts assembled, functional, organized, and local, with *mutually conscious coordination between all members.* They know each other (vs. 15, 16); they cooperate together (vs. 21-24); the purpose or goal is unity (v. 25).

There is no reasonable way to avoid the conclusion that the Pauline "*body*" in the disputed passage is a New Covenant assembly, localized and functional wherever it is found.

If, therefore, the baptism in the disputed text, as we have shown above, is not a part of regeneration or salvation, does this mean then that the charismatic doctrine of the baptism of the Holy Spirit as a second work of grace is correct? By no means; we must not establish one error to defeat another. But before we are prepared to interpret the disputed text, a few more basic matters must be recognized.

A Few Facts About Baptism. There are a few facts concerning baptism, typically overlooked, that we need to consider. The word baptism is mentioned six times designating the Holy Ghost as the medium. In each of these it is distinguished from John's baptism by designating water ("I baptize you with water, but ..."). Then Jesus mentioned a special ordeal which faced Him, His death, and referred to it as a baptism. But in almost all other cases where baptism is mentioned, it is merely called baptize, or baptism, etc. (at least 50 or so times), with no mention of the medium or element into which the subject is baptized.

Why?

The above objective biblical usage indicates that in the mind of the apostles and people of the early church environment, when they heard baptism, with no qualifier, they didn't think Spirit baptism; they thought water baptism. By all the evidence, water baptism was universally practiced among them – a thing that Paul could say "we all" had. If a person in the apostolic environment refused water baptism, he would not be considered among the "we all." In the apostolic environment there is no category recognized for saved people who would not receive baptism and joyfully take a responsible place in the institutional church. They knew no other church. It was not because they thought baptism was necessary for salvation, but the ordinances of baptism and the Lord's supper actually identified those *within* the communion of the New Covenant churches (Acts 2:41; 1 Cor. 5:8, 11-13). Today, this thinking is foreign to very many Christians.

After Pentecost, the baptism of the Holy Spirit was expressly mentioned only once (Acts 11:16), and that referred back to Pentecost. Among the people, the baptism of the Holy Spirit was a phrase not commonly used; the gifts or manifestation of the Holy Spirit was frequently mentioned, but when the people heard *baptism*, as established above, they thought *water*.

We know that Paul was saved on the Damascus road; but it was three days later before he received the miraculous manifestation of the gifts of the Holy Spirit, and only then after Ananias, a disciple of the church at Damascus, had laid his hands on Paul (Acts 9:9-21). This is reminiscent of the occasion at Samaria when James and Peter deliberately went up from Jerusalem to lay hands on Philip's converts (Acts 8:12f); likewise, it has some similarities to the occasion of the Gentile converts at Cornelius' home (10:44f). From these and other passages it is clear that the Paraclete, in launching and empowering the infant church, was acting in a sovereign manner choosing the right action for every situation. But it also shows that the baptism of the Holy Spirit does not occur in salvation. It is a church-related phenomenon not a salvation-related phenomenon.

The message Ananias was to deliver to Paul (9:15) might have caused any man to feel as though he was an institution unto himself. But God took care of that from the beginning. He taught Paul that he couldn't even *see* until that humble disciple from the church which Paul was planning to destroy had laid his hands on him. As soon as he could see, he was *baptized* (with *water*, no medium mentioned), and then the Paraclete began to empower him to preach and confound the Jews "proving that [Jesus] is very Christ."

When was Paul baptized with the Holy Ghost? That is a little ambiguous, but what is not ambiguous is that he certainly was manifesting the gifts of the Paraclete immediately after his *baptism* (in water).

Now, one more objective reality: according to Acts 2:41, baptism is the ordinance of God by which He inducts an obedient believer into the church, the body:

> Then they that gladly received [Peter's] word *were baptized:* and the same day *there were added unto them about three thousand souls.* And they continued stedfastly in the apostles' doctrine and fellowship, and in breaking of bread, and in prayers.

In the great commission, baptism is the ordinance of God wherein a believer is identified openly with the *"name of the Father, and of the Son, and of the Holy Ghost ..."* (Matt. 28:19). From Acts 2:41 we learn that this act also identifies the obedient believer with the church. Thus it is a blessed truth that *they all* were "baptized [in water] into the body of Christ," the church.

The apostolic churches did not recognize, nor do the epistles acknowledge a class of Christians that refuse baptism or remain aloof from the gathered baptized churches.

Now we should think seriously before embracing a doctrine that creates a change in God's eternal salvation or invents a special second work of grace. Neither of these theories is theologically adequate to satisfy the second-work-of-grace theory of the charismatics, nor the salvation theory of evangelicalism, nor the mystical church/body theory of Augustine and the reformers.

Interpreting the Disputed Text. Armed with the above objective truths, we are now able to understand how the apostles and people within the New Covenant church environment were thinking and how they would understand each other. Also, we have briefly discussed some long-disputed issues which are somewhat novel to the majority of evangelicals today, but many Christians of the 19th century would have been more at home with them. These issues, we believe, will help us think more clearly as the people of the apostolic churches thought, and prepare us to more accurately interpret the disputed text:

> For in one Spirit were we all baptized into one body, whether Jews or Greeks, whether bond or free; and were all made to drink of one Spirit (1 Cor. 12:13, ASV).

IN ONE SPIRIT. We will first consider the phrase "in one Spirit" (ἐν ἑνὶ πνεύματι). Throughout the New Testament the phrase "in the Spirit" is used, meaning that some attitude, purpose, or action is in accordance with or prompted by the Holy Spirit. For example, in Acts 19:21, we have this: "Paul purposed *in the spirit* (ἐν τῷ πνεύματι) when he had passed through Macedonia and Achaia, to go to Jerusalem ..." His purpose was in accordance with, led, or prompted by the Holy Spirit.

There are actually *dozens* of examples of this usage in the New Testament with slightly different structure depending on the context. For example: Simeon "came *by the Spirit* into the temple ... ." (Luke 2:27). "Praying always with all prayer and supplication *in the Spirit,* and watching thereunto ... ." (Eph. 6:18).

It was in this same attitude of harmony with the Holy Spirit, being commanded by Him, taught by Him, and led by Him as the Paraclete, that "we all" were baptized (in *water*, no medium mentioned because it is understood and experienced by all of Paul's audience) "into one body" the church (generic), i.e., any local[196] church.

---

[196] Though we use "local church" for clarity in our present theological climate,

Finally, lest anyone should be disturbed that the text reads "in *one* spirit" (ἐν ἑνὶ πνεύματι) instead of "in *the* spirit" (ἐν τῷ πνεύματι or ἐν πνεύματι), we have an exact parallel in Philippians 1:27: "… that ye stand fast *in one spirit* (ἐν ἑνὶ πνεύματι), with one mind striving together for the faith of the gospel." And another parallel is in Ephesians 2:18: "For through him we both [Jew and Gentile] have access by one Spirit (ἐν ἑνὶ πνεύματι) unto the Father." The emphasis in both of these parallels is unity, one spirit, one mind, just as in 1 Corinthians 12:13.

Summarizing, then, people can:

1. Purpose to do something in the Spirit (Acts 19:21).
2. Enter the temple in the Spirit (Luke 2:27).
3. Pray in the Spirit (Eph 6:18).
4. Stand fast in one Spirit (Phil. 1:27).
5. Have access to the Father in one Spirit (Eph. 2:18).
6. Be baptized (in water) in one Spirit (1 Cor. 12:13).

ONENESS. In our disputed passage (1 Cor. 12:13), starting with verse 4, Paul begins an emphasis on *unity*. He mentions the Spirit (v. 4), the same Lord (v. 5), the same God (v. 6), back to the Spirit in verses 8, 9, and 11. And in verse 12, referring to the church with many members as a unified body, he says, *"so also is Christ"* (v. 12).

Then the context following verse 13, through verse 27, focuses upon the real, visible, coordinated, unity that is to be exemplified in a real assembly, a body. Now this context (and indeed the rest of the Scriptures) proves that Paul was not thinking about a mystical, unobservable, dismembered entity comprised of all the saved of the earth, to which has been attached the unfortunate term "body" – calling it the church. No, we cannot lay this matter at Paul's feet; this is the work of subsequent theologues.

PARAPHRASING FOR CLARITY. Now, based upon the objective truths discussed above, we can better understand just how the early disciples were thinking about the church and how they would

---

its use is redundant. Every *ecclesia* is local, because every assembly must have a locus. To say "local church" is like saying "hot fire," or "cold ice."

understand the teachings of the Lord still fresh among them. This will allow us to understand (2000 years later in a very doctrinally confused environment) exactly what Paul meant by these words:

> For as the body [generic, any local assembly] is one [a single unit], having many members – and all the members of that one body, though many, still comprise but a single unit – that is also the way Christ is (1 Cor. 12:12, authors' paraphrase).

> For in one Spirit [universally understood to be the Spirit's leadership or prompting, e.g., Phil. 1:27; Eph. 2:18] we all were led to be baptized [in water, no medium expressed], into or unto one assembly, an undivided body [generic, any church], regardless of ethnic origin, Jew or Gentile; or social status, bond or free; we have all been made to drink[197] of the Holy Spirit (1 Cor. 12:13, authors' paraphrase).

This paraphrase supplies the information that would have been commonly understood by moderately knowledgeable disciples living in the early church environment, as is evident from the brief study above.

The message of 1 Corinthians 12:13 thus becomes very simple: 1) Christ is not divided, 2) therefore in a unified Spirit all obedient believers were led to be baptized into a unified body, the church. 3) The members thus form a unified, coordinated, functional body.

Every member is known and needed, even those we think to be "less honorable." Upon those "we bestow the more abundant honor," and the whole body is seen as more comely. There must be *no schism* in the body, but every member should have the same

---

[197] This clause could be consistently interpreted in either of two ways: 1) It could be a reference to receiving the Spirit in normative regeneration as the indwelling life principle: *"in him a well of water springing up into everlasting life"* (John 4:14). Or 2) it could be a reference to the *empowering work of the Paraclete* bringing forth from the believer to others the living waters of the Gospel: *"out of his belly shall flow rivers of living water. (But this spake he of the Spirit, which they that believe on him should receive: for the Holy Ghost was not yet given; because that Jesus was not yet glorified)"* (John 7:38, 39). Both are true but not the same. In the first, one receives or drinks of the indwelling Spirit in regeneration. In the second, one receives or drinks of the gifts and power of the Paraclete after His advent (Acts 1:8) and gives out the Gospel as a river of living water in the great commission.

care for one another. If a member suffers the others know it and suffer too, if one is honored, the others know it and rejoice.

The above interpretation preserves the ancient soteriology, the contextual integrity of the passage, and the integrity of New Testament ecclesiology without violating any of the linguistic features of the passage. Once this background is accepted and understood, the meaning is reasonably simple.

But the typical moderately savvy Christian or pastor in today's environment comes to this passage loaded with an entirely different set of presuppositions, i.e., the mystical body theory. This theory has been reinforced by the strong influence of two otherwise divergent views: 1) Reformation theology via Protestant academia, and 2) dispensational theology via Darby, Scofield, and fundamentalist academia.

A SHORT BUT LUCID PARAPHRASE. A recent book by James Carlin, in which the biblical concept of the church is set forth, includes an insightful discussion of 1 Corinthians 12:13 written by Charles Blair. He gives an intuitively simple paraphrase true to the meaning of the first part of the verse. He wrote:

> Verse 13 may be paraphrased as: "The same Holy Spirit Who led you, as a saved person, to be immersed and to be added to a given church, in the same way led me to the same experience, wherever we were."[198]

The directness of this statement, once we understand the nature of the apostolic churches, captures the essence of Paul's statement with surprising clarity.

CARROLL ON 1 CORINTHIANS 12:13. But consider yet another variation in interpretation. Once the above background has been established, B. H. Carroll's interpretation of 1 Corinthians 12:13 likewise preserves the integrity of the doctrines of salvation and the church. In the disputed passage he regards the phrase "in one Spirit" to refer to the baptism of the Holy Spirit in his paracletic work, but he makes the point that "into one body" (εἰς ἓν σῶμα)

---

[198] From an article "E Pluribus Unum: One Kind of Body" by R. Charles Blair in: James B. Carlin, *Identifying the Lord's Kind of Churches*, 2nd ed. (Emmaus, Pa.: Challenge Press, 2006), p. 77.

must be understood as "unto one body," i.e., something like *in reference to* or *with respect to* one body. He argues that:

> The baptism in water may be "unto repentance," "unto remission of sins," "unto Christ's death," "unto the triune name." The baptism in the Spirit is "unto the church," [i.e., one body]. As no other objective, its object was to empower the church, to dower the church, to accredit the church.[199]

Since Carroll's interpretation rejects both the second-work-of-grace theory, the salvation and mystical body doctrines of Spirit baptism, and preserves the integrity of the context of the disputed text, we see no biblical conflict with his interpretation and regard it as an acceptable, perhaps the preferred, rendering of the passage.

CONCLUSION. "Now ye [you Corinthians in particular] are [in essence] body of Christ" (v. 27). This verse has no definite article. It refers strictly to the Corinthian church being whatever "*body*" is. This is conclusive proof that the Pauline body is a localized assembly, not a mystical entity.

Moreover, the whole chapter is about the gathered churches; and if we could all learn the lesson that there is no mystical body *called the church*, the interpretation would be simple and immensely valuable to churches today if applied according to the truth it is designed to convey.

The mystical body/church is another notion borne out of and sustained by *subjective* reasoning, because it is established by no objective biblical proposition. Unity is concrete, specific, objective, real within obedient churches. Jesus has no need for a dismembered mystical church. He left us on a real earth, to do real work together in real unity. If all God's people will let go of the mystical and focus on the objective message of Scripture, we will see powerful change for the better upon this earth.

Defining the Baptism of the Holy Spirit

It is remarkable how few of the standard works have made any serious attempt to develop a coherent biblical doctrine con-

---

[199] Carroll, *An Interpretation ...*, XII [Acts], p. 45.

cerning the baptism of the Holy Spirit. As we try to present a reasonably comprehensive interpretation of the baptism of the Holy Spirit and later of tongues, we will begin with the question which was on the mind of all the people as the amazing events of Pentecost unfolded.

What Meaneth This? Peter seized upon this question as a cue to launch into one of the great interpretive sermons of all time, but his answer has been misunderstood by many, resisted by others, and misinterpreted to support the subjective and charismatic abuses outlined in the first three chapters of this book. After the Holy Spirit made His advent known to the people, the visiting throngs were confused:

> And they were all amazed, and were in doubt, saying one to another, What meaneth this? (Acts 2:12).

The subjectivity and abuse of Scripture inherent in the misunderstanding of Peter's answer to this question have been among the most divisive in the history of the Christian faith. We need to get the answer right once for all.

Peter's Answer. Peter confirmed that the fulfillment of Joel's prophecy began with the remarkable events of that day. He confirmed that a special *empowerment* would characterize the "last days," continuing until the "great and notable day of the Lord" (Acts 2:16-21). This broad prophecy, concerning events to be fulfilled in the New Covenant era, comprehends, but is not limited to, the baptism of the Holy Spirit. The range of this prophecy, and thus the range of the "last days," extends from Pentecost to the terminal event of the present heavens and earth, or "the great and the terrible day of the Lord." Joel's prophecy as cited by Peter is as follows:

> But *this is that* which was spoken by the prophet Joel; And it shall come to pass in the *last days,* saith God, *I will pour out of my Spirit upon all flesh:* and your sons and your daughters shall prophesy, and your young men shall see visions, and your old men shall dream dreams: And on my servants and on my handmaidens I will pour out in those days of my Spirit; and they shall prophesy: And I will show wonders in heaven above, and signs in the earth beneath; blood, and fire, and vapour of smoke: *The sun shall be turned into darkness, and the moon into blood,*

before that great and notable day of the Lord come: And it shall come to pass, that whosoever shall call on the name of the Lord shall be saved (Acts 2:16-21; see also Joel 2:28-32).

The critical feature within this passage is that God would pour out *His Spirit*, and there would be several remarkable results:

1. It would be upon *all flesh*, both Jew and Gentile, not just Jews as before.

2. Both sons *and* daughters would prophesy, not just the sons.

3. Old men who had about given up hope would now *dream again of better things to come* for their descendents under the *New Covenant*.

4. Young men who typically would have little expectation for better things *would now see visions and be empowered for great things.*

5. Servants, ordinary working folks, *both men and women will be empowered by the Spirit of God* poured out upon them.

6. God would finally bare His mighty arm in power and judgment and make all His enemies His footstool: *"I will show wonders in heaven above, and signs in the earth beneath; blood, and fire, and vapour of smoke: The sun shall be turned into darkness, and the moon into blood, before that great and notable day of the Lord come"* (Acts 2:20; cf Matt. 24:29-31).

7. And the entire period of the last days will be characterized by worldwide evangelism by the church in accordance with the Great Commission (Matt. 28:19, 20). "And it shall come to pass, that *whosoever* shall call on the name of the Lord shall be saved."

It is clear from the broad teachings of this prophecy that the work of God which Joel called the *pouring out of God's Spirit,* is the same phenomenon which John called the *baptism of the Holy Spirit.* Jesus characterized the baptism of the Holy Spirit as an *empowerment* of the church for the long road ahead into all the world:

"But *ye shall receive power, after that the Holy Ghost is come upon you:*

and ye shall be witnesses unto me both in Jerusalem, and in all Judaea, and in Samaria, and unto the uttermost part of the earth" (Acts 1:8).

Thus, at this point in our study, we could make a valid, though limited, definition as follows: The baptism of the Holy Spirit is an act by Jesus Christ wherein He sent the Holy Spirit in a special role upon (submerging) the waiting church at Jerusalem and from there to all the churches to follow. This definition is concise and accurate, focusing only upon the arrival of the Paraclete.

The people waiting in this gathered church were saved, baptized, and trained. They had the Holy Spirit indwelling in His normative role through regeneration, but not in His special paracletic role. Now we must go further to fully define the future work of the Paraclete.

The Work of the Paraclete. Since the term Baptism of the Holy Spirit has been ill defined and misused for many centuries, it will be difficult to reorient the thinking of the millions of well-meaning but confused Christians concerning the advent and work of the Holy Spirit in His paracletic role. The works He does in this role are as diverse as they are innumerable. They began immediately upon His arrival, and some have been continuous among His churches throughout the centuries. And some will continue throughout the years of His tenure until "The sun shall be turned into darkness, and the moon into blood, before that great and notable day of the Lord come" (Acts 2:20).

The tenure of the Paraclete is essentially the same as the tenure of the session of Christ at God's right hand:

> And David himself saith in the book of Psalms, The LORD said unto my Lord, Sit thou on my right hand, Till I make thine enemies thy footstool (Luke 20:42-43).

The role was created for the expressed purpose of providing aid and assistance to the church, filling the void *in the absence of Christ:* "… if I depart, I will send him unto you" (John 16:7). Then we read in Peter's Pentecostal sermon:

> Therefore being by the right hand of God exalted, and having received of the Father the promise of the Holy Ghost, *he hath shed forth this,*

which ye now see and hear. For David is not ascended into the heavens: but he saith himself, The LORD said unto my Lord, Sit thou on my right hand, Until I make thy foes thy footstool (Acts 2:33-35; see also Psalm 110:1).

That which was "shed forth" on the people, which they were seeing and hearing, was because Christ was by God's "right hand exalted." When Jesus comes again, the role of the Paraclete will be finished. But until then He works on behalf of the churches to provide whatever they need to accomplish the great commission.

MANIFESTATION AND AUTHENTICATION. Therefore, when the Paraclete "arrived" He went straight to the work. The initial work was to manifest Himself in a way that His presence could be detected objectively by human senses, just as it was in the Tabernacle and the Temple:

> And suddenly there came a *sound from heaven as of a rushing mighty wind*, and it *filled all the house* where they were sitting. And there appeared unto them *cloven tongues like as of fire*, and it sat upon each of them" (Acts 2:2-3).

Audibly, the manifestation was a great sound like wind; visually, it was light like fire – but apparently not hot, for it sat on each of the 120 members of the waiting church

They were assembled in one place in one accord (1:13) where they had been waiting for a few days not knowing exactly when the Paraclete would come or how they would recognize Him. But like the people before the Tabernacle and the Temple, the church itself needed this objective manifestation. It would settle forever any disputes arising from feelings or other subjective claims. The Paraclete had come, and he had come to the assembly of the commissioned disciples of Jesus. This would be the very first help they would need: *Objective validation as the New Covenant representatives of the God of Abraham, Isaac, and Jacob; the God of David and his Son Jesus the Messiah; "the house of God, which is the church of the living God, the pillar and ground of the truth."*

FILLING. With this validation providing these great credentials before the throngs gathered at Jerusalem, they were now ready for their next challenge: to launch out on their commission. But they would need power. "And they were all *filled with the Holy Ghost, and began to speak with other tongues,* as the Spirit gave them utterance" (2:4).

What was this "filling" with the Holy Spirit? Was the *filling* unique to the coming of the Paraclete? We think not. Others before had been "filled": certain *Old Covenant* characters, also John the Baptist, Zachariah, Elizabeth. Since the filling of the Holy Spirit was known before the advent of the Paraclete, it provides a helpful clue: Either the *filling* is 1) part of the normative work of the Holy Spirit, 2) there is overlap in the normative work and the paracletic work, or 3) part of the work of the Holy Spirit on behalf of the Old Covenant people was paracletic in nature. We believe the latter is the most likely.

But the filling was certainly needed at Pentecost, and the Holy Spirit provided. Were these gifts coming as a matter of special righteousness, or as an ecstatic experience?

No.

The "filling" is not an infusion of the Spirit into the cells or organs of the body. It simply means that the Holy Spirit gives one *a full measure of all the help that he or she needs:* In any given moment limitless assistance or power to meet the demand of that moment is given for whatever the work God wants done. If the need is only the courage to speak a word of Gospel witness, it is there. If God wants a mountain moved, the power is there.

POWER AND GIFTS. On this unique occasion, they needed power to speak in languages they didn't know, and it was there. But that was not the baptism of the Holy Spirit. He had already come. Having arrived in that special role, He was simply giving power to do the work God wanted done at any instant.

There were at least fifteen countries, and probably as many or more languages, represented in the crowds at Jerusalem on that occasion. But the people of the church were not learned linguists. So the Paraclete miraculously empowered them to speak the languages. These were known languages, not ecstatic babble. Not only did they communicate the "wonderful works of God," but that very act was a sign further validating the witness of the church. Signs and wonders will be examined in further detail later.

Next, Peter needed special *knowledge* to answer their question: "what meaneth this?" The power was given; it was a "gift" of the Holy Spirit, but that was not the *baptism* of the Holy Spirit. Then he needed power to preach, and what a sermon. That also was a "gift," but that was not the *baptism* of the Holy Spirit, nor was it a sign and wonder. Then they needed power to baptize 3000 souls, quite a job. That too was assistance; but that was not the *baptism* of the Holy Spirit nor a sign.

Next, Peter and John came upon a lame man. God wanted to show His power upon him, and the Holy Spirit provided the power to perform this work; the power was there. That was a "gift," but not the *baptism* of the Holy Spirit; it was a miraculous sign and wonder, further validating the church and those speaking in the name of God. But that was not the *baptism* of the Holy Spirit.

The Paraclete had come. He was on the job for whatever work, small or great, that God wanted done. He had been "poured out upon" the institution that God, generically, calls His church. It was submerged, baptized, one time, 2000 years ago. He stayed. The churches multiplied. Today He is still here. He came down and remained to provide the churches with power for whatever God wants done.

Conclusion. The Baptism of the Holy Spirit:

1. Is not regeneration, not a part of regeneration, not concurrent with it, and not a component of salvation.

2. Is not a second work of grace.

3. Is not sinless perfection or a "victorious life."

4. Is not an ecstatic experience.

5. Is not speaking in tongues, whether in known languages or in unintelligible sounds.

6. Is not any of the myriad gifts conferred on individuals.

7. Is not receiving direct revelation from God.

8. Is not a subjective existential means of knowledge.

Having seen what the baptism of the Holy Spirit is *not*, let us wrap up this study by forming a concise definition of what the expression *baptism in the Holy Spirit* actually means or refers to. Out of the three persons in Scripture who actually used the phrase, the one that conveys the most information as to its meaning is the Lord Jesus. This brief but highly informative discussion is in the first chapter of Acts:

> And, being assembled together with them, [Jesus] commanded them that they should not depart from Jerusalem, but wait for *the promise of the Father*, which, saith he, *ye have heard of me.* For John truly baptized with water; but *ye shall be baptized with the Holy Ghost not many days hence* (1:4-5).

> But ye shall *receive power*, after that the Holy Ghost is *come upon you:* and ye shall be witnesses unto me both in Jerusalem, and in all Judaea, and in Samaria, and unto the uttermost part of the earth (1:8).

From this statement by the mouth of the Lord Jesus, we can derive the following conclusions:

1. The apostles were not to launch out on the great commission immediately, but to wait for an event.

2. The event was the fulfillment of a *promise* of the Father concerning which Christ had thoroughly briefed them (John 14-16). It was the advent of the "Comforter" (the Holy Spirit as the *Paraclete*) whom the Father would send in Jesus' name (John 14:26).

3. In Acts 1:5 Jesus quotes John's prophecy of the baptism in the Holy Spirit, unequivocally connecting John's prophecy with the promise of the Father. Moreover, He put time limits on the fulfillment of the prophecy: "… not many days hence."

4. Now, verse 8 tells the rest of the story. After the baptism of the Holy Spirit, the submergence of this assembly, *after* he came upon them they would "receive power" as functional members of the body – not for individual merit as first one and then another got a second blessing. They were gifted by His own sovereign choices to perform a multi-millennial task: "[Y]e shall be witnesses unto me unto the uttermost part of the earth" (1:8).

5. An indispensable aspect of the work and advent of the Holy Spirit as Paraclete was the once-and-for-all authentication and confirmation of His church and Word to the world. By the advent itself and the mighty signs and wonders given early in the ministry of the church, both the institution and the Scriptures, given through chosen members, have received the seal and signature of God upon them forever.

6. This event was also the launching of the Great Commission wherein Jesus promised "I will be with you alway, even unto the end of the world" (Matt. 28:19-20). Jesus therefore, from the right hand of God, is with them through the Comforter; the Holy Spirit as Paraclete continues to be with the obedient, water-baptized, disciplined witnesses that constitute the institution Jesus built and called "my church" wherever she is found upon the earth, and for as long as He remains at the right hand of God.

Therefore, the baptism of the Holy Spirit is the advent and continued presence of the Holy Spirit, in the role of Paraclete, upon the churches that continue in obedience to the New Covenant commandments, ordinances, doctrines, conditions, and commission; gifting and assisting them, in the absence of Jesus Christ, to carry out the purpose of God on earth in the "last days" from Pentecost until Christ's second advent at the "great and notable day of the Lord."

V.

The Doctrine of Tongues in Scripture

Having examined the biblical doctrine of the *baptism of the Holy Spirit*, we must now examine a kindred doctrine which in the charismatic view is integrally related to the baptism of the Holy Spirit, i.e., the *doctrine of tongues.*

It has been now well over a century since the current historical tongues movements revived with a vengeance. One reason, we believe, as discussed above, is a reaction against the cold and lifeless churches and Christians left in the wake of modernism and liberalism. Those joining this late movement were typically seeking a subjective fulfillment, "looking for action, excitement, warmth and love. [The charismatic] wants to believe that God is really at work in his life – right now and right there."[200] Yet, it is apparent from Scripture that God's purpose for tongues was limited to the early days of the church:

> Speaking in tongues was rendered useless when the New Testament was complete; tongues are mentioned only in the earliest books of the New Testament: and history records that tongues did cease.[201]

John MacArthur further points out that some charismatics will agree categorically with that statement, but will contend that "[Tongues] started up again because we are in the last days and God is giving us the final outpouring of His Spirit."[202] But there is no biblical authority for such a belief.

Others among the Neo-Pentecostals claim that tongues are a special language, known only to God, to be used in private prayers and devotions. It is used so that the devil will not know what they are praying for; and, so the theory goes, neither do those praying know what they are praying for in such cases. As remarkable as this may sound, it is not difficult to verify that many charismatics do pray in this special "prayer language," notwithstanding Paul's admonition that he would pray both with his spirit and with understanding.

With these and numerous other such biblically unsupportable beliefs and practices abroad, how shall we proceed to get at the exact biblical truth? Would it matter to the typical charismatic if we did? To prove or disprove theories that have no actual propositional treatment in Scripture, or are suggested only by innuendo, is difficult. But, fortunately, we can demonstrate by objective Scripture truth what *does* exist as a part of the revelation of God. Theories and behavior that are not expressly revealed in Scripture are of human or other origin and must be regarded as transgression or intrusion upon the will and purpose of God. That is the line

---

[200] John F. MacArthur, Jr., "The Charismatics, Part 3," *Moody Monthly* Dec. 1979: 82-85.
[201] Ibid.
[202] Ibid.

of thinking we will pursue in the examination of the doctrine of tongues in Scripture.

Tongues in the Scripture: A Review

A review of all the occasions when tongues were used or otherwise mentioned in the Scripture should shed significant light upon the phenomenon itself. There are not very many passages of Scripture that deal with this subject, and so we can take a good look at every one of them. When we have finished, a pattern will no doubt emerge which will shed great light upon God's use of this gift.

There are a few prophecies in the Old Testament that bear upon the understanding of this phenomenon encountered in the New Testament, e.g., Isaiah 28:11 and 33:19 which we regard as prophecies fulfilled by the gift of tongues as noted in I Corinthians 14:21. But the Old Testament contains no example of tongues-speaking, not even among pagans. So we will limit our study primarily to New Testament passages.

Tongues in Mark 16:17-20

The first place we find a mention of tongues is in the book of Mark. It reads:

> And *these signs* shall follow them that believe; In my name shall they cast out devils; they shall *speak with new tongues;* They shall take up serpents; and if they drink any deadly thing, it shall not hurt them; they shall lay hands on the sick, and they shall recover. So then after the Lord had spoken unto them, he was received up into heaven, and sat on the right hand of God. And they went forth, and preached everywhere, the Lord working with them, and *confirming the word with signs following.* Amen (Mark 16:17-20).[203]

This is a very significant passage as it relates to the subject of tongues. The various gifts mentioned here are catalogued under the category of signs, and the second mentioned of these gifts is that of *tongues.* Other gifts mentioned are casting out devils, immunity to serpents[204] and poisons, and the gift of healing.

---

[203] Some regard the final verses of Mark's Gospel as spurious, not belonging to the canon of Scripture. We, however, do not hold this opinion.

[204] An example of this occurred in the life of Paul during the shipwreck experi-

Then Mark gives a very enlightening summarizing statement: As they go abroad preaching, "the Lord," in the person of the Holy Spirit who would be with them as Paraclete, is working with them "confirming the word with signs … ." Thus these miraculous gifts are "signs and wonders" for the *confirmation* of New Covenant truth which was being divinely revealed through the apostles and prophets and was eventually codified as New Testament Scripture. To this agrees the fuller explanation of this process of confirmation found in Hebrews 2:3-4:

> How shall we escape, if we neglect so great salvation; which at the first began to be spoken by the Lord, *and was confirmed unto us by them that heard him; God also bearing them witness, both with signs and wonders, and with divers miracles, and gifts of the Holy Ghost, according to his own will?* (Heb. 2:3, 4).

Tongues, therefore, were one sign among many others to confirm the newly revealed New Covenant truth: the Word of God revealed through Jesus Christ (Heb. 1:1, 2) being validated by special gifts given by the Holy Spirit. Other passages agree with this conclusion.

> Now I say that Jesus Christ was a minister of the circumcision for the truth of God, *to confirm the promises made unto the fathers:* And that the Gentiles might glorify God for his mercy (Rom. 15:8, 9).

Christ is the living Word, the effectual sacrifice through the blood of the New Covenant, who during His personal ministry provided the validation and authentication of New Covenant truth through His own miraculous wonders. Afterward He sent the Holy Spirit as Paraclete, i.e., the baptism of His church in the Holy Spirit, to further confirm the truth until God's final revelation was complete.

Thus in every way God "Hath in these last days spoken unto us by *his* Son" (Heb. 1:2), and even after His ascension, He sent

---

ence off the coast of Melita (Acts 28:3-5). It should be noted that this incident occurred in the normal process of a difficult circumstance. The Paraclete was on the job. Paul did not deliberately handle a snake as some foolishly and sinfully do. "Thou shalt not tempt the Lord thy God." Snake handling is not to be sought after. Neither are tongues. All gifts are given, or not given, as the circumstance serves God's sovereign choice and purpose (1 Cor. 12:11).

the Holy Spirit in a *special role* to carry on the work of confirming the Word and empowering the church. Special gifts of the Holy Spirit were given to those to whom He would reveal the New Testament truth, validating their witness through many signs and wonders, of which tongues were but one gift among many. Tongues-speaking is not *uniquely* tied to the baptism of the Holy Spirit – no more so than raising the dead or any other gift. Neither is it a unique second work of grace.

Tongues in the Book of Acts.

We move next to the book of Acts where many instances of the actual fulfillment of Mark's prophecy are recorded. Here we see the process of confirmation continuing as God launched the New Covenant truth into the world through the churches under the oversight of the Holy Spirit.

Initial Confirmation of the Church. The first and most significant occasion of tongues-speaking in Scripture is in Acts chapter two. On this occasion the disciples were gathered in one accord in an upper room on the day of Pentecost. As we observed in the last chapter, the advent of the Holy Spirit in His special role had just occurred, manifesting Himself by a sound like wind and by cloven tongues like fire. Next, "they were all filled with the Holy Ghost, and began to speak with other tongues, as the Spirit gave them utterance" (Acts 2:4).

Now, here is the first occasion of tongues-speaking in the Bible, as it was experienced by the Jerusalem church in a partial fulfillment of the prophecy in Mark, and they spoke with "other tongues" (Acts 2:4). The word *other* in this passage comes from the same root as our word heterodox, meaning different. The church brethren began to speak with *different tongues,* not unknown tongues but simply *different languages* other than their native tongues. And by this miracle the visiting foreigners gathered at Jerusalem heard the language each of his own home town, though they were from many places in the world. These miraculous languages were for *communicating with foreigners* who did not speak the native Jewish tongue, not to feature the speaker or to show his righteousness or to give a second blessing or to manifest the baptism of the Holy Spirit. The latter had already been done by the sound of wind and flames of fire. The tongues were a *functional miracle* for actual communications, and as a sign to the Jews (1 Cor. 14:21, 22; Isa. 28:11).

The account continues, "Now when this was noised abroad, the multitude came together, and were confounded, because that every man heard them *speak in his own language*" (Acts 2:6). The term *language* (v. 6) and the phrase *"his own tongue"* (v. 8) – those two words, *language* and *tongue* – both translate the same Greek word, denoting a national language. From this word we get our term, dialect, i.e., our mode of speaking, the sound or phonetic utterance of a people that signifies a certain meaning, simply a different national language.

What then do we learn from this occasion? We learn that tongues were a supernatural work of God – a sign and wonder – to speak to these foreign Jews in their own languages (not in an unknown tongue). The Jerusalem Jews and Galilaeans, however, were not learned in those languages; thus it was a miraculous demonstration of God confirming this new work. It was one among many miracles that identified the hand of God upon His church. It was done before many thousands of people so that it could not be mistaken or faked. Charismatic unintelligible tongues of today are nothing like the miraculous spoken languages of that day.

Confirmation of the Gentiles: Acts 10. The second instance of tongues-speaking recorded in Scripture is in Acts chapter ten. Before considering specifically the act of tongues-speaking in this passage, it is important to understand the significance of the occasion itself.

It concerned one Cornelius, a devout Roman centurion living in Caesarea, a generous man who faithfully prayed to God. In response, God sent an angel who advised him to send men to Joppa where he would find Peter. Meanwhile, God was preparing Peter, and the Jewish church, to make what seemed to them a very radical change from their traditional experience. God was about to initiate a major change in the format of the House of God, the New Covenant church. This change was even of greater significance than the change from the Tabernacle to the Temple. Knowing that this would be a giant step for the Jewish brethren, severely testing their spiritual maturity, God planned to provide clear confirmation to prepare them for change ahead, assuring them that it was indeed according to His will and purpose. This preparation was two-fold.

First, God prepared Peter through a vision, recorded in Acts 10:9-16. Peter learned the lesson: "What God hath cleansed, that call not thou common" (10:15). Perhaps Peter had not fully understood his own text, Joel 2:28-32, from which he had preached the great sermon on Pentecost. The text had said, "I will pour out my Spirit upon *all flesh*" (Acts 2:17). Heretofore, Israel, God's *Old Covenant* people had always thought nationally; they were a national entity. But now, the church, God's *New Covenant* people, would know no national or ethnic boundaries. Now, the Gentile would be included, as well as the Jew, in the New Covenant Church. But to Peter and his fellow Jewish believers, this would be a major hurdle to clear. They would need to be assured of God's unequivocal sanction on this move.

Second, God assured them by a sign. He confirmed to Peter and the six brethren that were with him by the sign of tongues-speaking similar to that which occurred on the day of Pentecost, except that it was in reverse. It was the Gentiles who spoke to the people of the church:

> While Peter yet spake these words, the Holy Ghost fell on all them which heard the word. *And they of the circumcision which believed were astonished,* as many as came with Peter because that *on the Gentiles also was poured out the gift of the Holy Ghost.* For they heard them *speak with tongues, and magnify God.* Then answered Peter, Can any man forbid water that these should not be baptized, which have *received the Holy Ghost* as well as we? And he commanded them to be baptized in the name of the Lord (Acts 10:44-47).

These seven brethren were in the home of Cornelius, the first recorded Gentile convert, and the Holy Spirit enabled the newly converted Gentiles to speak another language in such a manner that the Jews could understand and recognize that they were speaking miraculously a true language which they had not learned. Had they merely babbled in an unintelligible utterance, it would have meant nothing, only confusion at best. No confirmation could have been demonstrated in that way. Here, as at Pentecost, a language was spoken. They were enabled by miraculous powers to speak a language for the purpose of authenticating to these astonished Jewish brethren the fact that God had indeed received the Gentiles to be included in the church. So they baptized them.

This, once and for all, confirmed to the Jews that the church was for both Jews and Gentiles. Moreover, whatever was done here, Peter recognized it as the same kind of thing done at Pentecost (see Acts 11:16, 17). If Peter had to think all the way back to the Pentecost event to remember a similar occasion, that means the tongues-gift was not at all frequently given.

When Peter came back to Jerusalem it was inevitable, and God had anticipated it, that he would be confronted by Jewish brethren for baptizing Gentiles, bringing them into the church. Apparently these brethren also had not read Joel 2:28 carefully and had missed the inference of "all flesh" as inclusive of the Gentile in the New Covenant church. But Peter now had the full answer, thanks to God's wisdom and forethought in preparing the seven brethren (not to speak of the churches down through the ages) for that inevitable confrontation. So Peter carefully re-hearsed the whole episode (11:1-16) and reached this unanswer-able conclusion:

> Forasmuch then as God gave them *the like gift as he did unto us*, who be-lieved on the Lord Jesus Christ; *what was I, that I could withstand God?* When they heard these things, *they held their peace*, and glorified God, saying, *Then hath God also to the Gentiles granted repentance unto life* (Acts 11:17-18).

Now let us suppose, for the sake of understanding and analy-sis, that the Gentile converts gathered at the home of Cornelius had uttered nonsensical, unintelligible, claptrap – or that this was purely an ecstatic, subjective experience. Could Peter's conclu-sion have been as it was? Could he have immediately identified this manifestation as being of the same nature as that of Pentecost when the brethren spoke to the multitude in their own languages? Since God cannot be the author of confusion (1 Cor. 14:33), such claptrap could never bear witness of a work of the Holy Spirit. To the contrary, it bears witness that the speaker of such meaningless language is *not* speaking by the Spirit of God.

Therefore, we know the Gentile converts were speaking in a standard language known to the Jewish brethren, which those specific Gentiles had never learned. It was a sign, manifestly a miraculous work of God, as at Pentecost. What language did they speak? We can only guess. Though it is irrelevant, a logical deduction might suggest Hebrew, or perchance Aramaic. Whatever it was, it served the very sound and practical purpose to confirm God's objective that the New Covenant church would include both Jew and Gentile.

Confirming Church Authority: Acts 19:1-7. The third instance in Scripture where tongues-speaking occurs is in Acts 19.

THE EPHESUS TWELVE. Paul, traveling in the vicinity of Ephesus, encountered about a dozen believers whose understanding of recent developments in the Christian faith was incomplete. We read:

> And it came to pass, that, while Apollos was at Corinth, Paul having passed through the upper coasts came to Ephesus: and finding certain disciples, He said unto them, *Have ye received the Holy Ghost since ye believed?* And they said unto him, We have not so much as heard whether there be any Holy Ghost. And he said unto them, *Unto what then were ye baptized?* And they said, *Unto John's baptism.* Then said Paul, John verily baptized with the baptism of repentance, saying unto the people, that they should believe on him which should come after him, that is, on Christ Jesus. When they heard this, they were baptized in the name of the Lord Jesus. And when Paul had *laid his hands upon them, the Holy Ghost came on them; and they spake with tongues, and prophesied.* And all the men were about twelve (Acts 19:1-7).

SAVED BUT NOT BAPTIZED. The common interpretation of this passage is that the twelve brethren simply were not saved. But this hardly does justice to the language of the passage, the situation, or to the lesson to be derived from the event. Paul's inquiry was whether or not they had received the Holy Ghost *having believed.*

How did Paul know they were believers? One can not discern that on sight. Neither does one walk up to strangers and initially pose a question that amounts to insider jargon: "Have ye received the Holy Ghost since ye believed?" There had no doubt been some initial conversation by which Paul found out they were believers. Only then would it have been appropriate to ask if they had received the Holy Spirit, having believed.

There were doubtless many saints scattered throughout the area who believed the promise of a coming Messiah, in the Old Testament sense, who may have never heard of the Holy Spirit, or for that matter the name of Jesus. Yet The Holy Spirit did His perfect work of regeneration in men and women of faith whether or not they knew His name (See Hebrews 11). As we have previously discussed, one normative work of the Holy Spirit in regeneration is permanent residence in the believer's heart (Rom. 8:9, 15-16; cf. 2 Pet. 1:4). No theologian of the stature of Paul would ever ask the question, "have ye received the Holy Ghost *since* ye believed [*having* believed, or *when* you believed]?" if he was inquiring about their salvation. If they had believed, of course, they had received the Holy Ghost in His normative work of salvation. Even belief itself is dependent upon the Holy Spirit. If one has believed, it is inevitable that he is "partaker of the divine nature" (2 Pet. 1:4), i.e., the Holy Spirit who regenerates. Certainly Paul knew that, for he wrote:

> For ye have not received the spirit of bondage again to fear; but *ye have received the Spirit of adoption*, whereby we cry, Abba, Father. The *Spirit itself beareth witness with our spirit,* that we are the children of God (Rom. 8:15-16).

All the Old Testament saints were regenerated by the Holy Spirit who dwelled within them long before the "baptism of the Holy Spirit," which first occurred at Pentecost. Jesus chided Nicodemus because he did not know these things about regeneration (John 3:10).

EARLY APOSTOLIC TERMINOLOGY. Paul's question, "Have ye *received the Holy Ghost*," refers to something other than regeneration. It refers to the Holy Spirit in *His role of Paraclete*, which,

Paul knew, always came subsequent to salvation, if at all. In regeneration the Spirit comes to dwell within, but in His paracletic role the typical language is to "come upon" as in this case (Acts 19:6).

"Come upon" is the term Jesus used to inform the waiting church of the power of the Holy Spirit coming in the baptism which occurred at Pentecost (Acts 1:8). "Fallen upon" is the term used concerning the brethren in Samaria (8:16). "Fell on" is used of the Gentiles in Caesarea (10:44). All of these refer to the manifestation of the Holy Spirit coming upon different groups in His role as Paraclete. Moreover, this terminology is reminiscent of the language of the Old Testament when the Holy Spirit would "come upon" different people in His special assistance of the Old Covenant saints. As previously discussed, this was a Paraclete-type work. But regeneration is a different work of God's sovereign grace.

So the term *"receive the Holy Ghost"* became a commonly used expression in the early days of the church after Pentecost, referring to His paracletic role. We will look at a few examples of this usage. First in Acts 8, Philip had gone to Samaria to preach, "But when *they believed* Philip preaching the things concerning the kingdom of God, and the name of Jesus Christ, they were baptized ..." (v. 12). Now these believers were saved but they had not *"received the Holy Spirit"* in His gift-giving role as Paraclete. God, in His sovereignty, had determined to make it clear to the Samaritans that only His church (which at that time was only at Jerusalem) was His representative on earth. Therefore, when the Apostles heard about the people being saved at Samaria, they deliberately "sent Peter and John":

> Who, when they were come down, prayed for them, that they might *receive the Holy Ghost:* (For as yet he was *fallen upon none of them*: only they were baptized in the name of the Lord Jesus.) Then laid they their hands on them, and *they received the Holy Ghost* (Acts 8:15-17).

In this particular instance, even though they were already saved, God required the laying on of the hands of Peter and John before the Samaritans received and were sanctioned by the Holy

Spirit in His gift-giving role as Paraclete.[205] This could by no stretch of theology have reference to regeneration. They were already believers, just as the 120 believers who had received Him at Pentecost long after they had been saved.

The terminology *"gift of the Holy Ghost"* is a similar phrase used to refer to the same paracletic work of the Holy Spirit. For example, in Peter's sermon on Pentecost he made this statement:

> Then Peter said unto them, *Repent*, and be *baptized* every one of you in the name of Jesus Christ for the remission of sins, and ye shall receive *the gift of the Holy Ghost* (Acts 2:38).

Consistently, therefore, *the gift of the Holy Ghost* typically[206] comes after *repentance* (in salvation) and after *baptism*, because baptism is the ordinance of entry into the church (v. 41). When one enters the church, he or she enters the institution which was baptized in the Spirit, the Pillar and Ground of the truth (1 Tim. 3:15), and thus may receive whatever unique gift the Holy Spirit may sovereignly bestow upon him or her.

---

[205] This biblical reality, as previously discussed, highlights *both the common errors* concerning the baptism of the Holy Spirit held today by evangelicals. The baptism of the Holy Spirit *is neither regeneration nor synonymous with it,* as most non-charismatic evangelicals believe. It does indeed come *subsequent* to salvation as believers are identified with a biblical church or its agents (e.g., Peter and John at Samaria, or Paul with the Ephesus Twelve). But it is not a "second blessing" upon specific individuals; neither does it confer sinless perfection, nor tongues, nor ecstatic unintelligible speech as charismatics believe.

[206] The normal and permanent sequence is salvation, water baptism, then the gift of the Holy Spirit in His paracletic role. This sequence is doubtless the reason for the unusual structure of Acts 2:38, which has led some denominations (e.g., the followers of Campbell, the Disciples, the Church of Christ, and others) to conclude that baptism is necessary for salvation. Peter's purpose was to teach that *repentance and humble obedience to water baptism was necessary before one may expect the "gift of the Holy Ghost" in His paracletic role, exercised only (so far as it is revealed) within an authenticated church. Yet there is one exception to this rule, because the gifts of the Spirit are under control of God to serve His sovereign purposes (1 Cor. 12:11). This *only* exception was the household of Cornelius, where it was the church itself which had to be persuaded, only once, to baptize the first Gentile.

We see similar terminology used also at the home of Cornelius (Acts 10). At some point in Peter's preaching these Gentiles believed, were normatively saved (which no bystander could observe). But then, at God's chosen moment, He "poured out *the gift of the Holy Ghost*" (v. 45) upon these Gentiles so that the church would be assured that it was appropriate to administer water baptism to Gentiles. This special instance is the only record we have where God granted this gift before baptism and without further intervention by the brethren of the church. But in this instance, it was the church itself that had to be instructed. So God intervened by sovereign action, and the Gentiles abruptly began speaking in a language they had not learned but which was recognizable by the Jews. They *"received the Holy Ghost,"* and His gift of tongues was observable to the bystanders.

Another very significant example of the terminology *"gifts of the Holy Ghost"* is used in Hebrews:

> How shall we escape, if we neglect so great salvation; which at the first began to be spoken by the Lord, *and was confirmed unto us by them that heard him;* God also bearing *them* witness, both with signs and wonders, and with divers miracles, and *gifts of the Holy Ghost,* according to his own will? (Heb. 2:3-4).

Here we have a broad witness that all the truth of God is attested, authenticated, and confirmed by *gifts of the Holy Spirit* of which overt miracles, signs and wonders are a part. It is very unfortunate that the non-charismatic evangelical brethren have made the baptism of the Holy Spirit synonymous with or a component of regeneration, while the charismatics have made it a unique second work of grace. But neither the linguistic usage nor the theology of the Scriptures supports either of these theories. They are both mere conjecture.

THE AUTHORITY TO BAPTIZE. Now it was this same phenomenon, the gift of the Holy Ghost in His paracletic role, concerning which Paul inquired of the twelve believers at Ephesus (Acts 19:2). It was not a question of their salvation at all. But they had not been properly baptized or related to the church, or even informed about it. Here were believers, but where did they come from? Were there other brethren of the church laboring in the area? Were they from the church at Ephesus? Obviously not. Paul was concerned to know their status. Believers should not be wandering around with no official connection with or sanction by one of the churches which had been established, commissioned, and empowered. So he enquired, "have you received the Holy Ghost [in His special gift-giving role] since you believed?"

In order to properly interpret the meaning of this occasion of tongues-speaking, it will be necessary to consider the implications in its broader context. The context of the passage, beginning in Acts 18:24, concerns the ministry of Apollos. The episode takes place in the vicinity of Ephesus where Apollos had been preaching. We are told, "This man was instructed in the way of the Lord; and being fervent in the spirit, he spake and taught diligently the things of the Lord, *knowing only the baptism of John*" (v. 25).

Since the limits of Apollos' knowledge apparently ended early in John's ministry, the details of the identity of Jesus as the Christ, possibly His death and resurrection, His establishment of the church, were not known to Apollos. Yet all the Old Testament saints were saved without that detail. Moreover, his personal baptism by John the Baptist was perfectly valid, even as that of the Apostle John, Andrew, and others who were never re-baptized. But Apollos, in his well-meaning zeal, was engaged in a ministry of baptizing with no official authority. He had no direct connection with "the house of God, which is the church of the living God, the pillar and ground of the truth" (I Tim 3:15). John the Baptist's authority to baptize was directly from God (John 1:33), but Apollos had not been so sent.

Meanwhile, Christ had established an official institution, His church, to represent His name. He had created it (Mark 3:13-14; Matt. 16:18-19; 1 Cor. 12:28), commissioned it (Matt. 28:19-20), and authenticated it before the world by the advent of the Paraclete and all His mighty signs and wonders (Acts 2, and beyond). The churches having multiplied under the guidance of the Holy Spirit, were the only officially authorized representatives of the New Covenant to the world. They were the new sending agency under the Holy Spirit. But Apollos, with all good intentions in his innocent zeal knew nothing of all this. Therefore, Aquila and Priscilla took him aside and *"expounded unto him the way of God more perfectly."* He heard them eagerly and later became a great servant of the Lord among the churches.

Though it is not an absolute certainty, the preponderance of evidence is very strong that Apollos was the one who had preached the Messiah to the twelve at Ephesus and had baptized them. It seems obvious that Apollos was working as sort of a freelance evangelist apart from the commission and authority God had vested in the church approximately 20 years earlier.

In today's world this would seem a trivial matter; the typical Christian or church would think nothing of it. But it was not trivial then because it was not God's plan, and it is not trivial today. Such individual and independent action creates schismatic movements which after twenty centuries have multiplied into literally thousands of diverse denominations, each teaching a different body of truth. God's principles of church authority, if observed, are designed to prevent such schism and will preserve the unity of the faith.

Among the last words of Christ was His great prayer for unity (John 17:17-23). Naturally, then, the Holy Spirit would not authenticate this unauthorized work of Apollos despite his good intentions. Moreover, the Apostle Paul sensed there was a problem and moved to make things right before it spread. If nothing had been done and the Apollos movement had grown and spread, as eloquent a speaker as he was, there could have eventually been a new denomination of the Apollosites. This problem was the very reason the Jerusalem church, years before, had "sent" Peter and John to Samaria to demonstrate that *God's authority was extended from the church at Jerusalem* which had been sanctioned by the advent and work of the Holy Spirit. Otherwise, there would have been three denominations: the Jerusalemites, the Samaritanites, and now the Apollosites.

So having learned that the Ephesus twelve had not received the gift of the Holy Spirit in His paracletic role, Paul knew they were not a part of an authorized church.

So he queried, "Unto what then were ye baptized?"

And they answered, "unto John's baptism."

Now, that, of itself was not a problem, because John's baptism was the baptism that several of the apostles had from the hand of John himself who had been sent by God to baptize. But these twelve men, twenty years after John's death, had not been baptized by John himself. "John was the harbinger of Christ. He had no successor; no man had a right to perpetuate John's baptism ..."[207] except the Lord Himself (John 4:1-3). But when John passed off the scene, Jesus received from John a "people prepared for the Lord" (Luke 1:17). Then the apostles, and others under Jesus' authority, continued baptizing, and they and some of John's converts became the Jerusalem church sanctioned by the Holy Spirit on Pentecost. Thus the Ephesus Twelve, though believers, were not scripturally baptized and therefore were out of the loop of the churches, not willfully, but innocently ignorant.

Like Abraham, they had *"believed in the Lord; and he counted it to them for righteousness"* (Gen 15:6; Rom. 4:3, 16). Their hearts, therefore, were right, and as soon as Paul explained the connection between John and Jesus, they recognized their duty to be baptized in Jesus' name and were eager to obey. So they submitted to Paul for rebaptism and to the authority of the church Jesus had established, which the Holy Spirit had authenticated.

Now, this situation was very unusual. Apparently these twelve did not know about the church; they didn't know Paul, and he didn't know them. But God stepped in and confirmed all possible doubts after they submitted to the commission of the church to be baptized. Then Paul laid his hands on them (similar to the Apostles at Samaria), and God gave them the gift to speak in a language they had never learned, and they "prophesied." Now, they recognized that this gift was from God, extended through Paul as an agent of the church by the laying on of his hands. Paul heard and understood their prophesying and knew God had accepted them. Thus every question was answered and confirmed, and

---

[207] Carroll, *An Interpretation ...*, XII [Acts], 349-50.

they all were unified, *unified* in the normative work of the church. Moreover it was recorded in Scripture so that we today may see the purposes of God and yield to them. This is a tedious explanation but what a lesson for the thousands of modern Apolloses.

In all this there was not a hint that the tongues were unintelligible ecstatic babble. Such a thing would have served no purpose, confirmed no doubts, solved no problems. Had this been mere gibberish, what confusion it would have brought to an already difficult matter. But God is not the author of confusion (1 Cor. 14:33). We must, therefore, interpret this as a true language consistent with all other occasions and conclude that biblical tongues were real human languages, and all other tongues, so called, are imposters.

Concerning Spiritual Gifts: 1 Corinthians 12-14

The next, and last, time we encounter a discussion of tongues in the Scripture is in 1 Corinthians 12-14. Here we are apprised of the temporary nature of some spiritual gifts, and here a problem arises concerning the abuse of the gift of tongues. Given the propensity of fallen human nature to seek experiences involving tongues, etc., as demonstrated in the early chapters of this book, it is not surprising that a counterfeit version of the legitimate gift of tongues would soon appear. Paul finds it necessary to devote considerable space in the Corinthian letter to deal with this abuse.

Tongues: One Gift Among Many

But before we consider Paul's discussion of the abuse of tongues in chapter 14, we must first take a look at the important issues concerning spiritual gifts, and especially the gift of tongues in chapters 12-13:

> But the manifestation of the Spirit is given to every man to profit withal. For to one is given by the Spirit the word of *wisdom*; to another the word of *knowledge* by the same Spirit; To another *faith* by the same Spirit; to another the gifts of *healing* by the same Spirit; To another the working of *miracles*; to another *prophecy*; to another *discerning of spirits*; to another divers kinds of *tongues*; To another the *interpretation of tongues*; But all

these worketh that one and the selfsame Spirit, dividing to every man severally as he will" (I Cor. 12:7-10).

It has been established (above) that Christ sent the Holy Spirit upon the church to serve in the role of helper or Paraclete to empower the church for the task ahead until the "great and notable day of the Lord." One of the ways He empowers the church is by giving special gifts to individuals as these gifts are needed for the progress of the commission given the church (Matt. 28:19-20). The list, obviously not intended to be exhaustive, is as follows:

Wisdom,
Knowledge,
Faith,
Healing,
Miracles,
Prophesy,
Discerning of spirits,
Kinds of tongues,
Interpretation of tongues.

Not all the gifts listed here need be considered miraculous; certainly not all are to be considered as "signs and wonders." But all are needed at one time or another in the execution of God's purpose, and all are given by the Holy Spirit, not to everyone, but individually according to His sovereign choice, not necessarily the choice of the individual. Therefore the current charismatic practice of singling out the gift of tongues, particularly seeking it as a manifestation of the baptism of the Holy Spirit is wholly arbitrary. The practice of "teaching" novices to speak in tongues has to be of the "flesh" or worse.

Now notice; another list of gifts is given in verse 28:

And God hath set some in the church, first *apostles*, secondarily *prophets*, thirdly *teachers*, after that *miracles*, then gifts of *healings, helps, governments, diversities of tongues*. Are all apostles? are all prophets? are all teachers? are all workers of miracles? Have all the gifts of healing? do all speak with tongues? do all interpret? (1 Cor. 12:28).

This list repeats four gifts that are in the first list and four that are not, namely *apostles, teachers, helps,* and *governments.* The point of this list is to pose the argument, by rhetorical questions, that all these gifts are not intended for or available to everyone. Moreover, from this listing we are able to discern that not all the gifts given to the early church are intended to be permanent gifts available for all time. We will consider that in greater detail below.

What Kind of Tongues?

We have previously seen that on all three occasions where tongues-speaking occurred so far in Scripture a standard human language was spoken miraculously by persons unlearned in the language. Over against this there is not a hint that any tongue was an unintelligible utterance. Is the gift of tongues mentioned in 1 Corinthians 12 also the ability to speak a standard language; or does it refer to an unintelligible babble as lately presumed?

In both verses 10 and 28, the expression for "kinds of tongues" refers to any ethnic group bound together by a common tongue or language. Specifically, in this context, it means different national languages. Thus again, the gift of tongues-speaking here is the ability to speak languages that have not been learned on those occasions when the Holy Spirit so indicates and empowers one to do so.[208] This agrees with and strengthens the conclusion reached on all the previous occasions; thus the biblical gift of tongues as defined in Scripture does not exemplify or permit a Christian doctrine of unintelligible speech. We saw none of that in Acts, and we should expect none of it here.

Provisional Gifts: 1 Cor. 13:8-13.

As we noted briefly above, not all the gifts given to the early church are intended to be permanent gifts available for all time. In the latter verses of 1 Corinthians 12, we are alerted to this fact by the listing of the apostolic office among the other gifts of the Spirit (see also Eph. 4:8-12 for apostolic gift). And it is elementary that the gift of apostleship is time delimited by the nature of

---

[208] The gift of interpretation of tongues is obviously the inverse of that process.

the office. The qualifications for an apostle, as one who had been eye-witness of the resurrected Christ, necessarily delimits that gift in time to the lifespan of the last apostle. We will see that other gifts also are delimited in time for different reasons.

Paul, at the end of chapter 12, tells us of a "more excellent way." Few things pique human interest more than the sensational and miraculous. Yet to be preoccupied with those gifts is not God's highest calling. There are gifts which register higher than those on the scale of divine purpose; and if we aspire to reach them, the fellowship with God at these levels overshadows any "felt need" for psychic or ecstatic stimulation of the false and carnal "gifts" sought by modern charismatics.

In chapter 13, emphasizing the superiority of love, Paul deliberately led the thinking of his readers away from the sensational but temporary gifts. He was preparing them to aspire to the "best" gifts as he outlined the qualities of the greatest of all the gifts – *love*. The best gifts are not "signs and wonders." Listed first as a fruit of the Spirit (Gal. 5:22), love is at the peak of the process of personal sanctification. This is the bright red cherry that surmounts the delicious "sundae" of personal Christian growth. After outlining the process in Colossians 3:5-14, Paul points to the climax with these words: "And above all these things put on *charity (love),* which is the bond of *perfectness*" (Col. 3:14).

Some will question whether love is a fruit of the Spirit or a gift.[209] But does it matter? Paul tells us that the "love of God is shed abroad in our hearts by the Holy Ghost," referring to regeneration (Rom. 5:5). That is certainly a gift. Moreover, faith is listed both as a gift (1 Cor. 12:10) and a fruit (Gal. 5:22). The Holy Spirit who regenerates is also the Paraclete; there is bound to be some overlap.

Temporary vs. Permanent Gifts. So, in 1 Corinthians 13:1-7 Paul introduces and defines love, concluding with the truth that "Love never fails" (v. 8a). Then, abruptly, in verse 8b, he returns

---

[209] How different is a fruit from a gift? Exactitude is very important in handling the Scripture, but can we get so technical that we lose the essential truth in a matter?

to the contextual theme by pointing out the inferiority, limitations, and transitory nature of certain provisional gifts (namely, the gifts of prophecy, tongues, and knowledge) in stark contrast to love and the "best" gifts. He expressly foretells (13:8b) the ultimate demise of these three special revelatory gifts, and by implication probably others:

> Love never fails. But whether there are *prophecies*, they will fail; whether there are *tongues*, they will cease; whether there is *knowledge*, it will vanish away (I Cor. 13:8).

Singled out for demise are: 1) revelatory prophecy, 2) miraculous tongues (i.e., languages), and 3) revelatory knowledge; these will fail, cease, or vanish away (v. 8, 10). It is perfectly clear that these three named gifts are not permanent gifts in God's scheme of things; they will cease. However, the time of their passing depends upon the arrival of something called *"perfect"* (v. 10), the identity of which is not specifically named.

Thus a long-standing controversy centers around the time and occasion of the cessation of these gifts and the identity of that which is called perfect (v. 10).

We would expect this matter to be controversial because the entire rationale for tongues and the modern charismatic movement stands or falls on the identity of this "perfect." When the primary doctrine of nearly half of evangelical Christianity hangs upon such a tenuous thread, we can expect that thread to break under the stress sooner or later. And great will be the fall thereof.

D. A. Carson discusses three theories as to what the *perfect* is: Some argue for the maturity of the church. Others argue for the completeness of the canon of Scripture, and a third group argues that "'perfection' is related to the parousia"[210] (i.e., the presence, or second coming of Christ). Carson himself falls into the latter group and lists seven insightful points in defense of that position. Nevertheless, after all the evidence is carefully weighed, we must dissent in favor of the second group that the reference is to the *complete canon of Scripture*, entire and fully realized. Please

---

[210] D. A. Carson, *Showing the Spirit,* pp. 68, 69. We should point out that Carson regards the "perfect" as the "state of affairs" after the parousia.

note, however, that we identify the "perfect" or "complete" with Scripture itself, not with the conditions around it or the responses to it.

Identifying the "Perfect." To identify that which Paul calls perfect, we note that he draws a contrast between the *incompleteness* (or as Carson put it, the *"in-part-ness"*) of the three temporary gifts and the *completeness* of that which was to come.

> For we know *in part*, and we prophesy *in part*. But when that which *is perfect* [τέλειον, *complete*] is come, then *that which is in part* shall be done away (1 Cor. 13:9-10).

There must be a good reason why Paul did not simply tell us what the coming event or occasion was. Why was he so cryptic about the matter? Why did he not say: "But when Jesus, or the parousia, the mature church, or the complete canon of Scripture is come, these incomplete gifts will cease"? The fact is, it probably never occurred to Paul that there was any ambiguity at all in the statement. Of course the Holy Spirit knew and planned it just as it was written, but Paul, absorbed with the context and the content of the three named gifts as three aspects or "vehicles" of divine revelation, probably thought it would be immediately obvious to all. It probably never occurred to him that any reader would begin to think of things as irrelevant to the context (which we will discuss below) as, for example, the parousia or related conditions would be.

If we try to place ourselves in the context of the times and issues facing Paul, his thought process, under the guidance of the Holy Spirit, will become obvious. He was about to distinguish between two identical essences, concepts, or factors. The only distinction actually stated between the two factors is that the first is *incomplete* or *in part* and the second is *complete* or *whole*. It is elementary therefore that the two factors are of the *same essence* having only the distinguishing difference of fractional vs. whole. They must be of the same *intrinsic nature* or else a comparison on this one distinction is wholly meaningless.

For centuries engineers and mathematicians have known you can't equate apples to oranges, or equate five dogs with two miles, and have a meaningful equation. However, if one compares *half* an apple with a *whole* apple by saying one is *incomplete* and the other is *complete*, the essence of the two items is crystal clear: they are both *apple*.

One may say to a friend: "Here is half an apple for you. Tomorrow, I will bring you something which is distinguished from this half an apple by its completeness." By every rule of language and logic it would be understood that the item coming tomorrow is a *complete apple*. If the item in mind were a *complete elephant* you would have communicated nothing, no intelligible information, to your friend. He wouldn't have a clue what to expect. There are so many distinctive differences between an apple and an elephant that the comparison would be meaningless – irrelevant, arbitrary – having no correlation and impossible to decipher. Next day, your surprised friend would look at you quizzically and exclaim, "What has half an apple to do with an elephant?"

Now following this elementary rule of communication, if we know the intrinsic nature of the first, the *incomplete* factor, in Paul's discussion, we automatically know the intrinsic nature of the second, the *complete* factor. Paul set up the "equation" so that *completeness* is the unknown counterpart of the known *incompleteness*; this is the only stated distinction. The *incomplete* factor is known by name: prophecy, tongues, and knowledge. All of these are known by Paul's audience to be forms of *revelation* from God. The "complete" factor is *unknown* and must be extrapolated from the *known*.

Now, concerning the first or *known* factor, we know from both the immediate context and the larger context of Scripture, that the *incomplete* or partial factor was the knowledge of *divine revelation;* i.e., the *intrinsic essence* of the *content* of the prophecy, tongues, and knowledge was *divine revelation*, but it was *incomplete*. Therefore, the counterpart, the *intrinsic essence* of the content of the second factor must also be *divine revelation*, but it was *complete*. That "perfect" which was to come, therefore, can be none other than the *completed canon of divine revelation, the Scriptures*. And when it came, the gifts of revelatory prophecy, tongues (miraculously spoken languages), and specially revealed knowledge did, in fact, vanish away. Now, when we compare "apples to apples" it all makes perfect sense; we repeat: That which is "perfect" in this passage is *God's perfect revelation to man, the Scriptures.*

The "perfect" is neither our understanding of Scripture, nor the church's obedience to Scripture. The "perfect" in this passage is not Jesus Himself because "perfect" is in the neuter gender. It is not the parousia or "the state of affairs brought about by the arrival of the parousia,"[211] as many believe, because the parousia is wholly irrelevant to the context. The gifts of incomplete prophecy, tongues, and knowledge just have no correlation with the parousia (more on that later). That would be apples and oranges – or worse. Nay, the counterpart of *incomplete revelation* in this passage is *complete revelation*, the "perfect" canon of Scripture.

God's revealed truth to man, now complete, has been "...confirmed unto us by them that heard [the Lord]; God also bearing them witness, both with signs and wonders, and with divers miracles, and *gifts of the Holy Ghost,* according to his own will..." (Heb. 2:3, 4). Some of the biblical gifts, such as revelational prophecy and knowledge, functioned as temporary measures to guide God's people while the completed canon was developing. Signs and wonders such as tongues (also containing revelation), healings, or resurrections were given to confirm the authenticity of those chosen by God to write the Scriptures.

Illustrations: Incomplete vs. Complete. After making the

---

[211] To fully explore whether or not the conditions after the parousia would qualify as either "perfect" or "complete" would depend upon which view of eschatology is biblical. Though we will make no attempt to explore that question here, the eschatology that places Jesus on this present earth after the parousia for a thousand years ruling with a rod of iron over sinful flesh-and-blood humanity, being born and dying, would bear some serious scrutiny. And if the resurrected church-age saints, as co-regents with Christ, are intermingled on this present earth with natural Israel (as some believe), we must seriously question whether these conditions would qualify as being either perfect or complete.

prophecy of the demise of the three gifts (vs. 8-10), Paul made three statements to illustrate the contrast between the *incomplete* and the *complete*. For ease of reference, we will outline the three illustrative passages (vs. 11-12) and assign reference labels to each phrase:

11a. "When I was a child, I spake as a child, I understood as a child, I thought as a child:

11b. "but when I became a man, I put away childish things.

12a. "For now we see through a glass, darkly;

12b. "but then face to face:

12c. "now I know in part;

12d. "but then shall I know even as also I am known."

IMMATURE VS. MATURE. In v. 11a-b, Paul likens the distinction between the incomplete and the complete to the distinction between a child and a mature man. Both are human, but the child has bits and pieces of knowledge. His understanding is incomplete, and when he speaks it is childish, immature communication lacking in coherency and fullness of thought. But the complete or perfect is like a learned man with full and coherent speech. Thus the childish speech must be abandoned. It ceases when maturity comes.

SEEING DIRECTLY: IN BLACK AND WHITE. Verse 12a compares the *partial revelation* received through temporary gifts to a dark and murky view one might see in an imperfect mirror or perchance a polished metallic reflector. The knowledge or revelation any individual might hear through these gifts of prophecy was at best spotty, even to those fortunate enough to hear some of it. Normally it was not written down or collected.[212] While the individual prophecies were true, the big picture was fuzzy, dark, incoherent and incomplete. God's revealed truth appeared amorphous, could not be clearly seen, and the boundaries were ill defined.

But in 12b, when the canon was complete and gathered, it was plain. The complete Bible has a beginning and an end. One can look directly on its pages, search through the whole, com-

---

[212] Though Papias, an early church father, collected some of it and seemed to prize it above the written Scripture.

pare Scripture with Scripture, check and double-check, and get a coherent view of the whole revelation of God. It has shape and wholeness, like looking directly into the face of a friend, seeing clearly, *face to face*. To possess God's complete and final Word in black and white makes an immense difference in comprehension. With partial revelation we saw *indirectly, dimly* (12a), but with the complete written Word we see *directly, face to face* (12b). Both are seeing, but the difference is in the *way* we see – how clearly.

KNOWING IN THE MANNER KNOWN. The illustration in 12c-d seems to be the most misunderstood part of the entire passage. On the surface, it would seem to support the parousia theory a little better, but upon deeper examination it really does not: "now I know in part (12c); but then shall I know even as also I am known" (12d).

The *partial-knowledge* factor (11a, 12a, and 12c) is *constant* – identical in meaning in all three illustrations. But popular tradition interprets the whole passage (8-12) in the light of 12d. The popular assumption is that after the parousia we will have knowledge about equal to the knowledge of God. That of course will not be the case, not then or ever. We will never have that degree of knowledge in all eternity.[213] Omniscience belongs only to God. Therefore the parousia view vs. the canon view, in verse 12b, requires a little more discussion to sort out.

We do not contend that there are no advantages for knowledge in the post-parousia environment. We hold only that the statement of 12d is not sufficiently lucid and definitively restrictive to overturn the more rigorous data of verses 8-12c. Since verse 12c consistently retains the first factor in the "equation," namely, the *incomplete*, and since that is the *known* factor, a valid interpretation of 12d must yield the same conclusion as all the preceding data from v. 8-12c:

1. The initial rigorous proposition presented in verses 9 and 10 (see above) we will show (below) to be incompatible and irrelevant to the conditions following the parousia.

---

[213] Carson acknowledges as much, *Showing*, p. 70.

2. The two other illustrations presented in verses 11-12b are two superb illustrations fitting the canon view more naturally.

3. Then the same incomplete counterpart is presented in 12c, which must yield the same conclusion as the other illustrations. Thus the ambiguous (12d) is to be interpreted in the light of the more rigorous (vs. 9-12c).

Weight of the Argument

The weight of the argument for the identity of the complete, the unknown factor of verses 9 and 10, being the finished and gathered canon of Scripture is in our opinion unequivocal, based on all the data given.

Summarizing. The first illustration, childhood vs. manhood (v. 11a-b), clearly supports the canon view better, more naturally than the parousia view.

The second illustration (v. 12a-b) supports it equally well if not better overall. When people all over the world hold the Scriptures in their hands, seeing the Word of God directly in black and white, face to face, in contrast to the few bits of revelation a few people may hear from prophets, verse 12a-b is a superb illustration of that great reality.

The third illustration seems to present a bit more of a problem only because on the surface it appears to suggest a condition of omniscience for man. However, a correct translation appearing in the KJV and the NKJV both properly highlight the *manner* of knowledge and not the *degree* of knowledge: e.g., "I shall know *just as* [NKJV; or *even as* KJV; i.e., *in the manner that*] I also am known." That is, the Holy Spirit knows us *directly*, as it were face to face, not *indirectly* as through another channel:

> Whither shall I go from thy spirit? or whither shall I flee from thy presence? If I ascend up into heaven, thou art there: if I make my bed in hell, behold, thou art there. If I take the wings of the morning, and dwell in the uttermost parts of the sea; Even there shall thy hand lead me, and thy right hand shall hold me (Psa. 139:7-10).

Thus God knows by direct, objective firsthand knowledge. In a similar manner, when we have the complete canon of Scripture before us, we can *see* God's revelation directly and objectively first hand. We have direct access to the whole of it, in black and white, for ourselves. The third illustration, therefore, has the same basic meaning as the second: seeing God's revelation directly, first hand, face to face. It speaks of the manner of knowing, not the degree of knowledge.

Since we will never be omniscient, in this world or in the next, embracing the parousia view does nothing to solve that problem or improve or strengthen the argument over the canon argument. The same problem exists for both the canon and the parousia views. In fact Carson's argument from 12c-d for the parousia view works equally well for the canon view. He says:

> Most important is verse [12c-d]. Perfection entails a state of affairs where my knowledge is *in some way comparable* with God's present knowledge of me: "then I shall know fully,[214] even as I am fully known [sc., by God]." *This does not mean that Paul expects to be granted omniscience* [emphases added], but "that in the consummation he expects to be freed from the misconceptions and inabilities to understand (especially to understand God and His word) which are part of this present life... ." [Carson's quote is from Grudem, *Gift of Prophecy*, 213].

We contend that the combination of 1) the complete and gathered canon of Scripture 2) in the hands of a regenerate person, having been made "partaker of the divine nature" (2 Peter 1:4), and 3) accompanied by the assistance of the Paraclete (John 16:13-15) to illuminate the understanding, is also sufficient to make us free "from the misconceptions and inabilities to under-

---

[214] Carson's quote from the NIV uses the word "fully" (as do others) describing both man's knowledge and God's knowledge; some might gather from that translation that Paul was claiming omniscience for men as well as God. This could not be the case – ever; though God is omniscient man will never be. Both the KJV and NKJV translate ἐπιγινώσχω simply to "know" with no modifier. Thayer's definition does not use "fully" as such, but "know thoroughly, know accurately, know well." None of these necessarily imply more knowledge than would be the case of a man with the entire Scripture before him. A good translation would be "I shall know well *in the manner* that I am well known." The word that unveils Paul's meaning is (καθὼς) "in the manner that" (Wigram). "Now I know in part, but then I shall know *just as* [in the manner that] I also am known" (NKJV).

stand (especially to understand God and His Word)" *despite* the limitations of this present life. In this present circumstance there is no lack of information; we have the complete Word. Moreover, most of the true knowledge about the person, attributes, and purposes of God will yield only to spiritual discernment, not necessarily to observation and personal presence, and may well require the study of Scripture even after the parousia.

Again, we do not argue that there will be no advantages for knowledge after the parousia, particularly within the sinless environment of the new heaven and new earth (NHNE) and the ongoing heavenly process of learning. We hold that 1 Corinthians 13:8-12 when all things are considered – 1) the context, 2) the initial statement of the proposition (vs. 9, 10), and 3) the three illustrations – do unequivocally support the *completed canon* interpretation as "that which is perfect," and that the parousia and all other views fail. And since the Scripture was completed, at some point within the early period of church history, these gifts ceased. Therefore, in love, we beseech our Pentecostal and charismatic brethren to forsake modern charismata because the use of tongues, etc., in today's world is false, divisive, deceitful, and sinful, even though well intended.

Able to Comprehend (Eph. 3:18). But let us go further and consider the *potential* for knowledge in Scripture, the whole body of God's revealed truth. The potential for knowledge to be gained with the perfect and complete canon of Scripture before us and the illuminating ministry of the Paraclete at our side is immense. Although our direct awareness of the situation, environment, experience of sinlessness, and other such things in the NHNE will represent a quantum leap over our present understanding and general knowledge, it does not provide omniscience. But then the completion, availability, and study of the whole canon of Scripture also represented a quantum leap in knowledge over the former condition, but not omniscience.

Thus the parousia theory has no decisive advantage to explain the meaning of the passage. However, the weighing of this matter raises some other questions:

Will our knowledge continue to "grow" in the NHNE?

Will the knowledge of truth which one has gained from Scripture in this life be an advantage after the parousia?

Will a Christian who has neglected the study of Scripture all his life suddenly be zapped full of its grand mysteries so that they are suddenly equal with Paul, John, or even Spurgeon and other spiritually mature and biblically astute Christians of history?

Will Scripture be studied in the NHNE, for those who never learned the wonders of God's person and works revealed therein, or of the invisible attributes of God which may be understood best (or only?) through the revelation of His interface with sinners in the history of this earth? Will all these things be automatically and instantly known?

We do not know the full answers to these questions, but if one would at least ponder them it could help tone down some of the shrill rhetoric[215] surrounding the almost universal *assumption* that after the parousia there will be virtually nothing left to learn. But more meaningful than that, regarding the text before us, an approach that is more contextually driven would help us to avoid two serious errors in the interpretation of this passage:

First, it could prevent the error of *overestimating* the measure of our spontaneous knowledge and comprehension in a post-parousia environment.

Second, it could prevent the error of *underestimating* the measure of knowledge and comprehension possible through the completed canon of Scripture as we learn under the tutelage of the Holy Spirit as Paraclete.

When we examine the magnitude of knowledge, comprehension, and spiritual communion which are available to us through faith, which comes by the "word of God" (Rom. 10:17), under the guidance of the Paraclete sent for that very purpose, we need

---

[215] For example, Carson cites Turner quoting Calvin who thought it was "stupid" for people to think of this passage as other than a reference to the parousia, and Turner thinks that to interpret it differently is to accuse Paul of the "wildest exaggeration." *Showing the Spirit,* p. 71. Such an opinion surely derives from a rather low view of Scripture and the Holy Spirit's illuminating assistance.

not worry that Paul has engaged in the "wildest exaggeration." It would be hard to exaggerate the value of Scripture. Jesus Himself promised:

> Howbeit when he, the Spirit of truth, is come, *he will guide you into all truth*: for he shall not speak of himself; but whatsoever he shall hear, that shall he speak: and he will show you things to come. He shall glorify me: for *he shall receive of mine, and shall show it unto you* (John 16:13-14).

The deeper truths of God, His intrinsic attributes of *truth, love, holiness,* and more, are not insights that necessarily yield to "sight," experience, or visual presence. The angels have long had sinless access to the presence of God, yet they did not fully understand the wonders of the Gospel preached to us, "which things the angels desire to look into" (1 Peter 1:12). Why were they – brilliant, sinless, created a little higher than humans – still desiring to look into these mysteries if life in the presence of the Triune God suddenly imparts full knowledge?

These are things, as Paul said, of the "inner man." When God's *complete revelation* to man is objectively before us and He, as the Paraclete, is *actually present* and actively teaching, how would the actual bodily presence of the glorified Christ, however much we may long for it, be so superior in terms of fullness of knowledge? The fact that we do not "study" (2 Tim. 2:15) and take full advantage of this privilege is no fault of Scripture or the Holy Spirit. Were not the Apostles in the presence of the glorified Christ after the resurrection? And yet Christ said to them, "It is *expedient for you that I go away*: for if I go not away, the Comforter will not come unto you; but if I depart, I will send him unto you… . [And] when he, the Spirit of truth, is come, *he will guide you into all truth* …" (John 16:7, 13). Paul, therefore, did not hesitate to pray for what seems to be an almost unbounded fellowship and comprehension in the "inner man" of "all the fullness of God" possible through Scripture:

> For this cause I bow my knees unto the Father of our Lord Jesus Christ …That he would grant you, according to the riches of his glory, to be strengthened with might by his Spirit in the inner man; That Christ may dwell in your hearts by faith; that ye, being rooted and grounded

in love, May *be able to comprehend* with all saints what is the breadth, and length, and depth, and height; And to know the love of Christ, which passeth knowledge, that *ye might be filled with all the fulness of God* (Eph. 3:15-19).

Now, in light of these things, it is a pity that charismatics and other subjectivists continue to focus upon subjective experience and pursue bits and pieces of direct revelation, no longer available, when the entire reservoir of God's revealed truth is available.

It seems clear that the case for the parousia is far from an open-and-shut case. We therefore return to the one rigorous principle which resolves the issue in 1 Corinthians 13:8-12: We could call it the *contextual coherency* principle. Carson actually invokes this principle to reject one false view, namely, the view that "'perfection' refers (as in Ephesians) to the joining together of Jews and Gentiles ... . That theme is irrelevant in the context of 1 Corinthians 13."[216] That is, of course, a valid conclusion. However, the parousia view must be rejected for the same reason.

Parousia not Relevant to Context. How relevant is the post-parousia environment to the concept of termination of the gifts of prophecy, tongues, and knowledge? Although the case has already been made for the canon view, the fact remains, at the end of the day, that the parousia is wholly irrelevant to the cessation of the gifts of prophecy, tongues, and knowledge. It is a total misfit when forced into the context of 1 Corinthians 13:8-13.

As the earth itself melts with a "fervent heat" (2 Pet. 3:10), these three gifts are not exactly the first things one would think about as being terminated at the parousia: of course they would cease. Any number of things will cease that are far more central to life in this present age. For example, there is God's wonderful gift of marriage and human reproduction which will cease at the parousia. More relevant yet, is the termination of this present earth itself:

For if they escaped not who refused him that spake on earth, much more shall not we escape, if we turn away from him that speaketh from heaven: Whose voice then shook the earth: but now he hath promised, saying,

---

[216] Carson, *Showing*, p. 71.

> Yet once more *I shake not the earth only, but also heaven.* And this word,
> Yet once more, signifieth the *removing of those things that are shaken,*
> as of things that are made, that those things which cannot be shaken may
> remain (Heb. 12:25-27; see also Matt. 24:29-31; 2 Thess. 1:6-10; 2 Pet.
> 3:10).

Of all the innumerable, obvious things crucial to life on earth which will terminate at the parousia, why does Paul single out these three spiritual gifts: prophecy, tongues, and knowledge? What about healing, miracles, governments? To belabor gifts of the Spirit given in His paracletic role would be purely arbitrary; the work of the Paraclete Himself will be finished then.

The termination of the three gifts of prophecy, tongues, and knowledge, would not be news – not even to the Corinthians. Even they would know about the finality of all the things of this world at the parousia; at least they would know by reading two more chapters in this same letter. For in chapter 15 *parousia* is associated with the end (vs. 23, 24), when all God's enemies are destroyed, including death itself (v. 26). The session of Christ is ended. Then, not only the *gifts* but all the gift-giving work of the *Paraclete* Himself is finished because the work of the church on this earth is done.

People urgently need to know *now* which gifts were provisional and temporary and which were permanent and universally essential to God's purposes. Those are exactly the questions partially answered in 1 Corinthians 13:8-13.

Truly, the parousia view rather trivializes Paul's astute argument. It renders the passage sterile. Neither the Corinthians nor modern Christians could learn anything from it not already known – the elephant labors and brings forth a mouse. It was well known that virtually all things in life as we know it would end at the parousia.

Paul would not belabor an obvious answer that no one needs, or answer an elementary question that no one is asking. When Christ appears, of course these gifts would cease (if still operative). They would not "vanish away"; they would instantly and abruptly halt. As Carson also asks, "what possible service could they still render?"[217]

What Abides? What Goes? Moreover, as Paul concludes his discussion of the temporary gifts, he also lists certain permanent gifts that remain: "And now abideth *faith, hope, charity,* these three; but the greatest of these is charity" (1 Cor. 13:13). These three gifts are said to *remain* in contradistinction to prophecy, tongues, and knowledge which cease, but *faith* (listed as a gift in 1 Cor. 12:9) and *hope*, in the strict sense of their meanings, are not eternal.[218] They will, to be sure, become obsolete at the parousia; faith, by definition, will give way to sight (Heb. 11:1), and hope will give way to actual experience (Rom. 8:23). Therefore, if even some gifts that "remain" end at the parousia, the reference point for those that are temporary *must be at a prior event.* Thus, "that which is perfect," on this point also, *proves not to be the parousia.*

But on the other hand, if there were an event coming *before* the parousia that would supersede certain gifts and render them obsolete, then that would be valuable and highly relevant news. The completion and gathering of the canon of Scripture was such an event. It did supersede partial, bit by bit, revelation. Moreover, it is the *only* event that is relevant to and compatible with all that is said in 1 Corinthians 13:8-12. Again, when all things are considered: 1) the context, 2) the initial statement of the proposition (vs. 9, 10), and 3) the three illustrations (vs. 11-12), the preponderance of evidence unequivocally supports the *completed canon* interpretation. Therefore the gifts named: *prophecy, tongues,* and *special knowledge* have long since failed, ceased, and vanished away. The behavior that passes today for those things, revelatory prophecy, tongues, and the ubiquitous word of knowledge, is at

---

[217] Ibid.

[218] As for love, it is eternal and eternally functional; perhaps that is one reason why it is the greatest of all gifts. Moreover, once Christ appears in "power and great glory," and faith turns to sight, there will be no more salvation, because salvation is "by grace through faith" (Eph. 2:8) not by sight. And it must be by faith that it might be by grace (Rom. 4:16).

best the result of the fallen human psyche not yet sanctified by the Word.

The Reproach of Subjectivism. The great tragedy is that God's invaluable message in the six verses of 1 Corinthians 13:8-13 is lost through misinterpretation by those still trying to make room in Scripture for modern charismata and other subjectivist tendencies. What a different world this almost certainly would have been if the true meaning of 1 Corinthians 13:8-13 had been universally embraced by Christians throughout the centuries. What sad and melancholy reproaches, misrepresentation, and discord could have been circumvented?

Reviewing the sad record detailed above in chapters two and three, we recall the excesses of the Montanists, the sporadic outbreaks of ecstatic tongues in the Middle Ages, the reproaches of the Mother Ann movement among the Quakers, the Irvingite movement, the degrading barks and other reproaches that troubled the revivals in the Great Awakening. These might have been prevented by a biblical understanding of the true gifts of the Spirit; most of the participants were probably not malicious, just untaught and misguided.

Then came the great divisive Pentecostal and charismatic movements and the ultra-subjectivism and borderline existentialism of multitudes of evangelicals. Into this soil were sown the seeds of hard-core existentialism, only a step away from postmodernism. Even these extreme developments of subjectivism also might have been prevented, or at least minimized, with unified biblical teachings concerning the objectivity of God's final revelation in Scripture and the truth about spiritual gifts that no longer exist. This sad record of extreme subjectivism has not served biblical orthodoxy or the name of Christ well.

And now the modern charismatic and other movements have made counterfeit gifts and various subjectivist philosophies "acceptable." In this development our original premise (see Chapter I) that the quest for the direct subjective experience of God as a characteristic of fallen human nature is further validated. Christians prone to subjectivist and charismatic views are perpetuating the deceptive myth of spiritual gifts that have been dead for centuries. These subjectivist philosophies range from theories of continued personal direct revelation[219] and tongues, to existentialism, to postmodernism and the negation of the very idea of objective truth.

Since nothing happens in a vacuum, it is reasonable to believe that the misinterpretation, abuse, and misuse of biblical spiritual gifts have contributed to a significant decline in influence of historic, biblically objective, doctrinal orthodoxy over the past two centuries. And this diminution of the authority of Scripture, in turn, has contributed to an immoral culture shock from which this whole nation is now reeling.

The Abuse of Tongues: A Rebuke – 1 Cor. 14

It is not wholly surprising to find a rather lengthy passage of Scripture devoted to an apostolic rebuke for the misuse of the gift of tongues. But ironically, 1 Corinthians 14 is perhaps the main body of Scripture typically cited by modern charismatics in support of the contemporary misuse of tongues. Some insist that the tongues discussed in 1 Corinthians 14 are unintelligible utterances or "angel language" to be used in private prayer or devotions.

The modern use of tongues hangs upon no direct statement of Scripture but upon the thinnest threads of *innuendo*, upon which a very active imagination desperate for a modicum of support might seize (e.g., Rom. 8:26; 1 Cor. 13:1; and, probably strongest of all, 14:1). But no study of the biblical doctrine of tongues would be complete without an analysis of 1 Corinthians 14, for what we actually find there does not support but rather rebukes modern charismata.

Preliminary Considerations. Before we launch into 1 Corinthians 14, we should review as background the larger biblical context of spiritual gifts, and tongues in particular.

1. What have we learned so far?

---

[219] According to R. Fowler White in *The Coming Evangelical Crisis*, p. 86, this category would include such men as Wayne Grudem and Jack Deer. O. Palmer Robertson, *The Final Word*, pp. 87ff., also discusses Grudem's view and presents a perceptive rebuttal of it.

Starting with the first mention of the gift of tongues, we have learned that speaking in tongues (among other gifts) was a sign which would function as confirmation of the word which was preached by the people of the early church (Mark 16:17-20; Heb. 2:3-4). The gift of tongues was used shortly after the arrival of the promised Paraclete, and the gift itself was the power to speak in an existing human language which had not been learned by the speaker so that a native of that language could understand (Acts 2). The content of the language spoken was both intelligible and revelational, "… we do hear them speak in our tongues the wonderful works of God" (v. 11). There are two other accounts of tongues in Acts both of which, by all reasonable evidence, are of the same order as the first (Acts 10 and 19). Paul himself was witness to the latter.

Moreover, we have learned that the gifts of tongues, revelatory prophecy, and special knowledge would terminate upon the arrival of the completed canon of Scripture.

2. What was Paul's understanding of the meaning of tongues in 1 Corinthians 14?

Paul did not address the Corinthian tongues problem as one who was unfamiliar with the gift and its historical and theological background. It is evident that chapters 12-14 are a triad dealing with the general subject of spiritual gifts or spiritual matters, and it appears that there had been questions on this subject addressed to Paul from the Corinthians themselves. From 7:1, which mentions a letter from them, we learn that other matters had been addressed with the introduction of "Now concerning …" as in chapter 12. If we knew what the question was, it would doubtless help us to understand chapter 14 better. However, the Holy Spirit decides what the writers of Scripture are to exclude from Scripture as well as what to include. And we thus know that what we have before us is all the Corinthians needed to hear and all God wanted the rest of us to know about the issue and no more – or maybe He wanted us to dig for it.

Actually, this lack of information is important because it makes us aware that the issue being addressed in chapter 14 was so well known both by Paul and the Corinthians in their environment that it seemed unnecessary to Paul to answer the question of just what specifically is meant by tongues.

Is it an angelic language which is unintelligible in any human language?

Or is it, as formerly defined in Acts 2, the miraculous ability to speak a foreign human language formerly unlearned?

Or could it be the pagan Greek mystery religions creeping into the church, as MacArthur supposes?

Or could it be a combination of these things?

Since both Paul and the Corinthians obviously knew exactly what was meant by "tongues," we must conclude that they learned it primarily from the common Christian practice. The common practice of tongues was the miraculous ability to speak a human language formerly unlearned; this is firmly established in Acts, and though the historical record in Acts is limited, it is not ambiguous. Paul, who was closely associated with Luke the writer of Acts, would surely have been fully aware of the contents of Acts;[220] and it is likely that Paul was himself the source of some of Luke's account, especially of the tongues in Acts 19:6. We must therefore conclude that Paul's usage of *tongues* always corresponds in meaning to the record in Acts: known languages miraculously spoken.

The claim of tongues as being unintelligible angel talk is based upon obscure inferences, which can never rise to the integrity of *faith*, undergirded by evidence (Heb. 11:1). Since "whatsoever is not of faith is sin" (Rom. 14:23), we must abandon that which is based upon innuendo. The introduction of such an error into evangelical Christianity on the basis of the thinnest inference has created a melancholy and divisive condition that will not soon be healed.

Therefore having studied (above) the background of tongues

---

[220] Paul was still alive at the close of the book of Acts (Acts 28:30-31), c. 63 AD, the most likely date for its writing. See, "Acts," *The International Standard Bible Encyclopedia.*

in Scripture, we are honor-bound to stand upon the substantive evidence previously established as we analyze chapter 14.

Three important facts: *First*, we know from previous studies that the biblical gift of tongues is the miraculous ability to speak a foreign human language formerly unlearned. *Second*, we know from 1 Corinthians 13:8-13 that the gifts of tongues, prophecy, and knowledge were provisional and temporary, scheduled to cease when the canon of Scripture was complete and gathered. *Third*, we know that the *Apostle Paul knew both these things* when he was writing 1 Corinthians 14.

Therefore, the angel-talk theory is manifestly a case of grasping at straws to save a practice desperate for support. If the tongues of 1 Corinthians 12-14 had been manifestly of a different sort, any writer of the skill and stature of Paul, not to speak of the Holy Spirit, would have informed his audience of a change.

Armed with these facts, we are now ready to consider chapter 14.

Intelligibility: the Indispensable Element. In the first five verses (14:1-5), there is a series of alternate statements contrasting prophecy with tongues. In verse 1, Paul again puts *love* as the principal pursuit and encourages his readers also to desire spiritual gifts. Perhaps that was to avoid any discouragement by his forewarning (13:8-13) that certain gifts would cease. Then he singles out the gift of *prophecy* for special emphasis (v. 1) probably because it could be understood in the native language of the people. He contrasts prophecy with the gift of tongues because a foreign language could not (without interpretation, see v. 5) be understood by the native congregation (v. 2). In verse two, however, certain things are said which charismatics interpret as a reference to some new type of tongue that is unintelligible to humans in any known language:

> For he who speaks in a tongue does not speak to men but to God, for no one understands him; however, in the spirit he speaks mysteries (14:2 NKJV).

This verse, from which only a vague inference may be drawn, is doubtless the strongest argument found in Scripture for the existence of a gift of unintelligible tongues. If that is the way God intends for us to understand this passage, then it is an extreme departure, without warning or explanation, from the intelligible languages so far described in Scripture as the gift of tongues. On the other hand, if we are to take the historic accounts of Acts, and Paul's awareness of them, at face value in Acts 19 and 1 Corinthians 12, and 13, then we must be prepared to interpret the usage here in 14:2 the same way. We must, in fact, account for all that is said in chapter 14 on the basis that Paul is using the word *tongues* in its historic definition as intelligible human language.

Any Alternatives? The alternative to treating this passage in accordance with the historic record in Acts is to defend the usage of tongues in 14:2 as an abrupt change in the character of the gift without notice, without reason, and without a previous clue that God has now changed the character of tongues to *unintelligible "angel talk."* And this we regard as indefensible. A sudden reversion to the unintelligible tongues and sounds spoken heretofore only by pagans is not the work of the Holy Spirit. He "is not the author of confusion" (14:33).

If there were a compelling reason to conclude that the tongues of 14:2 were unintelligible, then could it be that some of the pagan Greek tongues, the unintelligible ecstatic, psychic, or demonic babble of pagans as cited in an earlier chapter of this book, had now been smuggled into the church by some of the Corinthians? That could have been part of the Corinthian problem, but we think it unlikely that verses two or four could be a reference to pagan tongues because that is not a way to "speak to God" (v. 2) or to "edify oneself" (v. 4).

Yet, as previously mentioned, John MacArthur, Jr. makes an insightful case for pagan tongues being at least part of the Corinthian problem that is worthy of consideration. Corinth had been for centuries the scene of a very immoral culture, and, according to MacArthur,[221] one of the greatest threats of all was the

---

[221] John F. MacArthur, Jr., *The Charismatics* (Grand Rapids: Zondervan Publishing House, 1978), p. 109.

mystery religions that the Corinthians had practiced in the past. He says:

> ... [pagan] religious ecstasy creates a euphoria that lets the worshipper experience tremendously good feelings... . [he] truly believes he has communed with deity... . Charismatic believers who experience various states of euphoria attribute this to certain gifts of the Holy Spirit, particularly tongues. Their conclusion is, "I felt so good ... I never felt this way before ... it's got to be God."[222]

MacArthur continues, "the Corinthian church had become carnal, and a lot of this pagan activity kept creeping in."

It is quite reasonable that some of the tongues problems at Corinth could have had a pagan source, yet about the only direct evidence in the immediate text to support that conclusion is Paul's use of the word "mad" (14:23) as we discussed above which is in fact only a different form of one of Socrates' words (see Chapter II). Otherwise the evidence is mostly circumstantial. So we should acknowledge the probability that there were rare pagan influences in the church.

However, if pagan tongues had been the only, or even the main, problem Paul was addressing, he would certainly have come down hard upon it and his discussion in Chapter 14 would have been a short direct rebuke against paganism. But what we actually find is very different. Paul proceeds so cautiously there must be yet another factor, a better explanation for the primary problem that answers more naturally to Paul's discussion.

Identifying the Main Problem. If the primary problem was not a lapse of the Corinthians back into pagan ecstatic tongues, then could there have been another problem? We think that is almost certain. We begin with the question: What must we make of the usage of the word *tongues* in verses two and four?

It seems obvious that both Paul and the Corinthians mutually understood perfectly well what was meant by the expression *tongues*. So much so that Paul felt no need to explain. We must recognize that several years after Pentecost, with all Paul's expe-

---

[222] MacArthur, *The Charismatics*, p. 112.

rience and interface with the churches, the nature of tongues was widely known to be human languages miraculously expressed. According to Paul's own claim to speak in tongues (again with no explanation as to the meaning) was a very common experience to him (14:18). People knew what it was, and Paul would never have used pagan tongues.

This reality then permits considerable brevity in the way it was discussed, i.e., no definitions needed. In verse 2, therefore, it would be understood that if one spoke miraculously in a human language to an audience that did not speak the language, only God would understand. No man would understand, *unless* there were some present who knew that language. When Paul says a tongue-speaker "speaketh not unto men, but unto God: for no man understandeth him," this does not imply private worship with no one present but the speaker. The Corinthians, familiar with the contemporary practice, would know exactly what Paul meant. He meant simply that there were *none, or few, present* who would understand a foreign language. Therefore a person speaking in a tongue would not have been understood. Verse three confirms that Paul envisioned an audience present that would not understand a foreign language.

Moreover, by the same assumption, in verse four we learn that the tongue-speaker "edifieth himself." If he edified himself, he spoke in a language that he himself (and God) understood.[223] Yet, Paul says in the same setting (v. 4): "he that prophesieth edifieth the church." That means that *Paul had in mind an assembly where people were present,* but that they could not understand the language of the speaker because it was foreign to them.

This fact is made clear by verse five; because in the same setting if someone *interprets*, the people present immediately understand. These verses (2-5) may sound a little cryptic to us, but

---

[223] Some charismatics today claim a mystical "edification" not based on understanding the language, but not so with Scripture. In fact the most strongly argued point in chapter 14 is *understanding*: verses 6-19. And indeed the whole theology of *faith* (see Hebrews 11:1, 3; cf. Romans 10:17; 14:23b) bases edification upon objective understanding.

that is the way people would speak if everyone knew the exact meaning of tongues as universally used among the Christians of the day. It is cryptic to us only because we do not have full first-hand familiarity with the first-century environment.

THE PROBLEM. By these facts we can discern the nature of the problem Paul was attempting to correct: *Some of the learned Corinthians were speaking in a language that none, or only part, of a native Corinthian assembly could understand, and claiming it to be the gift of tongues.* That deduction satisfies all the data so far given:

1. The speaker understood his own speech. Thus it was a human language, not "angel" talk or pagan ecstatic language.

2. God, of course, understood his speech.

3. The general audience did not understand his speech as spoken.

4. If the speech were interpreted, the audience would then understand.

Now, having identified the basic problem Paul was attempting to correct, there are certain facts that become immediately clear: If every person in the Corinthian church who spoke in a "tongue" (other than the native Greek language of Corinth) had been truly *gifted* by the Holy Spirit, the issue of edification and interpretation would never have come up. We know this because the Holy Spirit would always have given both the gift of *tongues* and the gift of *interpretation* so the entire congregation would have been edified. It follows then, since Paul had to *insist* upon interpretation (vs. 5, 27-28), that some among the Corinthians were speaking a learned foreign language *on their own, not by the Spirit,* without interpretation. The whole church, therefore, did not understand and was not edified.

Now if the tongues had been unintelligible "angel" languages *given by the Holy Spirit* only for private prayer or devotions, how could it have been spoken in public? The Holy Spirit does not lead people to violate His own rules – to speak in the wrong place at the wrong time. Therefore it is hard to see how misusing a "gift" of angel talk could have been the problem, but if that *had* been the problem, Paul would very simply have placed a broad ban on the speaking in tongues in a public assembly.

Why didn't he? Two reasons:

1. The gift of "tongues" under discussion in chapter 14 was *not* unintelligible "angel" languages; otherwise, the Holy Spirit Himself would never have given that forbidden gift in public. That would have been an inappropriate setting. We can't have it both ways. A *true gift of the Spirit, miraculously given, cannot be misused.* The spiritual gifts are sovereignly given – *when, where, to whom, and for the exact purpose God chooses – to enhance, not to hinder,* the works of God. God's gifts are perfectly given or not given at all. Those who would abuse spiritual gifts cannot have them (Acts 8:18-22). However, some gifts can be faked. Conveniently, tongues can be faked; and isn't it remarkable that Paul had no trouble at Corinth with people abusing the gift of raising the dead?

2. The true gift of tongues, the miraculous ability to speak unlearned human languages, was still useful to the Holy Spirit in Paul's day. It was very much operative at that time for communicating with others, for the Scripture was not yet complete. Therefore, Paul did not dare give a blanket order forbidding the public use of tongues (14:39). He knew the gift would cease, but he did not know when.

Again, we are forced back to the basic problem: Some of the Corinthians were speaking, *on their own*, in a learned language that none or only a part of the people present could understand.

THE MOTIVE. Now why would they do such a thing? To put the best face on it, some may have simply been thoughtless, or ignorant of the careful ways of God. But it is far more likely that some who were learned in one or more other languages, and had heard or observed the true gift of tongues, actually spoke in a language not native to the assembly for personal glory or veneration.

We know that there were those among the Corinthians who

were "puffed up." Moreover, we know that some in the modern charismatic movement have admitted to babbling in tongues for the same reason – personal glory in the eyes of other misguided souls. Thus faking is not above human nature.

Then, again, this raises the question: why did not Paul simply rebuke the impostors directly? Again, two reasons:

1. It is not always easy to detect an impostor or a fake from the real thing: In such a case, the risk of a false accusation is too great and disruptive to challenge, especially when no one of Paul's stature and discernment was present.

2. To challenge those who claim to be speaking in the Spirit could intimidate and discourage those to whom God was giving the genuine gift.

SOLUTION: RULES FOR ORDER AND EDIFICATION. Therefore, Paul's wise discourse initiated several rules as a solution:

1. He taught that edification was the true purpose for communication and teaching (14:5-19, 26) and encouraged the use of the more directly edifying gift of prophecy – not necessarily miraculous.

2. He established some rules whereby an impostor could more easily be detected and more order maintained.

3. He limited the number of tongues-speakers and imposed a rule for speaking one at a time (14:27).

4. He required that in every case of tongues-speaking that *there must be an interpreter* (see vs. 5, 13, 27-28).

   If there was no interpreter, then the tongue was not a gift of the Spirit. The Holy Spirit does not break His own rule; therefore, "let [the speaker] keep silent in the church" (14:28). Anyone could speak to himself and to God (v. 28) in any language he understands – but not in the assembly. Therefore, if there were no verifiable interpreter present, the tongue is exposed as a fake. It worked then; it would work today if followed.

5. Paul set up a system among the prophets where someone could "judge" the proceedings, and he imposed rules of order on the prophets as well (14:29-33).

6. He imposed restrictions on women (14:34, 35) the same as in 1 Timothy 2:11, 12, which precludes women from teaching or preaching in the public assembly where men are present. Today, charismatics and feminists boldly trample on these rules also.

7. All these were "commandments of the Lord" (v. 37) – which subjectivists violate at their own peril – given to establish a godly atmosphere of order and edification in the assembly (14:37-40).

What We Learn from the Unlearned. A further proof that the Corinthian tongues were real human languages is that *learning* made a difference. In three places (vs. 14:16, 23-24), Paul indicates that *learning* makes a difference in whether an individual in the audience would understand someone speaking in a tongue.

If the Corinthian tongues had been unintelligible "angel" talk, a learned person would have no advantage at all over the illiterate. It follows, therefore, that if learning had anything to do with understanding a tongue, then the tongue being spoken would have to be an existing human language which a learned person might understand, even without an interpreter. This is pretty strong proof that some of the multilingual individuals were spouting off in Latin or some other language that unlearned native Corinthians would not understand.

A Very Careful Solution Required. The task before Paul, therefore, in dealing with the Corinthian problem was very delicate. He must 1) work out principles or procedures whereby every one present in an assembly would be edified, 2) without any danger of his advice impeding or conflicting the free work of the Holy Spirit in the likely event that the Spirit would need to give someone an *authentic gift* of tongues, and 3) to establish procedures whereby impostors may be detected without discouraging those with the authentic gift.

Paul knew, and had already made the case, that the gifts of prophecy, tongues, and knowledge were to cease. But he also knew that the time had not as yet arrived because the Scripture (which he and others were in the process of writing) was not yet finished. Therefore, the task of discouraging the abuse of tongues by carnal individuals on the one hand, without interfering with the authentic and sovereign gift-giving work of the Holy Spirit in their lives on the other hand, was a challenging task. This, plus other factors mentioned above, made the writing of chapter 14 a little convoluted. And all these things together, plus the misinformation spread abroad by modern charismatics, makes the full understanding of chapter 14 rather difficult for today's reader so far removed from the early church environment.

Understanding: The Mark of God's Endorsement. The rest of chapter 14 in light of the above makes perfect sense. After the introduction (vs. 1-5), Paul enters into a lengthy discourse (vs. 6-19) wherein he presents a blanket criterion for what a gift of the Spirit is intended to accomplish, namely, *understanding* (emphasized seven times in verses 6-20). He argues for "speaking in tongues" that is "profitable." To be profitable, tongues must contain either *"revelation"* or *"knowledge"* (i.e., divine truth miraculously unveiled); and these are conveyed by means of either *"prophesying"* or *"teaching"* (v. 6).[224]

Paul introduces here an important concept or insight into the nature of spiritual gifts. From this concept we are able to see that *a plurality of gifts may be interactive simultaneously in a single individual and in what may appear to be a single act.* The gifts, especially prophecy, tongues, and knowledge, seem to be highly integrated[225] and convoluted. Thus, a single individual may *prophesy* divine revelation thereby conveying *knowledge* all by means of a miraculous language or *tongue.* All three of these spiritual gifts may be simultaneously operative, but the object of either of them separately, or all of them working together, is to impart *un-*

---

[224] Jamison, Fausset, and Brown, *A Commentary* (Wm. B. Eerdman, Reprint, 1993) 1 Cor. 14:6. So also Carson citing Grudem, *Showing the Spirit*, p. 103.

[225] It is probable that the interactive nature of these gifts, since they all involve divine revelation, is the reason the three of them are singled out together for termination (1 Cor. 13:8-13) when the canon of Scripture is complete and gathered as previously discussed.

derstanding. Paul's point is this: if *understanding* is not conveyed within a process, then the process is unprofitable; and if unprofitable, conveying no edification, we may know therefore that it is not of the Spirit of God.

Paul further argues that intelligibility and understanding are purposes even for inanimate things, pipe, harp, trumpet, and reasons that a *tongue* also must be "easy to be *understood*" (v. 9). If it is not, the so-called tongue is not a gift of the Holy Spirit. The message is unmistakable; God's only gift of tongues is for *understanding and communication.*

The criterion of understanding is applied to all forms of communication, whether prayer, singing, or simply speaking (vs. 13-19). God is a God of consistent, objective understanding, and once objective understanding occurs it often produces valid subjective responses of "joy unspeakable and full of glory" (1 Pet. 1:8).

Conclusion. All in all there is a mountain of evidence that every place in Scripture, including 1 Corinthians 14, where the authentic gift of tongues is discussed, it was the *God-given power to speak in an existing human language which had not been learned by the speaker,* so that a native of that language, or another learned person, could understand. It is that and nothing more. Over against this there is nothing in Scripture that could be called evidence which teaches that God has ever given a spiritual gift to anyone to speak in an unintelligible language or "angel talk," either in public or private. The "angel talk" theory bears all the marks of a rather transparent effort to rescue a practice which grew subjectively out of the fallen human psyche, or worse.

We believe the case is made that there is only one concept of tongues as a gift in the Bible, the miraculous ability to speak a language unlearned by the speaker, with each instance under the sovereign control of the Holy Spirit. Therefore, the practice of speaking in unintelligible tongues and passing it off as a gift of the Holy Spirit, whether in the ignorance of self-deceit or otherwise, can only be regarded as sin.

On this basis we kindly and lovingly admonish our brethren

who are caught up in this sin to repent and forsake it and make whatever restitution is possible in healing the vast breach it has created among millions of Christians. And for all of us we urge a deliberate, joint search of Scripture for true unity in truth among all Christians around the world that we might focus together effectually on the proclamation of the saving Gospel of Christ.

VI.
The Signature of God:
Authentication and Confirmation
of Scripture

As we continue our examination of the ancient human quest for direct experiential knowledge of God, this last chapter will focus on miraculous "signs and wonders." We will note briefly the transparent human efforts to duplicate them as some attempt to forge the signature of God upon their own particular cause. But primarily in this chapter we will focus positively upon the genuine wonders of God and His purpose for performing them.

FORGING THE SIGNATURE OF GOD

Large numbers of Christians in recent history have been focused primarily upon four illegitimate goals: 1) receiving a mis-interpreted experience of the baptism of the Holy Spirit, 2) speaking in unintelligible tongues, 3) receiving direct revelation, and 4) performing or receiving spectacular and miraculous signs and wonders. But these modern gifts, especially tongues-speaking, are easier to counterfeit than biblical miracles. In other words, it is easier to babble than to raise the dead. For this reason the charismatics have not been quite so successful in the realm of credible signs and wonders as with their own brand of tongues. Nevertheless, many are the claims of sensational wonders per-formed among them, but when it comes to verification of a specif-ic claim, at least in our experience, the great wonder turns quickly into a will-o'-the-wisp.

Jesus was unable to keep His wonders secret, though He urged the recipients of them not to tell. Yet, modern workers of wonders do just the opposite. They emblazon their dubious suc-cesses abroad and give wide media publicity to their sensational claims. But none of them have, to our knowledge, been thronged in the streets with people trying to touch the hems of their gar-ments. So different, however, were the works of Jesus and the apostles that people spontaneously found out, and there were times when Jesus had to escape the crowds just to get a chance to eat or sleep.

This difference should be our first clue that modern wonders are of a different sort; the vast publicity machines of modern won-der-workers produce nowhere near the results of the secret works of Christ.

Feeble "Wonders" are a Reproach

We realize that many of our modern charismatic brethren sin-cerely believe they are doing God a service by claiming invisible or unverifiable "wonders" and subjective, unintelligible tongues.

They do not seem to realize that a poor or questionable "wonder" is no glory to God, or that a feeble "sign" is actually a reproach.

Moreover, even non-charismatics today seem to delight in making a "miracle" out of every molehill. And in some churches or movements, if there is not an on-going cavalcade of "miracles," at least two or three times a week, then nothing is going on, and life in God's universe is rather dull. The fact is, it rather dishonors His name and shows His people to be gullible or untrustworthy to be always interpreting God's every-day blessings, or "common grace," as miraculous. God works no feeble, ambiguous wonders. When He is ready to bare His mighty arm, He needs no publicity. He makes His own publicity as He goes.

Undermining the Uniqueness of Scripture

It is unlikely that many, if any, of the adherents to the charismatic movements or subjectivist evangelicals consciously realize that their emphasis on so-called miracles, tongues, and other "wonders" actually undermines the uniqueness of Scripture. God's work of confirmation, which He reserved for those times and persons He used for producing the Scripture and authenticating the church, loses its uniqueness if later persons can duplicate the same signs and wonders.

The so-called "signs and wonders" of the charismatics are transparently contrived, possibly by well-meaning people hoping to add credibility to the faith. Probably few of them realize that if the signs and wonders claimed were truly of God, this fact would put the wonder-worker on a par with the original writers of Scripture; it would open again the canon of revelation and the words of those so confirmed would become new Scripture.

Then there are certain leaders who do realize this and desire to be on par with the apostles and other writers of Scripture. Satan would like nothing better than to destroy the uniqueness of the writers of Scripture. He would delight to call in question the very Word of God; then there would be no infallible standard of truth by which to test all other claims.

THE MATRIX OF SCRIPTURE'S UNIQUE AUTHENTICATION

We have already shown negatively that the revelations and tongues of charismatics and subjectivists are not of God. But now we want to show positively that God's design from the beginning was to create an infallible canon, an iron-clad authority, an objective standard of absolute, unchangeable truth with unique unequivocal credentials. He would produce a written Word revealing the persons, works, and purposes of the Triune God.

The works of God, including mighty signs and wonders, form the historical matrix out of which the Bible was produced with unique authentication. And if the Bible is and remains unique since its completion, the wonders that have conferred this uniqueness upon it have never been and must never be repeated. By these broad truths, and the works and words of Christ Himself, we can know that all works claiming to be of the same character as the original unrepeatable wonders of God are counterfeit.

Identity Requires Uniqueness

There is a broad and important doctrinal principle that permeates the whole of Scripture which appears not to be clearly understood by many interpreters of Scripture. The principle is this: *The works of God in the authentication and confirmation of His Word and its writers through many signs and wonders have uniquely identified the Bible as the only body of absolute truth.* In other words, if God were not its ultimate author, the Bible we have could not exist. In this truth we have a great weapon against the forces of darkness. We should be boldly and uniformly declaring this principle against the claims of postmodernism that there is no body of absolute truth.

Since there is a body of infallible truth that God has revealed to mankind, He must then have devised an infallible means of *identification* of that truth. A body of infallible truth would be of no advantage to mankind if it were impossible to distinguish it from all other impostors claiming to have the truth. We can be sure that an infinitely wise God would not, and did not, miss that point.

If humanity in its weakness is to be able to identify the Word of God, then God Himself must take the initiative and provide the distinguishing uniqueness that will allow a means of identity.

The Problem of Identity. A certain problem of identity applies to *everything*. If so-called identical twins were truly identical, even their mothers could not tell them apart. But in every case, there is something *unique* about each one that allows identity. Identity, then, depends upon *uniqueness*; each entity must have at least one unique feature to establish its identity. The Word of God is no different in that regard.

Yet the identity of the Word of God is further complicated by its own nature. It is intrinsically the highest in authority, in purity, and in accuracy; consequently we have no standard by which to measure it. Since God gave the Scriptures, by design, to be the supreme standard of truth and righteousness for all mankind, it cannot be authenticated by any lesser standard than itself.

Though more acute, this is not a problem wholly unknown in other human affairs. In the early days of the U.S. space program it became necessary to improve the timing standard for all the systems that were networked together, so the "atomic clock" was developed. By chance this writer, at that time, was working with a team of engineers and technicians assigned the task of testing the accuracy of this clock. But, alas, the problem was that the atomic clock was far more accurate than any timepiece or standard that existed; therefore, we could not directly measure its accuracy. We were, however, by observations over long periods of time and by calculations and extrapolations, able to determine that it was far more accurate than any other timing device we had. So it became the standard.

In a much smaller sense, this is the type of problem God faced in the authentication of His Word. How would He give His revelation so that an inferior being would be able to identify it as God's Word and distinguish it from all other claimants? Among men, there is no scholar, authority, or standard that could possibly validate its superior authority, purity, or accuracy as it came from the hand of God.

Is the Bible the infallible revelation of God? Among men, there is no one to ask.

Is the Bible historically accurate in every detail? No one was there in the beginning. No historian could possibly sit in judgment of the transcendent God who created and presides over history. God not only knows every bend, ripple, and eddy in the stream of history; He dug the channel in which it flows.

Is the Bible morally pure in all things commanded? To whom shall we turn for the answer? Is there a holy man who can detect a flaw in the God who alone defines morality? Shall we ask a modern subjectivist who claims God has spoken to him?

Neither man nor an angel from heaven can either pronounce judgment upon or validate the Word of God. Then where shall we look for its identity but to God Himself? And His answer is in the Word itself.

Self-Validation. Let us look at this problem from another perspective. Consider a fine diamond. Typically, it will come with a certificate of authenticity which is presumed to guarantee its genuineness. However, crooks can, and often do, produce certificates. Where, then, does the final proof of its genuineness actually reside? *It resides in the diamond itself; it bears its own witness as to its genuineness.* Its own intrinsic qualities are its final authentication.

Thus it is with the Word of God; the Holy Spirit, who inspired and accompanies it, has built into the Scriptures its own unique authentication. God has performed many mighty miraculous works, signs and wonders, throughout the Bible to which there were many eyewitnesses. Although the eyewitnesses are all dead, their testimony, nevertheless, became a vital part of the record.

For what purpose?

These wonders with their eyewitness accounts, by the deliberate design of God, are now indispensable ingredients forming the character of Scripture – as it were a diamond: clear carbon molecules fitting perfectly, symmetrically, and seamlessly together forming the hardest, most indestructible material commonly known to man.

So the Scripture, like a diamond, is what it is by the design of God, bearing its own authenticity within itself. It is imperative to understand that *these wonders are unique to the God of Scripture,* witnessed by innumerable observers, good and evil, and by chosen agents of God through whom the Scriptures were given.

If we affirm it to be the Word of God, we add nothing to it. If we denounce it as the word of impostors, we take nothing from it. We cannot change this "diamond."

There have been other "holy books" with claims of some miraculous wonders. These too have internal characteristics that witness to their identity.[226] Clearly their "wonders" are all too human, often pointless, contradictory, speculative, or even silly. None of them offer a transcendent, personal, rational creator God except those that borrow from the Bible, e.g., the Koran. Examine them; none is a realistic contender as a plausible, objective revelation from God.

A Word About *Knowing*. The comparison of Scripture against other documents suggests, on the surface, a principle which we have already rejected – that no human can sit in judgment to decide, of himself, whether or not the Bible is God's Word. This takes a little explanation lest we fall into the humanistic trap, as the ultimate judges of truth, along with the postmodernists.

Postmodernism seems to be, so far, the ultimate expression of human subjectivism and the exaltation of human judgment. Human subjectivism is comprised of feelings or persuasions drawn from within and regarded as the final criteria for truth. Postmodernism is subjectivism carried to its logical conclusion: the claim that truth is whatever each individual experiences it to

---

[226] The Vedic writings of the ancient Hindu bards, for example, form the basis of most of the Eastern religions, but those scriptures have no directly expressed declaration, let alone a confirmation, of a creator God. They are clearly agnostic in nature. The following lines from the Song of Creation in the Rig-Veda illustrate this vast gulf between other holy books and the Bible: "Who verily knows and who can here declare it, whence it was born and whence came this creation? ... He, the first origin of this creation, whether he formed it all or did not form it, Whose eye controls this world in highest heaven, he verily knows it, or perhaps he knows it not."

be, and one person's belief is as valid as any other. This resolves to the claim that absolute, objective truth does not exist.

Little do humanists seem to realize what they have done to themselves by embracing this philosophy. Where there is *no absolute,* there can be *no knowledge.* When a person thus negates God as the absolute, he surrenders a priceless gift, i.e., credibility as a rational being – stripping himself of *knowledge* itself.

The Christian must begin with the presupposition that he himself is a creation of the rational God of the Bible. God is the only sufficient grounds for human rationality. Without God, One has no right to demand a place in the league of the rational. *He has disqualified himself by his chosen pedigree – the offspring of chance.*

The humanist, as an evolutionary naturalist, begins with the presupposition (though he may deny it) that he is a product of *chance.* Having thus relegated himself to chance, the realm of the chaotic and irrational, he has no place to turn for the *validation of his thinking processes – having no principle upon which to base rationality* because *chance is irrational.*[227] Thus, upon this basis he cannot *know* anything.

The theme of this book asserts that a body of *absolute truth* does exist – it is God's revelation in Scripture – and that we can *know* it.

But how?

We know because the God of the Bible is a Person – a rational, intelligent, communicating Person. He created the *reality* and *order* of the objective universe, the opposite of chance. Then He created man in His own image as rational, intelligent, communicating persons. He created the mind of man originally as a *reliable receptor,* to *know* the objective truth that is God, His Word, and His universe. He who created reality created also the receptor of reality: the mind of man perfectly designed for the task. Then God communicated. He revealed to us what we needed to *know.* And we understood because *we were designed to understand.*

---

[227] For a fuller discussion of this subject see: Willard A. Ramsey, *Facing Eternity* (Simpsonville, SC: Millennium III Publishers, 1999), pp. 10-18.

Having validated our rationality, presupposing ourselves creatures of the God of the Bible, we may now test the presupposition by evidence. That leads us to the concept of faith. Faith, however, is not what the humanist wants to make it – a blind leap in the dark. Neither is it what the typical subjectivist believes it to be, i.e., believing where there is little or no proof. On the contrary:

> …faith is the substance (convictions, objectively undergirded and supported) of things hoped for, *the evidence of things not seen… .* Through faith *we understand* that the worlds were framed by the word of God, so that things which are seen were not made of things which do appear (Heb. 11:1, 3)

God, above all, would never ask His intelligent created beings to believe something for which there is no evidence: God designed the mind and heart to receive "the evidence of things not seen" (Rom. 10:17; Psa.19:1). That is faith. Thus faith confirms our basic presupposition and we *understand reality:* the truth that is God (Gen. 1:1), His Word (John 17:17), and His universe (Psa. 19:1-3). This makes *knowledge possible,* and *faith reliable.*[228] He who rejects this God-designed arrangement, can *know nothing.*

But now, we can *know* that the Bible is the Word of God, and identify all other claimants as impostors: "For God has not given us a spirit of fear, but of *power and of love and of a sound mind"* (2 Tim. 1:7).

Miracles vs. Signs and Wonders

A miracle is an act that suspends, overrules, modifies, or reverses one or more of the laws of nature by a supernatural power. Since the laws of nature were created and ordained in their courses by the transcendent God, no other power of its own volition can alter them except by God's consent. Only God is supernatural in the ultimate sense. God has given other beings miraculous power, but always limited to His own consent and purpose. The transcendency of God as the first cause of all things and all be-

---

[228] This is not to deny the Holy Spirit in His work of enlightenment, another element in the equasion, but the focus here is upon the God-created human rationality.

ings consequentially renders Him the sole source, controller, or superintendent of all supernatural works. Thus, *all* miracles are ultimately by His power, even if through a hostile medium.

Moreover, since identification of any entity requires *uniqueness*, the authentication and confirmation of the Bible as the Word of God would require associated phenomena that are unique to God. God's uniqueness resides in His transcendency. Nothing exists that He did not create, and no created being can alter nature or anything that He created except by His permission and power. *Thus, all things supernatural are necessarily under God's control.* Therefore, nothing is more *unique* to God than miraculous, supernatural, signs and wonders; they are His signature alone.

For this good reason, the miraculous powers of God are exercised guardedly. It is a sin for a human to *require* or *seek to perform* a miraculous sign in order to believe or serve God, for "A wicked and adulterous generation seeketh after a sign" (Matt. 16:4; Acts 8:18-20). Nevertheless, God has graciously and effectually used signs and wonders to confirm His Word and to shut the mouths of the skeptical and unbelieving.

God's miraculous works provide all the *uniqueness* necessary to identify God's Word from all other imposters. That is why mighty signs and wonders were associated with the giving of the completed revelation, the Bible; and then they promptly ceased, so that no one else might claim to receive new revelation after the close of the canon of Scripture.

But having said that, lest anyone should misinterpret us, we hasten to add: Although *signs and wonders* have ceased, *miracles* have not ceased.

A Distinction. This necessitates that we draw a distinction between signs and wonders and other miracles. We offer this explanation:

1. All *signs and wonders are miracles.*
2. But all *miracles* are not *signs and wonders.*

The more general term *miracle* is not exactly synonymous with *signs and wonders.* A sign, or wonder, as used in the Scripture, is indeed a miracle. But God quietly performs innumerable miracles in the lives of His people, in answer to prayer and for their benefit, that are not signs and wonders.

Therefore we do not mean to leave the impression that miracles have ceased today. This is not the case. But we shall presently see from the Scriptures that signs and wonders have ceased – and for a very good reason. But first we want to illustrate the distinction between a miracle that is a sign or wonder and a miracle that is not.

God's purpose for signs and wonders, as stated in the books of Mark 16:20, Hebrews 2:4, and implied in Romans 15:8, was to *confirm* God's revelation to man. A sign or wonder then would be a *special event* – a miraculous work of God that is *visible, spectacular, and easily discernable* to men as miraculous. If an event or phenomenon is unmistakably identifiable as an overruling of natural processes by supernatural power, a miracle, then we know the event is of God; because the power of God is uniquely behind every miracle. The purpose of *signs* is to demonstrate visually or otherwise to the senses of observers that a matter or event is a work of God. The event itself may be a wonder that accomplishes many other purposes, but the *sign* aspect of the event is God's signature, as it were, the "the finger of God" (Ex. 8:19).

For example, in the case of Moses and Pharaoh, God purposed to demonstrate to Pharaoh and the world that Moses was representing the most high God, creator of the universe with power to overrule the processes of nature. Therefore He turned the wood of a shepherd's rod into a living, writhing serpent. That was a miraculous wonder and thus a sign authenticating Moses' words before Pharaoh, because it was unmistakably identifiable as the intervention of supernatural power unique to God.

There are other events, no less miraculous, which would not have been signs or wonders. If God had miraculously created a snake in a dark corner somewhere, and had it slither out in front of Pharaoh's throne, all the observers would have assumed that a snake had simply wandered into the palace. That would have been a miracle, but not a sign and wonder because it was not unmistakably identifiable as the intervention of supernatural power.

Have Miracles Ceased? We want to be careful to make sure we are not misunderstood. *Miracles have not ceased.* We believe God works quiet, unobtrusive miracles every day.

God hears the prayers of His saints on a daily basis, and it is His good pleasure to answer some of them with a miracle. The woman with an issue of blood (Luke 8:43-48) was apparently a godly woman of faith with a desperate problem. She decided on a plan of action, probably unnecessary, to get close to the Lord in the crowd and quietly touch the hem of His garment believing she would be healed while drawing no attention to herself.

She was in fact miraculously healed and might have gone on her way privately rejoicing, giving thanks to the Lord by silent prayer. We do not doubt that innumerable similar scenarios work themselves out daily around the globe.

Many a saint has rocked a feverish child in the wee hours of the morning praying to God for healing with every rock. They have been to a physician (a gift from God) who has prescribed some medicine. Still the fever climbs. The medicine should have worked by now, and the saint lays his heart on the line in importunate prayer. Two hours later the fever breaks. Who healed the baby, the doctor or God?

Did the medicine work according to God's natural laws?

Maybe. Or maybe it didn't.

Let's suppose the medicine worked according to nature. Is that somehow an inferior blessing? Is it not of God? Who made nature? Who made the doctor who prescribed the medicine? Does it really matter? A non-miracle is as much a work of God as a miracle! Every "natural" process is a miracle performed long ago. In every event we are only one step away from a miracle.

But maybe God, to save the baby's life, performed a quiet, unobtrusive miracle in response to the prayers of His faithful servants. Even so, the world goes on in unbelief and is never the wiser. But in either case the mature saint pays the doctor and gives thanks to God!

We cannot get away from miracles, but we seldom know for

sure when one has occurred. The mature saint is satisfied with that. But those who are experience-oriented cannot be satisfied; they must see a sign. And God will have none of it.

A scenario similar to the above might have been the case with the woman with the issue of blood, except that the Lord chose to turn this particular miracle into a sign and wonder.[229]

Thus He opened it up to the public by inquiring who touched Him, and the *quiet miracle* became a *sign and wonder*, to this day still confirming the authenticity of Christ and His Word.

As we pray to the Lord, He often works for our safety, our healing, our financial situations, and innumerable other things. He resolves them according to His own sovereign purposes. If it works out naturally, we have our answer; if it takes a miracle, that's not a problem. Do we really need to know which it was? God still works miracles today. But which is greater, a miracle or a natural process? Neither can exist without His supernatural power. It's all of God.

Miracles have not ceased, but signs and wonders have ceased. They were designed to be detected by one or more of the five senses and reserved for the unique confirmation and authentication of the agencies and Word of God. But now His revelation is complete; the canon is closed; signs and wonders have ceased.

God did perform many signs and wonders, spectacular displays of His power in developing the credentials of Scripture, its writers, and His covenants so that there is now *one* and *only one* body of truth in the world that carries the *unique signature of God.*

Those today who try or claim to duplicate the signs and wonders of Scripture succeed only in undermining the uniqueness of Scripture and its writers with the effect, whether intended or not, of usurping that uniqueness for themselves.

---

[229] After all, one of Christ's ministries to the "circumcision" was to confirm the promises made to the fathers (Rom. 15:8), and here were the circumcision all around Him, a perfect opportunity for a sign and wonder.

Launching Scripture – Establishing the Concept of an Infallible Canon

We tend to forget that approximately two and a half millennia of earth history had lapsed before God initiated a formal, definitive, inspired, authenticated canon of Scripture. The Bible began with the initial five books penned and assembled by Moses.

God had made Himself known "at sundry times and in divers manners," throughout the early centuries of earth history. He had judged the earth with a universal flood, had dispersed the people by confusing their languages, destroyed Sodom and Gomorrah, and performed many other wonders. But it was during the life of Moses that He would confront the major centers of world power with a revelation of Himself and His former works from the creation of the universe, and initiate a formal body of revealed truth, the Bible.

Authenticating Moses. As God prepared to launch the initial installments of the canon of Scripture, it would be necessary to build an aura of supernatural authority around Moses that the world may know that he spoke for God. Not only must the writings of Moses be authenticated as the Word and revelation of God, but *the very idea of a literal, tangible document from God Himself* must be established in human consciousness and authenticated. Such a document, available to humanity, detailing the long-pondered mysteries of origins and destinies from a single, transcendent, sovereign, personal deity was at that time virtually incomprehensible, let alone universally authoritative. To establish such a document would take some remarkable exploits.

The Word of the Most High God was to be initially delivered through Moses. Thus God would unequivocally demonstrate – at the highest order of human culture – that Moses was commissioned to speak for Him. God would start at the top – with Pharaoh.

> And the LORD said unto Moses, See, I have made thee a god to Pharaoh … I will harden Pharaoh's heart, and *multiply my signs and my wonders in the land of Egypt* (Ex. 7:1, 3).

By the time God got through with Pharaoh, He had established Himself as transcendent above all gods and all nature, and the name of Moses would be forever burned in the consciousness of the world as an agent of God. The humbling of Egypt and the Exodus of the Hebrews are events rooted in history, not in mythology or folklore. Creation is historical because the transcendent God and all His works are real. Therefore the character of Scripture is woven around and anchored solidly to historical events. Skeptics have been wrestling with the passage of Israel through the Red Sea for centuries. But God put Israel on the map; she is anchored to the soil and the name of Moses with her. Thus in producing the opening chapters of God's revelation to man, both Moses and the covenant people are irrevocably identified with the Creator of the universe and His Word to man. Only the blindness of arrogance can fail to see it.

A Million Eyewitnesses.[230] After the Egyptian wonders, while the fame of Moses and Israel was spreading from the Nile to Mesopotamia, they arrived at Mount Sinai. There God launched His revelation to man in earnest by giving the Ten Commandments verbally in audible words (see Ex. 19:19; 20:1, 19, 22; Deut. 9:10) to the whole congregation gathered at the base of Sinai. God later wrote these commandments in tables of stone with His own finger (Ex. 31:18; Deut. 9:10), and then Moses, having broken them, chiseled a second set in stone. These Ten Commandments were incorporated into the five books written by Moses which became the initial installments of the authenticated canon of Scripture confirmed by mighty signs and wonders during the life of Moses.

Thus was born the phenomenon of an infallible standard of truth and righteousness through a writer designated by the voice of God (Ex. 20:22) before a vast multitude of ear- and eyewitnesses numbering, probably, over a million.

A Nation Convinced. There are skeptics today, as there were in Moses' day, saying, "Well, we have Moses' word for it that God spoke to him. So what's new? Every guru claims to receive rev-

---

[230] The exact population of Israel at the time of the Exodus is unknown, but some learned estimates place it as high as 2.5 million.

elation from God." But God anticipated every skeptic, and though they will not believe, He leaves them without excuse.

God did not leave it to Moses to make his own case; He went before the people Himself and with great signs and awesome wonders of fire and smoke on the mountain, and the sound of a trumpet until the earth trembled.

"Just a volcano and an earthquake," says the skeptic.

But God spoke to them by voice, out of the fire, in their own language: "And God spake all these words, saying, I am the LORD thy God, which have brought thee out of the land of Egypt, out of the house of bondage... ." (Ex. 20:1, 2). Then the Ten Commandments – audibly, from the lips of God – were spoken.

"Well, sure, Moses *wrote* that God spoke to them," retorts the skeptic, "but all we have is Moses' word for it."

Well not quite; we do have a bit more than Moses' word. God had Moses write one small statement, easy to pass thoughtlessly over, which has the logical effect of validating the entire process of divine revelation to every thoughtful reader from creation to the end of time:

> And the LORD said unto Moses, Thus thou shalt say unto the children of Israel, *Ye have seen that I have talked with you from heaven* (Ex. 20:22).

Now, this little statement highlights a *huge* principle of truth. It integrates the whole of the works and words of God, both the historical prologue before the event and historical epilogue since the event, into one epochal ratification of Scripture truth. In other words, God said to Moses: *go say to them*, a million eyewitnesses, *"Ye have seen that I have talked with you from heaven."*

That line is written in the *Word* that is said to be from God, but if God had not *actually talked* with them it would have been a dead giveaway. They would have immediately known that the so-called Word of God was false. That is why the entire nation was brought before the mountain; no one could successfully dispute the record that God spoke by voice. But if they had not heard, they would all have known that Moses was a false leader, simply trying to establish his own control over them, and history from that time forward would have been a very different matter. The Pentateuch could never have been received by this multitude of eyewitnesses as the Word of God if indeed they had not been actual eyewitness to these events.

Moreover, all the plagues of Egypt, frogs, locust, the death angel, walking through the Red Sea with walls of water on both sides, and finally the Sinai experience, would have been to them wholly preposterous.

Had the multitude not *experienced these events* firsthand, never could they have received the record of these incredible stories as the Word of God! A nation of eyewitnesses received these writings of Moses as the Word of the most high Creator of heaven and earth. Like all humanity, they were weak and often disobedient. But never did they argue: *"We didn't see any such wonders as these Scriptures say we saw."* They were witnesses to the reality and power of God.

No Way Out. The skeptic who wants to get free of the obligation to reverence and obey the God of Scripture, has no rational way out. When God launched His written Word into the world, He built into it the proofs of His authorship. All one needs to know to trust the accuracy of the Bible is that God is behind it; and as discussed above, an inferior instrument or authority cannot become the standard for a verdict over a superior instrument or authority. God's transcendent signature is all over the Bible; it is God's Word. And if God's Word, it is *infallible* because God cannot speak a fallible word.

Moreover, the validation God gave to His Word through the events of the life of Moses and the multitudes who witnessed these events is extrapolated both *backward in history to the creation of the world* and *forward through prophecy until the end of the world*. Numerous fulfilled prophecies along the way add proof upon proof that the phenomenon of Scripture is a work of the most High God. And the greatest of the prophecies are of the coming of the Messiah (Gen. 3:15; 12:2-3; 49:10; Deut. 18:18-19; 2 Sam. 7:12-29; Psa. 22; Isa. 9:6-7; Mic. 5:2 and others). As history developed, the Scriptures grew, prophecies multiplied, and signs and wonders were used discretely as God guided the process, building the canon of Scripture toward a complete, final body of *absolute truth* despite the claims of postmodernism.

Signs and Wonders: The Signature of God

Most signs and wonders are brief, temporary events, and most people say, "Alas, I never saw one." But take heart, there are some signs and wonders that are *perpetual*, that everyone may see. Most people do not recognize these as miraculous signs and wonders. Some of the most powerful factors for identifying the Word or works of God are perpetual in nature and are ever before us.

Perpetual Signs and Wonders. As we open the pages of Scripture, we are confronted with the greatest "sign and wonder" of all, *the creation of the universe.*

God's work of creation described in the first lines of Scripture has, so far, been perpetual. Other attempts to explain the wonders of the universe, atheistic or evolutionary theories, are nowhere near adequate, scientifically or otherwise, to account for what is observed daily in creation. The origin of nature is a supernatural event because nature bears its own scientific witness that it cannot self-create, and Scripture confirms it (Heb. 11:3). Creation was a display of immense power verifying our environment as a work of God, and every human is an eyewitness to its reality:

> The *heavens declare the glory of God;* and the firmament showeth *his handywork.* Day unto day uttereth speech, and night unto night *showeth knowledge.* There is no speech nor language, where their voice is not heard (Psa. 19:1-3).

We ignore this vast display of the transcendent power of God and the unavoidable knowledge of it at our own peril:

> Because that which may be known of God is manifest in them; for God hath showed it unto them. For the invisible things of him from the creation of the world are clearly seen, being understood by the things that are made, even his eternal power and Godhead; so that they are without excuse (Rom 1:19-20).

Therefore, Paul said to the Greek philosophers:

> We also are men of like passions with you, and preach unto you that ye should turn from these vanities unto the living God, *which made heaven,*

and earth, and the sea, and all things that are therein: Who in times past suffered all nations to walk in their own ways. Nevertheless *he left not himself without witness*, in that he did good, and gave us rain from heaven, and fruitful seasons, filling our hearts with food and gladness (Acts 14:15-17).

The creation itself shouts to us every day and manifests the supernatural power of the eternal Spirit.

Within one sentence, in the opening words of the Bible, God is identified as a *transcendent* and *rational person.* And in the opening lines of John's Gospel the same identity is invoked by the same wonder of creation and firmly linked to Jesus Christ. Thus the God of Genesis and the Christ of the Gospels are unequivocally identified as the transcendent God of creation. The great supernatural work of creation has *uniquely* identified the Bible with the God of creation and the Christ of the Gospel. We will all be held accountable for the conclusions drawn from this great sign and wonder.

Goal-Oriented Continuity. Among the first hints of supernatural wonder about the Scripture is the *continuity*, over the course of millennia, from creation to Christ. It has a goal-oriented continuity through many generations of writers, unknown to each other, spanning many centuries. And yet they form a coherent whole and reach a harmonious conclusion. This also is a perpetual sign and wonder. Out of a mountain of coherency, there are a few details in Scripture that are hard to understand, an acknowledgement suggested in Scripture itself (2 Peter 3:16), but none insurmountable or contradictory.

This wonder of continuity is continuously observed by those alert enough to see it, and it has no plausible "natural" explanation. In this feature also, the Bible is unique and unrivaled.

Genealogy in Reverse. Another perpetual sign and wonder, to which any reader of Scripture may become an eyewitness, begins in the early pages of Genesis and continues intermittently into the New Testament. Not many people are aware, when reading the genealogies which begin as a formal listing in Genesis chapter five, that they are an eyewitness to a perpetual miraculous, sign or wonder.

These genealogies, continuing throughout the Old Testament Scriptures including the two books of Chronicles, follow a genealogical path through approximately four millennia. This genealogical path aims at a certain individual designated in Genesis 3 as the seed of a woman, the future person who would engage in a winning struggle against the deceiver of Eve. This genealogy terminates on that very person, Jesus of Nazareth, and then it stops. No more genealogies are kept in Scripture.

Moreover the genealogy of Jesus is given by two independent persons, Matthew and Luke. Yet, there is obviously no collusion between them: Matthew's genealogy leads to the head of Jesus' family, Joseph, the "husband of Mary." The other leads to Mary's family because Jesus was the seed of the *woman,* a virgin.

Now, some are asking, "What is so miraculous about a genealogy?" People develop genealogies every day, but with one major difference: they start with the individual whose genealogy they wish to generate and work backwards through historical records; nothing miraculous about that. But try it from the other end of history. To predict at every generation, before the fact, the right individual leading to someone yet unborn, 4000 years into the future, and hit the right individual is a supernatural wonder! Do this, and you have a miraculous wonder of the first rank! The Bible is, in one sense, a genealogy in reverse from Adam to Christ.

To generate a genealogy in reverse is the work of a transcendent God. The statistical opportunities for error in achieving this are astronomical, the probability of success is virtually zero. And although there are a few ambiguities (though nothing inexplicable) in the genealogical records, these are nothing to compare to the statistical mountain of data that is correct (inexplicable in its setting except as a work of God), which verifies and authenticates the whole.

If one has read the Bible, he should not say, "I have never witnessed a sign and wonder."

The Final Word – Confirmed and Authenticated!

In the time period when the canon of Scripture was formally

initiated, during the life of Moses, there was an unusual eruption of supernatural signs and wonders. As discussed above, God was asserting Himself into human affairs at the highest levels of human civilization and power. He was, then and for all time, placing His name before humanity:

> And God said unto Moses, I AM THAT I AM: and he said, Thus shalt thou say unto the children of Israel, I AM hath sent me unto you. And God said moreover unto Moses, Thus shalt thou say unto the children of Israel, The LORD God of your fathers, the God of Abraham, the God of Isaac, and the God of Jacob, hath sent me unto you: *this is my name for ever, and this is my memorial unto all generations* (Ex. 3:14-15).

The name of God would be placed before the world forever. Moreover, He would initiate a written revelation of Himself, His law, and His future purposes; and He would place upon it His signature by mighty signs and wonders. Accordingly, there was an upsurge of supernatural wonders to establish the initial credentials of His official canon. This was the *period of initiation*[231] of the canon of Scripture.

Then, centuries later, as the central figure in Scripture, the Messiah, came into the world and the canon of Scripture was approaching completion, another eruption of signs and wonders occurred. This was the *period of completion* of the canon of Scripture.

Jesus Confirms the Promises – Romans 15:8. In Romans we read, "Now I say that Jesus Christ was a minister of the circumcision for the truth of God, *to confirm the promises made unto the fathers*" (15:8). This work, a major aspect of Jesus' ministry, was to confirm the fulfillment of the truth of the promises or covenants made to the fathers in the Old Testament. Thus, by signs and wonders, He not only validated *again* the early promises of Scripture, but He unequivocally asserted His own personal deity, demonstrating the same transcendent powers that validated the

---

[231] This fact does not preclude the possibility that Moses may have had access to some written sources. But this was the time that God began to formalize, consolidate, serialize, and validate a specific canon, superintended and inspired by the Holy Spirit. Moses was His choice for the first installment.

first installment of Scripture. The signature of *Yahweh* upon the early Scriptures and of *Jesus* upon the final Scriptures is the same identical signature!

Now let us consider the wonders of Jesus as works of confirmation (Rom. 15:8). The Gospels are filled with the wonders of Christ ranging from power to still a storm to the resurrection of the dead. In John we will note that the confirming work of Christ goes even beyond what is recorded: *"And many other signs truly did Jesus in the presence of his disciples, which are not written in this book"* (John 20:30).

These Gospel wonders were done in partial fulfillment of His ministry of confirmation: 1) of Himself as Messiah, 2) of the foundation of the church, and 3) of the ones who would write the New Testament Scriptures.

The Last Word. Just as *Yahweh* confirmed His own Name to the world before giving His Old Testament Word through the Old Covenant people, so *Jesus Christ* confirmed Himself before giving His New Testament Word through His New Covenant people, the church. Thus the *final revelation* to man is through Jesus Christ:

> God, who at sundry times and in divers manners spake in time past unto the fathers by the prophets, *Hath in these last days spoken unto us by his Son, whom he hath appointed heir of all things, by whom also he made the worlds* (Heb. 1:1-2).

From His birth, especially during His personal ministry, Jesus Christ spoke to mankind confirming it through the renewed wave of supernatural wonders. Then Jesus sent the Holy Spirit, in His role of Paraclete, who continued, by signs and wonders, to authenticate the New Covenant church and those who wrote the late Scriptures. Thus Jesus continued to speak through the Holy Spirit:

> Howbeit when he, the Spirit of truth, is come, he will guide you into all truth: *for he shall not speak of himself; but whatsoever he shall hear, that shall he speak:* and he will show you things to come. *He shall glorify me: for he shall receive of mine, and shall show it unto you* (John 16:13-14).

As we have considered in detail in an earlier chapter, the

Holy Spirit was sent to empower, accompany, give gifts, superintend, and authenticate the work of the church and the completion of the canon of Scripture. But the basic process of authentication and confirmation of Scripture by signs and wonders did not change in principle until the canon was complete.

Confirmation through the Paraclete. As we continue to follow the principle of confirmation and authentication of the Word of God by means of signs and wonders, several New Testament passages are especially relevant and set forth the principle very clearly.

An important passage, as we have noted above is Mark 16:17-18, 20. Let us review verse 20: *"And they went forth, and preached everywhere, the Lord working with them, and confirming the word with signs following."* As they went preaching the Word, the Lord was working with them through the Holy Spirit for the purpose of *confirming the Word* which would be canonized as Scripture. This was done with signs and wonders, God's *unique signature* upon revelation.

Bearing them Witness – Hebrews 2:3. Perhaps the most relevant passage expressing the deliberate process of the confirmation of Scripture by signs and wonders is in the book of Hebrews. It is clear that God was working according to a plan or principle to validate and establish the truth of His Word. This passage says:

> How shall we escape, if we neglect *so great salvation;* which at the first began to be spoken by the Lord, and *was confirmed* unto us by them that heard him; God also bearing them witness, both with *signs and wonders and with divers miracles, and gifts of the Holy Ghost,* according to His own will? (Heb. 2:3).

This passage gives a brief summary of the work of God in the confirmation of His Word. We have a sequence of events: 1) This "great salvation" – the Gospel and truth of God's New Covenant which by prophecy was foretold – is the message which "first began to be spoken by the Lord," personally. 2) It was passed on to those who "heard Him," His immediate disciples, especially the apostles. 3) Then it "was confirmed unto us," i.e., those who heard the Word from the apostles, and at every step God openly and visibly "bore them witness" with signs and wonders, that what they preached and wrote was God's truth.

The people of the churches, often in great multitudes of thousands, began to receive the writings of the apostles. These writings contained the record that the people were witness to great signs and wonders just as it was in the days of Moses. For example:

> And by the hands of the apostles were *many signs and wonders wrought among the people* ... . There came also a multitude out of the cities round about unto Jerusalem, bringing sick folks, and them which were vexed with unclean spirits: and *they were healed every one* (Acts 5:12-16).

> And it came to pass in Iconium ... that *a great multitude both of the Jews and also of the Greeks believed...* .Long time therefore abode they speaking boldly in the Lord, which gave testimony unto the word of his grace, and *granted signs and wonders to be done by their hands* (Acts 14:1-3).

> Truly the *signs of an apostle were wrought among you* in all patience, *in signs, and wonders,* and mighty deeds (2 Cor. 12:12).

This short sampling makes the point that the churches were eyewitness to these wonders, i.e., to *the signature of God* upon these New Covenant churches, the apostles, and upon the New Covenant Scriptures the churches were receiving. These same Scriptures clearly declare that the multitudes *saw* these wonders, and the multitudes *received these writings as the Word of God* because they knew they actually did see these wonders. Otherwise, they would have laughed them to scorn.

Again, here is the same built-in self-validating principle: If the people *did not see* these signs and wonders, then they would have known immediately that the writings were false, and could not be the Word of God as claimed. The apostles and Scripture writers would have been found liars. There were many contemporary enemies of the truth, but they did not argue that the wonders did not occur, that the dead were not raised nor the sick healed:

> But when [the Jewish leaders] had commanded them to go aside out of the council, they conferred among themselves, Saying, What shall we do to these men? for that *indeed a notable miracle hath been done by them is manifest to all them that dwell in Jerusalem; and we cannot deny it* (Acts 4:15-16).

Even Gamaliel, "a doctor of the law, had in reputation among all the people," made no arguments against the claim of supernatural wonders observed by the numerous eyewitnesses.[232] He said only, "*... let them alone: for if this counsel or this work be of men, it will come to nought: But if it be of God, ye cannot overthrow it; lest haply ye be found even to fight against God*" (Acts 5:33-39). Great advice, and now we know how it turned out.

The New Testament content was originating concurrently with this new eruption of signs and wonders, extending from the ministry of Jesus until the completion of the canon of Scripture.

Then the signs and wonders (but not miracles) ceased – making the Scriptures *unique*.

Moreover, the continuity of these authenticated works of God, from Moses' *Genesis* to John's *Revelation*, create such an impregnable network of reinforced, intertwined strands of truth, events, history, wonders, and eyewitnesses that the minuscule objections of skeptics[233] are so weak and groundless they are actually silly.

Thus God has continuously confirmed by "signs and wonders" the Word which is now complete.

Confirmation of the Church and Apostles. Though we have noted above the work of the Holy Spirit, as Paraclete, with the church and the apostles, this area deserves a little more specific attention. Much as Moses was visibly identified with God in preparation for the giving of the Pentateuch, so were the apostles identified with Jesus in preparation for their unique, temporary role in the progress of the church and New Testament Scripture. After the resurrection of Jesus, the work of confirmation was focused mainly upon them. Peter on the day of Pentecost spoke these words:

---

[232] Josephus himself acknowledged that great wonders had been done by the followers of Jesus, though his statement has been challenged as has every fact that supports God's Word.

[233] Especially empty are the arguments of objectors who claim to believe the Bible, but who wish to find exemption from some specific commandment by pointing to a handful of obscure texts, difficult translations, or commandments they do not like.

> Ye men of Israel, hear these words; Jesus of Nazareth, *a man approved of God among you by miracles and wonders and signs,* which God did by him in the midst of you, *as ye yourselves also know* ... (Acts 2:22).

Peter said the people themselves knew about the signs and wonders of Jesus. If the people had never seen them, this would have destroyed Peter's credibility. Christ did these wonders publicly, as God's sanction upon His life, work, and message. Lazarus, for example, was raised before many witnesses, as were the son of the widow of Nain and the daughter of Jairus. Likewise, the blind men in Jericho and the lame man let down through the roof were healed, and a multitude was fed before many witnesses. Even the unbelieving Jews, just as the enemies of Moses, made no attempt to deny the reality of these events. That would have been intellectual suicide because innumerable people saw them, including both believers and unbelievers.

But now, after Jesus' ascension, the apostles having been inseparably associated with Jesus in all these things, are ready to take the lead. Therefore, being empowered by the Holy Spirit, the apostles pick up the work and the narrative continues: *"... and many wonders and signs were done by the apostles"* (Acts 2:43).

Then further on we find the church praying *"that signs and wonders may be done by the name of thy holy child Jesus"* (Acts 4:30). And again *"... by the hands of the apostles were many signs and wonders wrought among the people"* (5:12). Here are examples of the principle expressed in Hebrews 2:3, that God confirmed the words of them that heard the Lord.

Continuing now with our survey of signs and wonders, we find Philip in Samaria: "Then Simon himself believed also: and when he was baptized, he continued with Philip, and wondered, *beholding the miracles and signs which were done"* (8:13). The confirmation continues through Paul: "Long time therefore abode they speaking boldly in the Lord, which gave testimony unto the word of his grace, and *granted signs and wonders to be done by their hands"* (14:3).

These wonders comprised a progressive, cumulative body of proof in confirmation of the words of those who heard the

Lord – primarily the apostles who gave us the New Testament Scriptures.

The Apostle Paul said, "For I will not dare to speak of any of those things which Christ hath not wrought by me to make the Gentiles obedient, by word and deed, *Through mighty signs and wonders, by the power of the Spirit of God; so that from Jerusalem, and round about unto Illiricum,* I have fully preached the gospel of Christ" (Rom. 15:18,19).

Finally, revisiting I Corinthians 14, we have gone full circle: *"Wherefore tongues are for a sign not to them that believe, but to them that believe not"* (14:22). Now, with this data behind us, it is easy for us to see that tongues were only one of many signs and wonders performed as God used the broader principle of signs and wonders, dazzling and sensational miracles, for the once-and-for-all confirmation of His Word.

The continuity is now complete from Moses on Sinai to the Apostle John on Patmos – From Genesis 1:1 to Revelation 22:21. We repeat what we said on page one. God has delivered an authenticated canon of truth clad in impenetrable armor, barricaded and buttressed, cross-braced and anchored, within an indestructible bulwark of proof, unique and complete.

This Word, to change the metaphor, is an ocean of absolute truth, and no man can swim its breadth nor fathom its depth. With this in hand, how could a person of faith ever feel "dryness" of soul? Or why would an ungrateful soul agonize before God for yet another beggarly crumb of revelation when he has not mastered what has been given? Rejoice, God has spoken!

The Sham of Modern Charismata

How transparently anti-climactic it is to point to today's personal "revelation" from God, or obscure "wonders" such as an "unknown tongue" when God's complete and sufficient Word is before us.

When we can so readily relive by faith God's opening the Red Sea, bringing enough water from a rock to satisfy a million thirsty throats, His audible voice from the top of Sinai, His stopping the universe for Joshua, why do we go away hungry?

When we can follow Jesus as He healed lepers, stilled the storms of the sea, raised the dead, settled our sin debt on the cross, rose from the grave and ascended to God's right hand, why should we seek a subjective "experience" in search of joy?

We have all that God is going to give us until we see Him in His glory, and we haven't received, comprehended, enjoyed or obeyed half of what we have.

God's Word is a chain of evidence that is impossible to negate, and it demonstrates that the Master of the universe is the author of the Bible.

It is therefore ludicrous for Christians of the twenty-first century to seek the same credentials that were given to the writers of Scripture. But it is especially inconsistent to single out unintelligible tongues from all the other possible signs and wonders, e.g., the healing of leukemia, walking on water, or raising the dead.

The reason is rather obvious: unknown tongues can be faked or psychologically learned by deceived and misguided people who are *not satisfied with the quiet but firm foundation of faith that now comes to us through the Word* which was fully confirmed long ago by mighty signs and wonders.

Therefore, in the midst of his discussion of the proper place of gifts, Paul tells us that there are certain gifts that will always remain and are to be sought after – faith, hope, and love (I Cor. 13:13). And he tells that certain gifts will fail, cease, and vanish away (I Cor. 13:8), and they have.

Now, we are shut up to faith, the objective evidence of the unseen. Love it, believe it, and your joy will spiral out of sight.

We should therefore never expect God to repeat these signs and wonders again unless there is more Scripture to be written. Since the canon of Scripture is closed (Rev. 22:18), any further use of these great signs of confirmation would destroy the *uniqueness of God's signature* upon the Scriptures and would place the words of individuals today on a par with those of Moses and Paul.

COUNTERFEITS – THE SIGNATURE OF SATAN

Along with these great works of God, there have been and will continue to be attempts to counterfeit these powers by Satan. We find, as a biblical principle, a second miracle-working force in the world *counterfeiting the miracles of God*. God is not the only one who works miracles; yet He is the only one who *controls* the working of miracles – where, when, and by whom. God, for His own sovereign purposes whenever He is pleased to do so, sometimes permits satanic or demonic forces to work miracles. The psalmist wrote, "Surely the wrath of man shall praise thee: the remainder of wrath shalt thou restrain" (Psa. 76:10), and strange as it may seem, God also causes the wrath of Satan to praise Him, which we will show below.

Satanic Duplication

An example of satanic duplication is seen in the contest between Moses and Pharaoh:

> And Moses and Aaron went in unto Pharaoh, and they did so as the Lord had commanded: *and Aaron cast down his rod before Pharaoh, and before his servants, and it became a serpent.* Then Pharaoh also called the wise men and the sorcerers: *now the magicians of Egypt, they also did in like manner with their enchantments. For they cast down every man his rod, and they became serpents: but Aaron's rod swallowed up their rods.* And he hardened Pharaoh's heart, that he hearkened not unto them; as the Lord had said (Ex. 7:10-13).

Here is a pretty clear instance of God permitting the emissaries of Satan to produce a miracle. The overall occasion was intended to validate Moses' claim to be an agent of God, and the ultimate result did in fact validate that claim. Nevertheless, God permitted the magicians to duplicate the miracle of Moses because He had a subordinate purpose to serve.

God knew Pharaoh's heart was bitter, searching for any little shred of justification to defy God, and thus He permitted Satan to provide it in the form of a miracle. By this means God "hardened" Pharaoh's heart and multiplied "signs and wonders in the land of Egypt" (Ex. 7:3).

When God permitted the magicians to throw down their rods, which also became serpents, Pharaoh quickly seized upon that very fact to vindicate himself. He said in effect, "See my people can do it too"; however, Satan was behind it. But Pharaoh ignored the fact that Moses' serpent swallowed up the others. Though a subtle distinction, it would have been more than enough to have convinced any man who was seeking the truth.

Satan's Interface with God

Satan's business is deception, and he misses no opportunity to press his cause before the Almighty. An example of his persistence is the classic interchange between Satan and God which is the basis of the book of Job (1:6-12). In this narrative, God, for His own sovereign purposes, gave Satan considerable latitude to bring numerous calamitous events into the life of Job and his family. The lessons here are somewhat complex, and we will not take the space to unravel the details. But they follow precisely Romans 8:28.

The relevant point in this present context is simply that Satan is sometimes allowed to do remarkable, even miraculous works, but always under the limitations imposed by God.

Another example of Satan's opportunistic interface with God is on the occasion of a meeting between Jehoshaphat and Ahab. God's patience with Ahab was wearing thin, and He was about ready to take him out. This occasion provides one of the most remarkable insights into the operations around God's throne in the Bible. The prophet Micaiah describes the event:

> I saw the LORD sitting on his throne, and all the host of heaven standing by him on his right hand and on his left. And the LORD said, *Who shall persuade Ahab, that he may go up and fall at Ramothgilead?* And one said on this manner, and another said on that manner. And *there came forth a spirit, and stood before the LORD, and said, I will persuade him.* And the LORD said unto him, Wherewith? And *he said, I will go forth, and I will be a lying spirit in the mouth of all his prophets.* And he said, Thou shalt persuade him, and prevail also: *go forth, and do so* (1 Kings 22:19-22).

You can read the rest of the story, but the point is that Satan's business is deception, and he works at it incessantly – even appearing at times to alter the affairs of history. *If Satan can appear to possess the transcendency of God,* which is made most apparent to humanity through supernatural works, *then he shall have usurped the signature of God.* By this means he can lead millions of subjectivist, feelings-oriented people into grievous errors.

The counterfeit forgeries of the signature of God would be Satan's ultimate weapon; he could use it to put *pseudo-scripture* into the mouths of prophets, preachers, and "Christians" – just as he did the prophets before Ahab who claimed to be receiving divine revelation. Then the misled, sometimes well-meaning multitudes who seek after signs will follow like sheep to the slaughter.

Lying Wonders. Satanic powers in the world under certain conditions are permitted to duplicate, or at least appear to duplicate, the miracles of God. Paul calls them "lying wonders." He writes:

> And then shall that Wicked be revealed, whom the Lord shall consume with the spirit of his mouth, and shall destroy with the brightness of his coming: Even him, whose coming is *after the working of Satan with all power and signs and lying wonders* (2 Thess. 2:8-9).

The Satanic forces strive to counterfeit, and actually do counterfeit as God permits, similar signs and wonders by which God has confirmed His Word. In Revelation we are alerted to these satanic powers: "And I beheld another beast coming up out of the earth ... And *he doeth great wonders, so that he maketh fire come down from heaven on the earth in the sight of men, and deceiveth them* that dwell on the earth by the means of those miracles which he had power to do in the sight of the beast ..." (Rev. 13:11-14).

With no further interpretation of the full meaning of these things, at least they show that Satan recognizes their value for deceit. If he can duplicate signs and wonders, he has reached the ultimate in deception because they most nearly imitate God. And with these powers, it is no problem for him to foster deception in those who are always looking for miracles, tongues, or other wonders and go about seeking to witness or perform them:

> O ye hypocrites, ye can discern the face of the sky; but can ye not discern the signs of the times? *A wicked and adulterous generation seeketh after*

a sign; and there shall no sign be given unto it, but the sign of the prophet Jonas. And he left them, and departed (Matt. 16:3-4).

The modern multitudes who feel a subjective need for something more than the completed written Word apprehended by faith are on dangerous grounds with their fascination with modern tongues, or other shadowy and obscure "wonders." Since these phenomena fulfill a psychological need for sensuous satisfaction, where faith in the Word itself is weak, they are tailor-made for deceit.

A Solemn Warning. Jesus forewarns of Satan's duplicity. Toward the end of the earthly ministry of Jesus, He gave His disciples a solemn warning that Satan would attempt to obscure, duplicate, and undermine His work of confirmation by means of counterfeit "signs and wonders" performed by *false prophets: "For there shall arise false Christs, and false prophets, and shall show great signs and wonders;* insomuch that, if it were possible, they shall deceive the very elect" (Matt. 24:24).

We must, therefore, sort out the "signs and wonders" of satanic origin from those of God, and the only way we can do that is to have a thorough knowledge of the teachings of the Scriptures concerning God's limited use of signs and wonders. They are 1) uniquely and totally under the control of God; 2) used in a limited way in Scripture to authenticate the works of God, Scripture, and those agents of God used to produce His completed canon; then 3) God terminated His use of signs and wonders to make them *unique* to His purpose of confirmation.

God then warned us that Satan would attempt to continue what God had terminated, hoping to deceive by usurping the unique signature of God. Attempts to counterfeit the wonders of God are going on today by some called Christian, deceiving those weak in the Scripture and thus in faith.

In the newspapers, some years ago, there was an account of a charismatic leader who said that Christ had appeared to him in his own private prayer room, or "secret chamber." He said he had seen Christ who had come and had spoken to him. If his statement were true, it would be a powerful reason for anyone who loved the

Lord to go and hear what Jesus had said beyond what is revealed in Scripture. But Jesus has warned us beforehand:

> For there shall arise false Christs, and false prophets, and shall *show great signs and wonders; insomuch that, if it were possible, they shall deceive the very elect.* Behold, *I have told you before.* Wherefore if they shall say unto you, Behold, he is in the desert; *go not forth:* behold, he is in the secret chambers; *believe it not* (Matt. 24:24-26).

"Believe it not," Jesus said; "go not forth." Remember, there will be very convincing false signs and wonders shown by deceivers who are not of God. That is a truth of Scripture. But *God will not undermine the uniqueness of the completed canon of Scripture* by perpetuating true signs and wonders.[234]

Identifying the Counterfeit. If Satan is busy attempting to usurp the signature of God, how then are we to distinguish his counterfeit works from the works of God? In this regard the Lord expresses a tremendously important and significant principle:

"Behold, I have told you before…" (Matt. 24:25).

We have the Bible filled with God's truth, the validity of which rests upon the confirmation of God by means of signs and wonders so that we can trust it and know that it came from God. If Satan then attempts similar "signs and wonders," would that not muddy the water and confuse the unwary as to whose word is God's Word? There are two sets of signs to contend with; one set was of God in the past and one set is satanic in the present and the future.

How can we know which is authentic?

The principle expressed by Christ in Matthew 24:25 warns us of events perhaps of later times, but John says the Spirit of Antichrist is already in the world (1 John 4:3, 2 John 7). *Therefore God has told us beforehand.*

Furthermore, the Word that was confirmed teaches us that the signs and wonders used to confirm the Word were unique:

---

[234] However, God still performs quiet, unobtrusive, and sometimes not-so-subtle miracles every day by the millions, in response to the needs and prayers of His people. But these are not immediately recognized as supernatural works.

1. This truth is extrapolated from the theology of the nature of God as transcendent; i.e., He alone is above all nature. This makes supernatural intervention solely His domain *uniquely*.

2. The occurrence of signs and wonders are clustered primarily in two relatively short periods: 1) around the *initiation* of the Scripture (during the life and times of Moses), and 2) around the *completion* of Scripture (during the life and times of the Lord Jesus and the apostles). Each period being about a century in duration, more or less.

3. That signs and wonders were for the confirmation of the Word of God is expressly stated in the New Testament Scriptures (by Christ, Rom. 15:8; and by the Holy Spirit, Mark 16:20; Heb. 2:3-4).

4. We are expressly told that certain miraculous gifts, particularly tongues as signs, were to cease when the canon of Scripture was complete. These and other wonders did in fact stop (see lengthy discussion above, Chapter V). There have been no spectacular supernatural wonders on the order of those in the lives of Moses, Christ, and the apostles that are verifiable and not many have been claimed since the death of the last apostle. But this has not been for want of trying, especially in recent times.

5. Christ rebukes those who seek after signs and wonders, and He says *no sign will be given them* except the "sign of Jonah," i.e., the resurrection of Christ, the greatest confirmation of the Gospel. Knowing, therefore, the Lord's stance on that matter, *there is zero possibility that signs and wonders would continue into the indefinite future as a typical Christian way of life.*[235]

6. Now that the Messianic promises have been established, the Scripture has been completed, the body of absolute Scripture truth has been identified and validated, and the mouth of every subjectivist and skeptic has been stopped. God owes no man

---

[235] There will be some signs in connection with the second advent of Christ, but we have been told. An eschatological discussion of them is beyond the scope of this book.

any further revelation than what is in the Bible. "The just shall live by *faith*," the proof of *things not seen*.

7. Then finally, Christ warned us of false wonder-workers. Thus when we see their claims and their "wonders," we know their works are not of God.

If God should grant to any person today the same signs and wonders He did to those who heard the Lord and who wrote the Scriptures, then that person's words would have the same credentials as the Scriptures. *This would clearly undermine the unique credentials of Scripture.* That is why the subjectivists and charismatics, though they mean well, are so strategically important to Satan today; their pseudo-signs cut at the very foundation of scriptural authority, though we believe most of those involved do not realize it and do not mean to weaken the authority of Scripture. Nevertheless, the subjectivist approach to Christianity has diminished the sense of authority and sufficiency of Scripture in the eyes of countless thousands of Christians today.

How is it then, that we are to make the determination of what is right and wrong? Here we are today and *we do not see the same kind of confirmation* that we read about in Scripture – not among the Pentecostals or anywhere else. They are not raising the dead nor instantly restoring the twisted limbs of lifetime cripples. They are seizing upon cheap, imitation miracles – healings that cannot be tested, or unintelligible language that cannot be tested, a "sign" that anyone can fake or learn. We are warned not to go after them.

We do not say that all who speak with "tongues" are deliberately faking. Older ones "teach" the younger ones to speak in tongues – a thing unheard of in the Scriptures. Most, we believe, have learned it as a psychological response and are deceived as to what it is. But they are asking others to believe that their tongues and other "wonders" are works of God, when we have seen that the very claim itself is contrary to the Word of God. Today, we do not look for signs for confirmation of what we believe. We follow a confirmed Scripture. From it we must conclude that God's signs and wonders are past, but that Satan is still in the business of deceit. And now we know.

The Last Word

Now, let us look back in time and summarize the marvel of what God has done over the centuries to establish an immutable foundation for His Word and for our faith. It is important to understand the fact that God has made His own case for the Scripture, and those miraculous wonders of the Gospels and the book of Acts are only the final extension of the work of confirmation that He began long ago. The confirmation and validation of the Scriptures span many centuries of history, and it is this long-term, unified confirmation that makes an unassailable case.

Reviewing the Big Picture of Confirmation

As we look back to Exodus we will see God, as He gave the first Scripture through Moses, beginning to validate and confirm the writers of His revelation.

Exodus Nineteen. In this chapter is recorded the occasion on which God gave the Law to Israel – the Ten Commandments. There God gathered the children of Israel around the base of Mt. Sinai, and came down upon the mountain to speak to them with an audible voice. God wanted to demonstrate for all time that He, not Moses, was the real author of the law and of the books Moses wrote. He would speak audibly as a wonder-filled sign to the people:

> And the Lord said unto Moses, Lo, I come unto thee in a thick cloud, *that the people may hear when I speak with thee, and believe thee forever* (Ex. 19:5).

This was to confirm Moses' writings *forever*, not just to those present. It was a sign that God used as He continued to confirm His name and His Word through Moses as a "memorial to *all generations*" (Ex. 3:15) – not just to those who heard it. God came down on Sinai so that *the people* could witness, hear, and see for themselves and *believe Moses forever*.

That is a remarkable statement; how could the people believe Moses' words *forever*? Most of the adults gathered there would be dead within forty years. Is that all that the language intended to imply – until death? There is more to this event than is immediately obvious. The occasion would, in fact, provide credible persuasion of God's covenant people *forever*, as long as the world would stand, and beyond.

It may be argued that this suggestion is an overstatement of the meaning of the language (19:5), and we could concede that linguistically. But when God speaks, using words that on the surface seem extreme, perhaps it would be wise to at least ponder the larger picture a little before dismissing it.

The event did indeed result in the people (those present at the event, their posterity, and many others into the future) believing Moses and his writings *forever*, and God of course knew and purposed that, whether or not the language rigorously conveys it. This fact is supported by God's purpose as expressed in Exodus 3:15, that He was beginning, through Moses, to put His *Name* in *memorial to all generations*. That objective would certainly involve the canon of Scripture which God was beginning to build.

Forever – A Timeless Witness. But how could the Sinai event cause people to believe Moses forever? There were, at least, several hundred thousand people gathered before Sinai. And here is the answer to the question: The book of Exodus is a record written down which relates the fact that the people *did hear the audible voice of God*. Therefore, if they actually heard God's voice, they knew Moses told the truth. Exodus was written in a day when these thousands of people were living[236] and able to hear the voice of God and believe.

---

[236] Jesus Himself certifies the validity of the Pentateuch and accepted the Mosaic authorship without question. By constantly using the expression "it is written," declaring that "one jot or one tittle" of the law shall in "no wise pass away," and that "the Scriptures cannot be broken," etc., He settled the matter for every person who believes in Jesus as the incarnation of God. For further discussion see Augustus Strong, *Systematic Theology* (Valley Forge: The Judson Press, 1907), p. 199, and on authorship and chronology of Exodus, see, "Exodus," *International Standard Bible Encyclopedia* (Grand Rapids: Eerdmans, 1939) Vol. II.

They could see and observe. Little children, peeping fearfully from behind their mother's skirts, would remember vividly. The multitude would carry these memories with them as personal eyewitnesses. Families would discuss them around dinner tables and upon their rooftops in the cool of the evening. The children, down to their old age, would *point to the account in Exodus* and tell their grandchildren how it was, "I was there; it was awesome. *We heard the voice; we saw the fire just as it says; it is a matter of history. This tells what we saw. This is the Word of God.*"

And we *still* speak of these very things today and *believe Moses*, knowing the implications of the eyewitness acceptance of what they saw written in books which claim to be from God. A people would never receive a document as true which says they saw and heard, if they didn't see and hear.

Moreover, this and the other great events of the Pentateuch will be discussed in heaven – and they (we) will believe Moses *forever and ever: "And they sing the song of Moses the servant of God, and the song of the Lamb, saying, Great and marvellous are thy works, Lord God Almighty; just and true are thy ways, thou King of saints"* (Rev. 15:3).

Moses wrote a record of the Sinai event and related experiences in the Pentateuch. The record says God came down and spoke to them with an audible voice – to many thousands of people – and if God did not do that, all of them would have known that Moses was a liar. They would never have received Moses' writings as authentic, much less as the very Word of God. They would have said to Moses, "No, we saw no such thing; we didn't hear the voice of God. You wrote that all the people were gathered before Sinai and heard God's voice, but that didn't happen. Moses, your name will go down in infamy." There would have been a great hue and cry throughout the nation saying, "Moses, you are a deceiver. You are trying to become the leader among this people by dreaming up this God as a tool to gain control of us."

But they did not say that; therefore, *we know even to this day that they actually heard the voice.* They knew it really happened. It was a sign and a wonder, and that nation received Moses' writings as the Word of God. Today, thirty-five centuries later, we cannot disannul that confirmation. There is no reasonable or logical way anyone can make the witness of several hundred thousand people, with their children, and their children's children, to be of no force.

They acknowledged that Moses' writings were accurate, which means they *did hear God's voice*. And if they heard God's voice, that means *God spoke through Moses* to bring the first codified, written, authenticated Scripture to mankind. These writings therefore contain their own authentication. God's witness has power. This witness stands today, and forever, as invincible proof of the authenticity of Moses' writings.

A Cavalcade of Corroboration. Similar proofs could be developed from many other such events, e.g., the crossing of the Red Sea, the sanction of the Tabernacle under Moses (Ex. 40:33-38) and later the Temple under Solomon (1 Kings 8:5-12), the walls of Jericho, Elijah's experience on Carmel, etc. Many such signs have been given in the Old Testament, each one compounding the witness and building exponentially the authenticity and authority of Scripture as the unique Word of God.

Once the phenomenon of divine revelation from God had been established with Moses, the question "has God spoken to men in Scripture?" was no longer at issue. The only question remaining was "by whom has He spoken?" But now that question also has been answered, as reflected in the complete and gathered canon. Now, the total sequence of God's witness to His Word by signs and wonders is complete, having been firmly established down to John, the last apostle.

Since then the mighty signs and wonders of God have been purposely and conspicuously missing.

Jesus, the Ultimate Confirmation

Now the final great and major phase of the confirmation of God's Word to us, as we have seen, was the ministry and work of the Lord Jesus Christ. The writings of the Gospels are laced with many events witnessed by and known to the people of the early first century.

Such events as the appearance of the angelic host to the shepherds and the star of the wise men are all signs and wonders to place the signature of God upon the colossal event of the incarnation. These things were not done in a corner. God confirmed each event as He went along, event by event, in a long succession of events aimed at authenticating to "all generations" God's two greatest gifts to mankind: The *Redeemer of the world*, and the *perfect revelation of God.*

Making a Statement. God's greatest statement to the world was made during the advent of the Messiah, the incarnation of God in Jesus of Nazareth. All such wonders, events, and witnesses are intertwined and enmeshed together forming one integrated fabric. All signs, like arrows, are solidly pointing one direction, yet with no collusion:

Caesar decreed the taxation.

The shepherds saw the angelic host, worshipped the Christ child, spread the news abroad, and doubtless rehearsed this event around their campfires as long as they lived.

The wise men saw and followed the star and discussed the birth of Christ with the learned men at Jerusalem.

Herod killed the babies.

Nothing was out of place – nothing crossed up. As skeptics cast doubt on one account, ten others rise up to take its place. The great body of truth remains unshaken.

God Speaks Again. Jesus, whose birth was confirmed by the witness of angels and the miraculous star, went to John the Baptist, a man called of God to identify the Messiah to Israel, seeking baptism. John baptized Jesus in the River Jordan where throngs of people were gathered from Jerusalem and all Judea. Then John baptized Christ; and as He came up out of the water the people heard a great voice out of heaven blanketing the land, saying, *"This is my beloved Son, in whom I am well pleased"* (Matt. 3:16, 17). God Himself, again *with His own voice,* just as He had spoken on Sinai, confirmed the life, the person, and the work of this individual, Jesus of Nazareth, of whom Moses had written (John 5:46), and declared Him to be His own Son.

Thousands heard this personal declaration of God the Father that Jesus was His Son.

And as they listened in astonishment they saw, descending from out of the blue as far up as the eye could see, the Holy Spirit in the form of a dove. Thousands watched as He got larger and larger and came and settled upon Jesus. On this unique occasion the manifestation of all three persons of the Holy Trinity appeared once again to human senses. They saw and they heard.

Some of John's own disciples, who later became apostles of Christ, were present. They (and doubtless others) later received the account in a book, that they themselves had heard God speak from heaven and accepted the account as the Word of God. If they had not heard the voice of God, they would never have received those writings as the Word of God. But not only did they receive them, they *died* for the message they contained. This is confirmation that cannot be answered to this day.

That same Jesus, after God's own verbal declaration, went about in Galilee and Judea performing miracles beyond nature – doing the things that can only be done by the power and permission of God: healing the blind, raising up people who were already in the coffin – dead people – bringing one out of the tomb after four days.

Truth to Die For. He confirmed His Word by His ministry and by His life. Then further confirming it through His death and His wonderful sacrifice, He allowed Himself to be crucified.

As Jesus hung on the cross, the sun became black and the land was darkened; there was a tremendous earthquake. The heavy veil of the temple was rent in two from top to bottom, and again the Word, the purpose and events of God's New Covenant were confirmed. Christ was a minister to "confirm the covenants" made to the fathers. Three days later, after having been sealed in a tomb by the authority of Rome, He came out of the tomb and showed Himself alive to many hundreds of people, and *His disciples saw Him*, touched Him, handled Him. *Then His disciples also saw* Christ bodily and physically ascending up out of their sight against the laws of gravity in front of many people.

Not only did Jesus suffer and die in fulfillment of the promises made to the Fathers, but as we have seen, His disciples also, particularly the apostles, were *so absolutely persuaded of the truth of the Gospel,* including the promises from the foundation of the world, that all twelve of them would suffer unspeakable persecution and finally a martyr's death (with the possible exception of one). And not one of them said, "There was no resurrection, I'm going home."

Jesus' disciples saw it all, and they acknowledged (and some wrote) the books that contained these accounts that they themselves had seen Jesus rise from the dead were indeed true – the Word of God. Peter insisted, *"we have not followed cunningly devised fables ... but were eyewitnesses of his majesty"* (II Pet. 1:16). Now if these men had not been eyewitnesses of these things, they would never have died in defense of truth that said they were eyewitnesses. The Word is confirmed absolutely.

Each of the apostles received the New Testament books being written in their lifetimes as they became available, recording the accounts of these wonders and featuring them as eyewitnesses, as the Word of God. Central to the validity of the Gospels is the atoning death and resurrection of Christ, and this is the message which was preached by all the apostles. It was for this message that they suffered and died. We know therefore that they were convinced. Being eyewitnesses, they held these truths with a tenacious conviction.

No man will leave his home and family to roam through a hostile and disinterested world suffering privation, scorn, and finally death for a cause they know to be false. It matters not how strong a brotherhood, a promise, or conspiracy may exist between twelve men, unless each of them was persuaded in his own intellect and heart *that he had seen, heard, touched, or witnessed these renowned events, including the risen Lord Jesus,* they would never have persisted in their suffering, continuing unto death, to proclaim what they would have known was a false claim.

Somewhere, sometime, someone among the twelve would have said: "I didn't hear God's voice from heaven; I didn't see

Him walk on water, feed 5000 with a few loaves and fishes, raise Lazarus, see Him alive after the death of the cross, or see Him ascending into heaven." Someone would have said, "This is too much. I've had it with this conspiracy. I'm going home."

No! Something happened in their experience; something objective, physical, tangible – a proof that persuaded them absolutely that Jesus was the incarnation of the God of the Scriptures. *This was a truth to die for.*

Some of those same apostles, with a few others, wrote the words God gave them in the New Covenant Scriptures. These words were confirmed in a manner similar to the confirmation of the Old Covenant Scriptures. And then all these events were complete. All signs and wonders, including tongues, came to an end, that the completed canon might stand with a unique authentication and authority.

Jesus included in these Scriptures the solemn warning that there would follow false prophets and false signs. He indicated that those whose words and deeds do not agree with this great body of truth in His revelation were to be rejected as false prophets. And *He told us beforehand* that there would be false signs in the latter days; thus the confirmed Word will judge them all.

Now, all these things are meshed and locked together by thousands of witnesses who never knew each other. They cover centuries in time. No natural explanation can account for all of them; they uniformly claim that the Bible is the Word of God – confirmed by supernatural events.

Then after the ascension of Jesus into heaven, He continued His confirmation through the miraculous power of the Holy Spirit. He continued the signs and wonders to validate the growing cloud of witnesses who were in this chain. He validated the work of the apostles and the church by continuing these signs and wonders until the Scriptures were complete. And so He tied the Scripture together from beginning to end – from Moses on Sinai to John on Patmos – by signs and wonders.

Then He cut these wonders short and made the Scriptures unique, and the final standard was born.

The Scriptures: God's Final Standard

Today we judge a work not by whether it is accompanied by miracles, or by signs and wonders, but now we judge "signs and wonders" by the uniquely confirmed Word. Thus we try the spirits, not by whether the spirits can speak in an unintelligible language but by whether the spirit behaves and speaks according to truth as verified by God's Word.

Today, if someone should come along and raise the dead, and do mighty wonders, we must not go after them. The mighty works of God have had priority over the deceitful counterfeits of Satan, and have served their purpose. *Christ has told us beforehand that there would be deceitful works to follow.* So we are forewarned. Therefore, knowing the confirmed Word, we do not look to the modern-day workers of "wonders" for truth. If you do not know the Word, you may go after them to your detriment. But remember Paul's warning to the Galatians:

> I marvel that ye are so soon removed from him that called you into the grace of Christ unto another gospel: Which is not another; but there be some that trouble you, and would pervert the gospel of Christ. *But though we, or an angel from heaven, preach any other gospel unto you than that which we have preached unto you, let him be accursed.* As we said before, so say I now again, *If any man preach any other gospel unto you than that ye have received, let him be accursed* (Gal. 1:6-9).

It would be hard to argue with an angel from heaven. But suppose you had gone to a charismatic meeting and all of a sudden you saw an angel from heaven coming through the roof, leaving no hole, and settling down in the midst of the people. Suppose the angel then began to preach things which are contrary to the Word which has now been confirmed by mighty works of God.

The angel begins: "I am a messenger sent from God, and God has sent me to you with a new revelation."

What should you do?

Do not believe him. *That is a commandment.*

It matters not that it is an angel from heaven; it does not matter what kind of sign or wonder he does. The Lord has told us beforehand; *go not after him.* It matters not what kind of miracle a person is able to perform, what manner of tongue he may speak, if he uses the language of *angels,* we test him by the finished, confirmed Word, the final standard.

If he says, "But this is according to the Word," then we do not need his message; let him turn to the chapter and verse and read it. If he says, "But there is a change or substitution in the Word," then he is diminishing from the Word, which is forbidden (Deut 4:2; 12:32; Rev. 22:19). If he says, "But I have new revelation for you," then he is adding to the Word, which is forbidden (Deut 4:2; 12:32; Rev. 22:18). God's Word is both complete and perfect, and if anyone pleads today that they have a direct revelation from God, *"Go not after them."*

Today it is not up to us to decide any issue concerning the will of God apart from the Scripture. All we have to decide is: What does the Scripture teach? Ours is to conform to the Word that is already confirmed. We must measure every spirit, doctrine, or behavior by Scripture. We analyze every movement by Scripture: Does the movement teach the things that are true? Is its body of doctrine truth? Is its behavior, manner, witness, and purpose scriptural? Does it conform to the will and purpose of God as expressed in the confirmed Word? That is all we need to discern.

The full confirmation of Scripture is not, after all, in a single miracle; it is in the consistent, inter-meshing integration of all the mighty works of God. Once that principle is understood, then the Word must be seen as the *sole standard for truth in all matters,* in matters of science, arts, business, entertainment, education, sports … *ad infinitum.* All these matters must be compatible with the biblical paradigm. That is because God is *transcendent* over all things. Nothing is beyond His jurisdiction; nothing is neutral.

All God's Word applies to all of life, for every one, all the time, everywhere; whether in heaven, in earth, on the moon, Mars, or in distant galaxies.

Without that long, intertwining chain – event after event confirming each other over centuries – a single miracle standing alone would hardly be decisive. It is the whole interlocking chain that unequivocally establishes the Bible – God's final answer to subjectivism, revelationism, existentialism, and postmodernism – as the one *unique body of absolute truth* against which all other claims are to be measured.

It is time for Christians to surrender to this reality and come together around this Word, deliberately weighing our doctrines and practices. Among the final words of Jesus was this prayer:

> Sanctify them through thy truth: *thy word is truth*... . That they all may be one; as thou, Father, art in me, and I in thee, that they also may be one in us: *that the world may believe that thou hast sent me* (John 17:17, 21).

And so today it is the Word itself that is the final Standard for truth on earth. We can continue to be split and divided by each one going about seeking his own special revelation from God, or we can make a deliberate choice to look to the objective Word as the only complete source of truth available to us and come together around it. Until we do, most of the six billion souls in the world will die in unbelief. But Jesus has plainly given us the solution for reaching them by reaching unity in truth.

The Bible is that Word of truth, which alone bears the *unique signature of God.*

Bibliography

Aldrich, Roy L. *Is the Pentecostal Movement Pentecostal?* Detroit: Detroit Bible Institute, n.d.

Armstrong, John H., ed. *The Coming Evangelical Crisis.* Chicago: Moody Press, 1996.

Bartleman, Frank. *How Pentecost Came to Los Angeles.* Self-Published, 1925.

Benedict, David. *A General History of the Baptist Denomination in America.* 1813. rpt. Lafayette, TN: Church History Research and Archives, 1980. Vol. 2.

Bettenson, Henry. *Documents of the Christian Church.* New York: Oxford University Press, 1943.

Burdick, Donald W. *Tongues: To Speak or Not to Speak.* Chicago: Moody Press, 1969.

Carlin, James B. *Identifying the Lord's Kind of Churches.* 2nd ed. Emmaus, PA: Challenge Press, 2006.

Carroll, B. H. *An Interpretation of the English Bible.* 17 vols. Nashville: Broadman Press, 1942. Vol. 12, 13.

Carson, D. A. *The Gagging of God: Christianity Confronts Pluralism.* Grand Rapids: Zondervan Publishing House, 1996.

__________. *Showing the Spirit: A Theological Exposition of 1 Corinthians 12-14.* Grand Rapids: Baker Books, 1987.

Colson, Charles, and Nancy Pearcey. *How Now Shall we Live.* Wheaton: Tyndale House Publishers, Inc., 1999.

Criswell, W. A. *The Baptism, Filling & Gifts of the Holy Spirit.* Grand Rapids: Zondervan Publishing House, 1973.

Davidson, C. T. *Upon This Rock.* Cleveland, TN: White Wing Publishing House and Press, 1973. Vol. 1.

DeGrandis, Robert. *The Gift of Tongues.* n.p., 1983.

Dillow, Jody. *A Biblical Evaluation of the Twentieth Century Tongues Movement.* n.p., 1972.

Elwell, Walter A., ed. *The Evangelical Dictionary of Theology.* Grand Rapids: Baker Books, 2001.

Euripides. *The Bacchae.* Tr. Geoffrey S. Kirk. Englewood Cliffs, N. J.: Prentice-Hall, Inc., 1970.

Faulkner, R. O., et al., Tr. *The Literature of Ancient Egypt.* New Haven: Yale University Press, 1973.

Gardiner, George E. *The Corinthian Catastrophe.* Grand Rapids: Kregel Publication, 1974.

Gephard, Keith. *The Folly of the Charismatics.* Greenville, SC: Bob Jones UP, 1981.

Green, Michael. *I believe in the Holy Spirit.* Grand Rapids: William B. Eerdmans Publishing Co., 1975.

Grudem, Wayne. *The Gift of Prophecy in 1 Corinthians.* Washington, D.C.: University Press of America, 1982.

Hammond, William A. *Spiritualism and Allied Causes and Conditions of Nervous Derangement.* New York: n.p., 1876.

Hawkins, William C., and Willard A. Ramsey. *The House of God.* Simpsonville, S.C.: Hallmark Baptist Church, 1980.

Hillis, Don W. *Tongues, Healing and You.* Grand Rapids: Baker Book House, 1969.

Himmels, John R. *Facts on File Dictionary of Religion.* New York: Facts on File, Inc., 1984.

Horton, Michael. *In the Face of God: The Dangers and Delights of Spiritual Intimacy.* Dallas: Word Publishing, 1996.

House, Paul R., and Thornbury, Gregory A., eds. *Who Will be Saved? Defending the Biblical Understanding of God, Salvation, and Evangelism.* Wheaton: Crossway Books, 2000.

Jenson, Robert. *America's Theologian, A Recommendation of Jonathan Edwards.* New York: Oxford University Press, 1988.

Johnson, Brad. *An Indictment of Pentecostalism.* Choteau, MT: Old Paths Gospel Press, n.d.

Kantzer, Kenneth S. "The Charismatics Among Us." *Christianity Today,* 22 February 1980: 29.

Kidd, B. J., ed. *Documents Illustrative of the History of the Christian Church.* New York: The Macmillan Company, 1933.

Kling, David W. *The Bible in History.* Oxford: Oxford University Press, 2004.

Latourette, Kenneth Scott. *A History of Christianity.* New York: Harper & Row Publishers, 1953.

Lindsell, Harold. *The Holy Spirit in the Latter Days.* Nashville: Thomas Nelson Publishers, 1983.

MacArthur, John F., Jr. *Charismatic Chaos.* Grand Rapids: Zondervan Publishing House, 1992.

MacArthur, John F., Jr. *The Charismatics.* Grand Rapids: Zondervan Publishing House, 1978.

Mackie, Alexander. *The Gift of Tongues.* New York: George Doran Company, 1921.

Mackintosh, Hugh Ross. *Types of Modern Theologies: Schleiermacher to Barth.* London: Nisbet and Company Ltd., 1937.

MacPherson, Dave. *The Incredible Cover-up.* Plainfield, N.J.: Logos International, 1975.

__________. *The Great Rapture Hoax.* Fletcher, N.C.: New Puritan Library, 1983.

__________. *The Rapture Plot.* Simpsonville, S.C.: Millennium III Publishers, 1994.

Mills, Watson E. *A Theological/Exegetical Approach to Glossolalia.* New York: University Press of America, 1985.

Mook, James Richard. "Basis of Neo-Pentecostal Ecumenicity." Thesis. Dallas Theological Seminary, 1980.

Morris, Henry, III. *After Eden: Understanding Creation, the Curse, and the Cross.* Green Forest, AR: Master Books, 2003.

Murray, Iain H. *Revival and Revivalism: The Making and Marring of American Evangelicalism 1750-1858.* Edinburgh: The Banner of Truth Trust, 1996.

Oldenbourg, Zoe. *Massacre at Monsequr: A History of the Albigensian Crusade.* Trans. Peter Green. New York: Random House, 1961.

Orr, James. *The Christian View of God and the World.* New York: Charles Scribner's Sons, 1879.

Pamphilus, Eusebius. *The Ecclesiastical History of Eusebius Pamphilus.* Tr. Christian Frederick Cruse. Grand Rapids: Baker Book House, 1955.

Pink, Arthur W. *The Holy Spirit.* Grand Rapids: Baker Book House, 1970.

Plato. *Plato Selections.* Rapheal Demos, Ed. New York: Charles Scribner's Sons, 1927.

__________. *The Works of Plato.* B. Jowett, Tr. New York: The Dial Press, n.d.).

Pyle, Hugh F., *The Truth about Tongues and the Charismatic Movement.* Murfreesboro, TN: Sword of the Lord Publishers, 1989.

Ramsey, Willard A. *The Fateful Lightning.* Simpsonville, S.C.: Millennium III Publishers, 2000.

__________. *Facing Eternity.* Simpsonville, S.C.: Millennium III Publishers, 1999.

Robertson, O. Palmer. *The Final Word: A Biblical Response to the Case for Tongues and Prophecy Today.* Edinburgh: The Banner of Truth Trust, 1993.

Sauer, Erich. *The Dawn of World Redemption.* Trans. G. H. Lang. London: Paternoster Press, 1956.

Schleiermacher, Friedrich. *The Christian Faith.* Ed. R. H. Mackintosh, and J. S. Stewart. Edinburgh: T. & T. Clark, 1928.

__________. *Brief Outline on the Study of Theology.* Trans. Terrence N. Tice. Richmond: John Knox Press, 1966.

Shedd, William G. T. *A History of Christian Doctrine.* New York: Charles Scribner's Sons, 1897. Vol. 1

Seel, John. *The Evangelical Forfeit: Can We Recover?* Grand Rapids: Baker Books, 1993.

Smith, Timothy L. "The Cross Demands, the Spirit Enables." *Christianity Today.* 16 February 1997: 22-26.

Sontag, Frederick. "Soren Kierkegaard." *Great Thinkers of the Western World.* Ed. Ian P. McGreal. New York: HarperCollins Publishers, 1992.

Speir, J. M. *Christianity and Existentialism.* Tr. David Hugh Freeman. Presbyterian and Reformed Publishing Company, 1953.

Stagg, Frank, et al. *Glossolalia: Tongues Speaking in Biblical, Historical, and Psychological Perspective.* Nashville: Abingdon Press, 1967.

__________. *The Holy Spirit Today: Biblical Teaching Applied to Present Needs.* Nashville: Broadman Press, 1973.

Strong, Augustus. *Systematic Theology.* Valley Forge: The Judson Press, 1907.

Strouse, Thomas M. *I Will Build My Church: The Doctrine and*

History of Baptists. Virginia Beach: Tabernacle Baptist Theological Press, 1995.

Sweet, William Warren. *The Story of Religion in America*. New York: Harper and Brothers Publishers, 1930.

Thiessen, Henry C. *Lectures in Systematic Theology*. Grand Rapids: Wm. B. Eerdmans Publishing Co., 1949.

Verduin, Leonard. *The Reformers and Their Stepchildren*. 1964. Rpt. Grand Rapids: Baker Book House, 1980.

__________. *The Anatomy of a Hybrid*. Grand Rapids: Wm. B. Eerdmans Publishing Co., 1976.

Index

268

Finney, Charles G. 55, 56, 57
Friends (Quakers) 40, 41, 56
Full Gospel Business Men's
Fellowship International
(FGBMFI) 67, 84

G
Gardiner, George 4, 43, 69, 84,
261
genealogy in reverse 231-232
Gentile(s) 127, 128, 166, 168-
175, 194, 239
gift(s) of the Holy Spirit 51, 62,
137, 147, 166, 167, 169, 174,
175, 178, 186, 203, 210, 235
Gnostic, Gnosticism 17, 19, 29
God-spoke-to-me syndrome
91-94
Great Awakening 48, 51, 52, 53,
72, 197
great commission 116, 129, 131,
144, 148, 151, 157, 160
Greek worshippers 23

H
Hippolytus 31
holiness 36, 54, 55-57, 61-65,
81, 193
Holy Spirit
  Old Covenant roles 122-127
Holy Spirit, normative work
111-116
House of God 122, 140, 168

I
indwelling, of Holy Spirit 29,
112, 115, 151, 156
inerrancy 85, 98, 102

infallible, infallibility 6, 9, 78,
83, 85, 89, 9-98, 114, 215, 216,
218, 227, 229
Institute for Creation Research
104
Irenaeus 34, 38
Irving, Edward 43, 45, 46, 47,
107
Irvingite Movement 43, 47, 48,
52, 53, 54, 61, 197

J
Jansenists 40
jerking, jerks 18, 42, 49, 50-54
John the Baptist 100, 116, 118,
120, 121, 128, 132, 136, 158,
176, 252
jumping 63
justification 8, 59, 82, 102, 113,
136, 242

K
Kierkegaard, Soren 72, 76-78,
87, 90, 91, 106
knowing (epistemological)
219-221

L
Lee, Ann (see Mother Ann)
liberalism and charismata 67, 69,
81, 83, 84, 86, 163
love 16, 43, 50, 55, 64, 74, 75,
93, 112-114, 136, 137, 141-143,
164, 182, 183, 191, 193, 194,
196, 201, 221, 240
lyddite 57

180, 183, 185-187, 194-197, 199, 201, 207-209, 229, 235
prophetess(es) 22, 30, 31, 33, 35
prophet(s) 18, 22-26, 29, 32, 45, 50, 77, 128, 130, 166, 180, 189, 207, 234-245, 255
provisional gifts 181-183
psyche, psychic(s) 5-6, 21, 23, 25, 26, 28, 33, 34, 42, 43, 46, 48, 51, 52, 66, 68, 89, 102, 103, 105, 110, 182, 197, 202, 210

Q
Quaker(s) 40, 41, 42, 61, 72, 197

R
regeneration 15, 16, 28, 29, 84, 111-116, 125, 133, 134, 136, 137, 146, 151, 156, 159, 172-175, 182
Regent Square 43, 46
revelation, direct 2, 4, 6, 8, 11, 13, 15, 32, 42, 47, 71, 82, 91, 93, 94, 96, 103, 159, 194, 198, 214, 257
revelation, divine 7, 41, 77, 91, 94, 97, 184, 185, 186, 209, 228, 243, 251
revelatory knowledge 183
revelatory prophecy 183, 186, 196, 199
revivalism 51, 53
revival(s) 39, 43, 45, 48, 50-53, 55, 59, 60, 62, 63, 64, 197
Roberts, Oral 66, 67
rolling 49, 50, 52, 54

S
salvation 54, 56, 111, 112, 116, 127, 132-138, 142, 143, 146-149, 152, 153, 159, 166, 172-175, 196, 235
Sartre, Jean-Paul 78, 106
Satan 12, 51, 63, 69, 95, 107, 215, 241-248, 256
satanic 21, 34, 52, 241, 243, 244, 245
Schleiermacher, Friedrich 72-78, 87, 90, 91, 107, 262
scientific creationism 104
Scofield, C. I. 45, 54, 135, 152
Second Vatican Council 85
second work of grace 54, 58, 61, 112, 132, 146, 148, 159, 167, 175
Seymour, William J. 62, 63, 64
Shakers 26, 41, 47, 81
Sheffey, Robert S. 61
Sibylline priestess 27
signs and wonders 4, 16, 17, 34, 46, 54, 161, 166, 167, 175, 176, 180, 182, 186, 213-216, 218, 222, 223, 225, 227, 230, 233-248, 251, 252, 255, 256
Sinai 1, 227, 229, 239, 240, 248-250, 253, 256
sinless perfection(ism) 3, 17, 25, 36, 37, 54, 56, 61
slain in the spirit 20, 52, 63
snake handling 66, 166
Socrates 22, 23, 24, 203
spiritual gifts 32, 33, 45, 46, 179, 195, 197, 198, 199, 201, 206, 209
Spurling, Richard G. (Jr. or Sr.) 58, 60, 61, 62, 65
Subjectivist Party (see Objectivist Party) 102